Blogs, Wikis, MySpace, and More

Library of Congress Cataloging-in-Publication Data
Is available from the Library of Congress.

Cover design: Emily Brackett/Visible Logic

First U. S. edition
Published by Chicago Review Press, Incorporated
814 North Franklin Street
Chicago, Illinois 60610
ISBN-13: 978-1-55652-756-2
ISBN-10: 1-55652-756-X
First published in Great Britain in 2007 by
Carlton Books Limited
20 Mortimer Street
London W1T 3JW

Printed in Singapore
5 4 3 2 1

Blogs, Wikis, MySpace, and More

Everything You Want to Know About Using Web 2.0 but Are Afraid to Ask

Terry Burrows

CHICAGO REVIEW PRESS

Contents

Introduction

It's been about 15 years since I first wrote professionally about technology, and in particular the Internet. Since that time, things—not to understate the case—have changed somewhat. Modes of social interaction that for most of us would have been pure sci-fi fantasy are now a mundane fact of life. Barely 30 years ago my parents were still in awe of color television—technology that my generation has largely taken for granted. Yet while my four-year-old son is adept at using a laptop and routinely surfs children's websites, I still marvel occasionally when I open a media-rich web page that loads almost immediately. Or when a colleague from the other side of the world e-mails an mp3 that he finished mixing only a few minutes earlier, and has taken barely a few seconds to reach my computer.

Here's a personal illustration of the scale of that change. Let's go back to spring 1995. At that time I was very heavily into the album *The Bends* by Radiohead, which had just been released. I'd read that it was possible to download a video of the band's new single, "High and Dry," and so decided to give it a try. I switched on my Apple Mac, and then an external 14.4 kilobyte modem. I first had to run a dedicated program to connect me to the Internet. After a few moments of high-pitched whirring and buzzing (a sound that now seems strangely nostalgic), I was told I was online. I then launched a web browser called Mosaic and typed in a URL. I clicked on a download button and then left it to do its thing. I returned to the computer about 30 minutes later, only to find that the Internet connection had failed. (It did this frequently.) I reconnected. Again—this time after about an hour—the connection failed. I decided to give it one final effort. I went back after one hour to find that the file still seemed to be transferring; a further hour later, and it still seemed to be working. Finally, after four-and-a-half hours I was able to view a tiny, glitchy, low-resolution film. It was, in all, an underwhelming experience. To add further perspective, not only was I paying around $30 a month to an ISP to have any sort of facility to connect to the Internet, I also had to pay the telephone company for about six hours worth of calls! And, of course, while I was hooked up to the Internet, my phone line was tied up.

Fast-forward now to summer 2007. I'm sprawled on a sofa, shiny new MacBook Pro on my lap. I've just launched a web browser and typed in the URL for the world's most popular video site, *You Tube*. Seconds later, and I type in the search: "**Radiohead High and Dry**." And I'm now watching that same video being streamed to me via an eight megabyte broadband line, via a wireless home

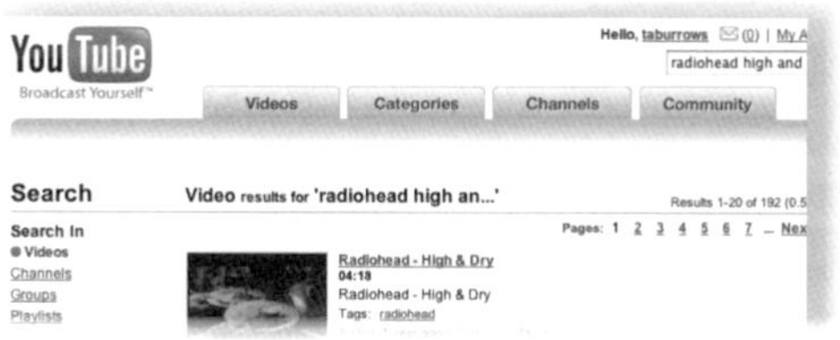

network. I still pay an ISP roughly the same monthly fee I did 12 years ago, there's no specific charge for using the phone line, *and* I can make and receive calls while I'm connected. It's a pretty amazing development really.

The fact that I can now watch videos on my laptop more easily and cheaply may not *seem* to be heralding a new way of life, but consider some of the implications here. If I can watch old music videos on demand, then why not entire TV shows or movies? Why do I need to buy DVDs? Why do we need TV channels? Or even a TV? If I can make video calls via my laptop, do I necessarily need a phone system?

So, if I'm still fortunate enough to be writing about technology (or anything else, for that matter) 15 years from now what can I expect to find? One thing's for sure, the more the Web becomes central to our lives, the more effort the business community will put into figuring out how to make us pay for its content—and media in all of its forms will be increasingly available online. One technical development we can expect is that most of the software we currently use will not have to be bought and loaded onto our computers, but will be built into websites and accessed via a browser. And that's really the starting point for this book.

We're now entering a period where, for a growing number of users, *everything* they want to do on their computers can be achieved through using application-based web pages. This evolution, along with the explosion of online social networking and shared community data, is often described under the flimsy, catchall banner of "Web 2.0." This term is pretty meaningless in any specific technological sense and more often than not is used by the business world to market new products as being "cutting edge." The media, too, have latched onto the term. But here it has grown into a kind of shorthand to describe the most popular developments and fashions in Internet usage. And that's probably the best way to view this book. Many of the applications you find in here would probably be described as Web 2.0. All of them, however, illustrate the way web technology is currently being used now, and areas in which it is likely to develop in the future. These are the early days of an ongoing revolution, but there's already plenty of amazing stuff out there from which you can choose. So have fun!

Terry Burrows
London, June 2007

A Brief History of the Future

At the turn of the 1990s, a phenomenon emerged from the margins of the computer world with implications on the way we would operate and interact in the very near future—implications that few could have foreseen. It was around this period that computer scientists, technologists, and other geeky types began to appear in the mainstream media telling us how an "information superhighway" was about to knock the planet off its axis. Like all new technologies, "the Internet," as it was called, didn't really work that well, and the early uptake was mostly among other geeky types. In truth, although this first wave of commercial Internet users may have talked about it with mind-numbing evangelical zeal, in practice they largely treated it as an alternative to a telephone or a fax machine.

A Changing World

Few of those early pioneering users could really have imagined how different a place the world would be barely 15 years later. Now we find that e-mail, instant chat, and text messaging are far more common means of communication than any printed medium. And when was the last time you were sent a *handwritten* letter? (And if you were, and it wasn't from an 80-year-old great aunt, wouldn't you think the sender was a bit . . . well . . . weird?) And what of the poor old fax machine? In the early 1990s it was just beginning to migrate from the office place to the home; now most will have been sent to a final resting place—and that would most probably be the local dump.

If we look at what now represents routine modern Internet usage, we really do begin to see how our lives have been altered. We routinely order all manner of goods—books and DVDs, underpants and groceries—using online shops. Often using "virtual" currencies like PayPal. We download our music, TV, and films, legally or otherwise, using peer-to-peer (P2P) software or digital music stores; we sell our old unwanted stuff on eBay or other auction sites; we make our innermost thoughts available to the world via blogs and web pages; and we use so-called social networking sites to communicate with and make new friends. There can be no denying that the Internet has made the world a very different place.

Let's also take a look at the changing face of the hardware. One major development is that computing has increasingly become a mobile activity. More and more of us are moving away from cumbersome desktop systems, aided by a new generation of powerful "Wi-Fi" laptops. Increasingly, we have wireless systems

in place in our homes, meaning that more and more computer activities have migrated from the desktop to the sofa. And if you live in any reasonably sized town you're likely to find plenty of hot spots where you and your laptop can get Internet access. Indeed, go into any café in London, New York, or any other major city and you're sure to find a handful of surfers dotted around the room. Some of this hardware has even begun to merge into a rather murky cloud: increasingly computers and mobile phones—that other revolution in social technology of the late 20th century—are crossing over. We can now make calls from our laptops, look at websites on our phones, and take photographs, videos, and audio recordings on both. And now Apple—ever at the cutting edge in aesthetic technological design—has brought us the iPhone, which starts to bridge the gap between phone, computer, camera, and mp3 player.

Where Did It All Come From?

The Internet was actually an spin-off of one of the U.S. government's late-'60s cold war initiatives—a stable, "packet switching" data communication system linking together military bases across the world that could withstand chunks of the system being taken out by some form of attack. On January 1, 1983, the U.S. National Science Foundation took this network further, constructing a university "backbone" that would become the NSFNet. Many commentators view this date as the true "birth" of the Internet. Although only two years later this was opened up to commercial parties, it remained principally in the realm of academia for the rest of the decade.

The initial users were attracted by three distinct types of application: user groups and forums, where people with like-minded interests could exchange views or post questions; e-mail, which was basically an electronic postal system; and the World Wide Web, feted as the world's largest information retrieval system. The first two of these, of course, remain fundamental online practices, and although the software may have evolved the basic principles are pretty well unchanged. The Web, however, is a different matter altogether.

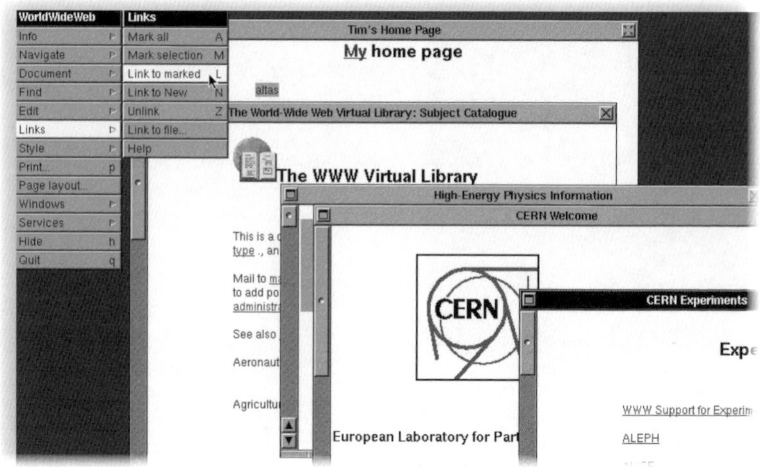

Evolution of the Web

Jokingly referred to in the early days as the "World Wide Wait," the Web has evolved beyond all recognition. Early websites may well have been written in the same HTML code that most still are today, but prevailing connection and transmission speeds meant that the image-rich pages we now take for granted barely existed back then. After all, who would want to type in a URL only to wait 10 minutes for a page to load with its associated pictures? (And, in truth, that's not a particularly exaggerated example.)

So where exactly did the World Wide Web come from? It was the brainchild of British scientist Tim Berners-Lee. While working at CERN, the world's largest particle physics laboratory, he proposed a project based on the concept of a hypertext markup language (HTML) to enable researchers to share and update information. It was on August 6, 1991 that Berners-Lee put the first website live. Its URL was **http://info.cern.ch/hypertext/WWW/TheProject.html**, and it looked pretty much like a web page in the modern sense (*see above*). Appropriately, "Tim's Home Page" provided an explanation of what the World Wide Web was all about, how one could own a browser called *WorldWideWeb*, and how to set up a web server. It was also the world's first web directory, since Berners-Lee maintained a list of other sites as they came into existence. From this historic birth, other innovators with more entrepreneurial vision made things happen.

Technical Evolution

The "Web," as it soon became known, evolved quickly. Browsers began to emerge with ever greater functionality and neat innovations, such as the ability to store (or "bookmark") websites, so that users didn't have to maintain a manual directory of web addresses if they wanted to revisit the site at a later date. However, it was with increased commercial connection speeds that the Web truly began to flourish. In 1995, the average Internet user went online via a 14.4 kilobytes-per-second modem link; nowadays, eight megabytes-per-second broadband connections are widely found in the home—that's over *500 times* faster. As these speeds increased, web designers were able to enrich with images and sounds what had previously often been dull, text-based sites.

Enhancing the Web Experience

The early websites suffered from one major drawback: they were static objects, with no way for the users to interact with the page. Much of this was due to the fact that browser functionality was limited by simply interpreting HTML instructions to perform basic operations. The solution to this issue took two forms: plug-ins and enhanced scripting. Both had the same goal in mind—boosting the power of the web browser.

Plug-ins were small add-on programs that were loaded into the browser to enable it to deal with specific types of media, such as animation or video. Many different plug-ins emerged, some of which were created with the sole aim of popularizing "non-standard" or advanced file formats. The most popular examples usually ended up integrated into new versions of the browser software; others quickly faded from view. Among the most significant plug-ins was Flash, which enabled movies and animations created using the Macromedia (now Adobe) Flash multimedia authoring system. This is now one of the most commonly used methods of projecting such media on the Web, and Flash programming skills are a standard requirement among web designers.

Other important developments have come in the form of programming enhancements to the HTML code used to create web pages. The most important of these is JavaScript. Developed in 1995 by Netscape, the company behind the Navigator web browser software—at that time the field leaders—JavaScript enabled web authors to design interactive sites with dynamic content. It was quickly integrated into the other major browsers. (Although Internet Explorer still only uses a subset of the language—JScript.) Its importance is still being felt, as AJAX—the Web 2.0 language—is itself a JavaScript-based technology.

Web 2.0

The term Web 2.0 is currently one of the hottest buzzwords in the media world. So what does it mean? Where did it come from? Will it really change our lives?

Birth of the Phrase

The concept of Web 2.0 came from an Internet media businessman named Tim O'Reilly. He and his colleagues coined the phrase in 2003, and it became public at the first Web 2.0 conference a year later. To begin with, though, it's important to understand that while the term Web 2.0 would suggest some sort of a new version of the Web, it does *not* refer to any kind of update to the technical specifications of the Web; it refers to changes in the ways designers have used the web platform, and in the changing behaviors of the end user.

The idea of Web 2.0 begins with the bursting of the so-called dot-com bubble following the collapse of the technology-heavy NASDAQ exchange in March 2000. Here, the Internet and its associated industries went through an inevitable "thinning out" process, as the markets began to realize that much of the heavy speculative investment of the previous five years had created a sector that was vastly overvalued. The highly publicized financial freefall that followed led some to proclaim the Internet and the Web had been one massive hype, and investors started to look elsewhere. However, it's fair to say that stock market bubbles are a part of any emerging trend, and while many prominent players fell by the wayside, what remained were the *real* success stories of the industry—the Googles, Yahoo!s and Amazons, which were left in an even stronger position than before. In fact, there's some evidence to suggest that when a market goes through this process it is sending out a signal that it has moved beyond up-and-coming fashionability into the realm of mainstream acceptance.

The concept of Web 2.0 came about during a conference brainstorming

Brainstroming

-------------- WEB 1.0 -------------		-------------- WEB 2.0 --------------
DoubleClick	------->	Google AdSense
Ofoto	------->	Flickr
Akamai	------->	BitTorrent
mp3.com	------->	Napster
Britannica Online	------->	Wikipedia
Personal websites	------->	Blogging
Evite	------->	Upcoming.org and EVDB
Domain name speculation	------->	Search engine optimization
Page views	------->	Cost per click
Screen scraping	------->	Web services
Publishing	------->	Participation
Content management	------->	Wikis
Directories ("taxonomy")	------->	Tagging ("folksonomy")
Stickiness	------->	Syndication

session. The basic tenet of the argument was that far from having collapsed, the Web was, in practical terms, more important than ever, with innovative new uses continuing regularly to make themselves known. Their conclusion was that the dot-com collapse could be seen as a turning point for the Web. They came up with specific examples that identified philosophical differences between the "old" Web ("Web 1.0") and the new (see box above) and then developed a series of specific themes. The three most important were the Web as a platform, the harnessing of collective knowledge, and the creation of a "rich" user experience.

The Web as a Platform

The basis for this idea was that instead of thinking of the Web as a place where browsers viewed data through small windows on the readers' screens, it was actually more broadly the platform that allowed people to get things done. Thus instead of needing to buy and install software for word processing, spreadsheets, presentations, and editing your photographs, it would be possible to perform all of these activities using applications that were built into the website and used through the web browser. Similarly, why would we need to download our entertainment content, such as music, films, or TV shows, when we could simply access it via a web browser?

Harnessing Collective Knowledge

A good deal of the interest in Web 2.0 issues has focused on aspects of social interaction, whether it be networking, sharing talents, and creating new relationships on MySpace; whether creating a dialogue through the use of blogs; whether tagging and sharing websites using Del.icio.us; or whether contributing collective knowledge by editing Wikipedia. Developments of this kind, some would argue, herald a new dawn for creativity, democracy, and community. A counter argument is that this will ultimately create a desocializing impact as we spend more and more of our time shouting into a huge online abyss with nobody actually listening.

Rich User Experience

Many of us were so amazed by the World Wide Web in its early years of development that we were quick to forgive its shortcomings. It was slow, unreliable, and clunky to use. But it was worth the trouble. We're now in a new era where web designers seek to re-create the interactivity of a computer desktop on the Web. This is largely accomplished using "new" technologies such as AJAX. These new tools enable web applications to behave in ways that are familiar to us from our use of traditional desktop applications. For example, this could mean something as simple as integrating drag-and-drop techniques. Formerly such operations would have been problematic, but now the time delays caused by server calls is largely mitigated by smaller amounts of information being sent asynchronously through JavaScript calls.

But Is It Really New?

It is. And it isn't. Let's start with the technology of the Web. Much has been made of the role AJAX has played in the development of Web 2.0 applications, but it *is* itself based on JavaScript, which has been around for well over a decade. A widely

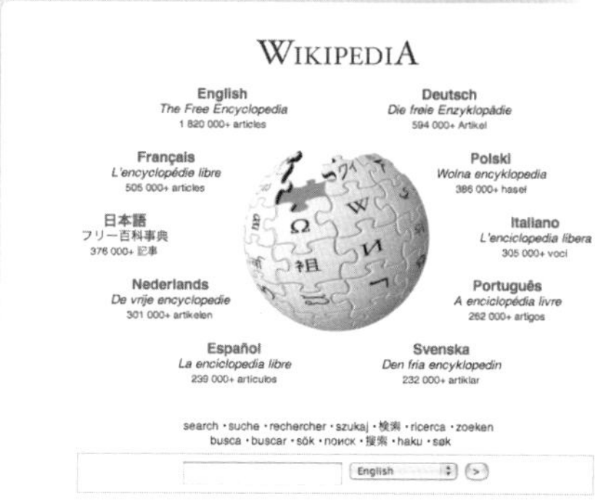

held view in the technical community is that AJAX is JavaScript that *works*. Certainly if you take a look at some of these AJAX-based sites you will quickly see (and feel) that it does make for a much smoother Internet experience.

Similarly, social networking and democracy are hardly new ideas as far as the Internet are concerned—it could even be argued that they were central tenets of its foundation and evolution. Personal websites have been around since the beginning the Web, and have always been used by some as a means to express personal views. On the surface, blogging would not seem to be too far removed, apart from the fact that the user can do it more easily and elegantly. However, there is this interactive aspect to consider. If we take two people speaking to one another as an analogy, the personal website is one person delivering a lecture to another; the blog at least opens up the floor to questions and then possible dialogue.

One genuinely innovative area that seems to have evolved out of the Web 2.0 debate is how data can be combined from different sources—even those over which the user has no control—to create what are known as "mash-ups." This has created many fascinating hybrids—some of which you'll come across in the book. So, for example, it could be possible to combine a gallery of bars tagged in Flickr with comments that people have written about those bars, and then connect the whole thing to Google Maps.

A Final Verdict?

Web 2.0 as a term has become inflated through media coverage and distorted by marketing people using it to sell their products. In fact, it has already become a somewhat meaningless buzzword. But the ideas underpinning the basic concepts are, in themselves, so fascinating that we can't help but ask ourselves how life online is going to evolve, and what impact it will have on the way we live our lives away from the Web.

Blogging

A blog is an online diary or journal. The term is a slang abbreviation of "web log." Most blogs take place on a dedicated blogging website. They are user-generated, and entries are usually displayed in reverse chronological order. Blogs are widely used as diaries or to provide commentary or news on specific subjects. A typical blog combines text, images, and links to other blogs or related web pages. An important feature of blogging is that readers are able to leave their own personal comments in an interactive format. There are now thought to be around 60 million active blogs in existence across the world.

The Early Days

The blog as we know it today evolved from the online web diary. Here, as the term suggests, people would keep a running account of their everyday personal lives. One particularly well-known example of an early news-based blog was the Drudge Report. Founded in 1994 by maverick political reporter Matt Drudge, his website consists largely of links to political news stories from the U.S. and

international media. It is particularly noted for being the first news source to break the Bill Clinton/Monica Lewinsky scandal to the public. Matt Drudge himself, however, is thought to dislike having his famed site referred to as a blog.

The first web logs were simple websites that were updated manually. However, soon tools began to appear that were able to facilitate the production and maintenance of articles posted in reverse chronological order, which opened the blogging process to a larger, nontechnical group of users. Ultimately, this resulted in the creation of the browser-based software that now predominates.

When Blogs Go Bad!

Given the popularity and personal nature of many blogs, it's not surprising that some have ended up with unexpected consequences for the bloggers themselves. Areas of legal concern have included the release of confidential information or making defamatory remarks. There are also an increasing number of well-documented cases of employees losing their jobs for publishing details of their working or personal lives. In fact, this is now sufficiently commonplace to have evolved its own specific term: to be "dooced" is to be fired from your job for something you've written on the Internet. This comes from the case of Heather Armstrong in Salt Lake City, Utah, who, in 2002, was fired from her job as a web designer for writing a satirical blog about her experiences at a dot-com startup company—she wrote under the pseudonym of "Dooce." She later offered would-be bloggers some sound advice: "I was fired from my job because I had written stories that included people in my workplace. My advice to you is BE YE NOT SO STUPID."

• In 2005, U.S. blogger Aaron Wall was sued by Traffic Power for defamation and publication of trade secrets. He exposed what he alleged were attempts to rig search engine results on Google. The case was keenly observed by bloggers because it addressed the legal issue of who is liable for comments posted on a blog.

• In 2006, Ellen Simonetti, a flight attendant with Delta Airlines, was fired for comments made on her blog, "Queen of the Sky," which also showed her posing in her work uniform. The company argued that a blogger's activities could be capable of adversely affecting an employer's brand.

• The same year, Jessica Cutler—"The Washingtonienne"—blogged about her sex life while being employed as a congressional assistant. She was dismissed after the blog was discovered, and later went on to write a novel based on her experiences.

• In 2007, Egyptian blogger Kareem Amer was sentenced to four-year prison term, having been charged with insulting President Mubarak and Islam, and inciting sedition through his blog.

• In Britain, college lecturer Tracy Williams anonymously contributed to a blog in which she referred to political candidate Michael Keith-Smith as a "Nazi." Her identity was easily traced by her ISP, and in 2006 she was successfully sued for £10,000 ($20,000) in damages and £7,200 ($14,000) costs.

Evolution of Blogging

As is often the case in any field of endeavor, there is no clear agreement as to who invented blogging. Certainly one widely quoted candidate is Justin Hall, who, in January 1994, while a student at Swarthmore College, Pennsylvania, created *Justin's Links from the Underground*. Starting as an early guide to the Internet, it gradually evolved to incorporate intimate details of Hall's own everyday life. In December 2004, *New York Times Magazine* referred to him as "the founding father of personal blogging." However, it was several years before blogging started to take off in a big way. To give an illustration as to how things developed, within a year of its launch in 1996, the website Xanga had only 100 online diaries; by the start of 2006 there were well over 20 million.

The popularity of blogging rocketed when the first hosted blog tools began to appear in the late 1990s, with OpenDiary being credited as the first blog community where readers could add comments to blog entries written by others. In August 1999, Pyra Labs launched Blogger, a free service that provided for the first time an easy set of tools for any nontechnical person to set up a blog.

The first blogs to make a big impression were political in nature, with names such as Andrew Sullivan, Ron Gunzburger, and Taegan Goddard coming to prominence. Indeed, in 2002, blogging was largely responsible for forcing the resignation of U.S. Senator Trent Lott from a leadership post, when a speech honoring former presidential candidate Strom Thurmond was interpreted by some as supporting racial segregation. The mainstream media only started reporting the story after it had arisen from the blogging community. This gave a boost in credibility to the idea of blogging as a serious medium of news dissemination.

Blogging evolved further during the recent war in Iraq, with Iraqi bloggers such as Salam Pax gaining widespread readership in the West. Additionally, many "warblogs" were created by serving military personnel, giving readers new perspectives on the realities of war, as well as alternative viewpoints from official news sources. Blogging is now more popular than ever, a recent study estimating that well over 30 million Americans were now regular readers.

Etymology

The term "weblog" was first used in 1997, coined by Jorn Barger in his influential early blog *Robot Wisdom*. The shorter form was introduced two years later by Peter Merholz, who jokingly cut "weblog" into the phrase "we blog" on his website. This was quickly adopted as both a noun and a verb.

How to Start Blogging

A blog can be a deeply personal document. You could think of it as being a cross between a personal telephone call and a newspaper column. You can share your favorite recipes, make public your most intimate thoughts, or, if so inclined, go off on the wildest of political rants. Of course, with millions of blogs now fighting for attention, yours will have to be something special to gain public attention, so it's worth putting some thought into what you are about to do. Here are some steps to getting on the blogging ladder.

Decide on your theme There are two general approaches to blogging. You can write on whatever subject happens to interest you at any moment in time—rather like a diary—or select a single theme and stick with it. If you want your blog to develop a following, the latter approach will be better—people with similar interests are more likely to keep returning for more.

Choose your service There are many developer-hosted blog sites from which you can choose. Among them are Xanga (**http://www.xanga.com**), Blogger (**http://www.blogger.com**), and LiveJournal (**http://www.livejournal.com**). These are all free to use. Other more sophisticated sites, such as BlogIdentity (**http://www.blogidentity.com**) and Bubbler (**http://www.bubbler.com**), charge for the service. Another possibility is to use a downloadable offline blogging client. This is in essence a word processor for blogging—you can write when you're not online and then upload your post when you connect to the Internet. BlogJet and Ecto are two such examples.

Customize your space Most blog spaces give you some control over the way they look. For example, you can decide on the colors, number of columns, and the overall look of your page. You may also want to consider other media, such as images, sounds, or video clips.

Get writing This is the difficult part. The best advice for novice writers is to keep posts brief, and write about what you know. If you have specialist information your blog is more likely to gain a following. Many bloggers begin with an introductory post, telling prospective readers why they have started their blog and the kinds of things they intend to write about. Be confident: if you're taking the trouble to create a blog, it's presumably because you want others to read your work.

Develop your persona Before you finalize your blog, take a look at as many others as possible. See what your rivals are doing, and note the things you like and dislike. You'll see quickly that there is more to most blogs than just the posts themselves. Many blogging applications allow you to add your own lists to your page. Here you can note the books you are reading or music you are listening to. You can also incorporate third-party services into your blog, enabling your readers to subscribe to your site.

Going public When you choose your blogging service, try to establish if it automatically "pings" the most important weblog tracking sites—most of them will do this automatically. This means checking if your service (or offline software) sends notifications to tracking sites to alert them that you have posted a new entry. This will open your blog to search engines. If your service does not do this automatically, you could use a third party such as Pingomatic (**http://pingomatic.com**), which allows you to choose which tracking sites you wish to update. You can also manually enter your pings—a list is shown in the box below.

Build a relationship with your readers There's only one way to gain a following and that's by making frequent postings. If people like what you write, they will come back; if there's nothing new to read, they will soon lose interest. At some point, it comes down to making a commitment and sticking to it. And don't forget, the more you blog, the better you'll become at it.

Manual Pings

Here is a list of websites where you can manually "ping" the most important weblog tracking sites:

http://api.my.yahoo.com/rss/ping
http://bblog.com/ping.php
http://bitacoras.net/ping
http://blog.goo.ne.jp/XMLRPC
http://blogdb.jp/xmlrpc
http://bulkfeeds.net/rpc
http://coreblog.org/ping
http://ping.blo.gs
http://ping.cocolog-nifty.com/xmlrpc
http://ping.rootblog.com/rpc.php
http://ping.syndic8.com/xmlrpc.php
http://ping.weblogs.se
http://rcs.datashed.net/RPC2
http://rpc.blogrolling.com/pinger
http://rpc.pingomatic.com
http://rpc.technorati.com/rpc/ping
http://rpc.weblogs.com/RPC2
http://topicexchange.com/RPC2
http://www.a2b.cc/setloc/bp.a2b
http://www.weblogues.com/RPC

Blogger

http://www.blogger.com

Launched by Pyra Labs in 1999, Blogger was one of the earliest dedicated blog-publishing tools, and it is widely believed to have helped popularize the format. In February 2003, Pyra Labs was bought out by Google. Blogs can now either be hosted on Google's server (on the **blogspot.com** domain), externally on a user's own domain, or on the user's own server.

Creating Your First Blog

Now let's take a look at how to use Blogger, and create a space of your own to produce your first blog.

• Enter the URL **http://www.blogger.com** in your web browser. In the Blogger home page, click on the arrowed button marked **Create Your Blog Now**. You first need to set up a Google account, so enter the requested details and click on the **Continue** button.

• The resulting screen enables you to set up your blog. First, create a title for your blog and then create a unique URL where it will reside—if you want that to be on the Blogger server, you must come up with a unique prefix for the blogspot.com domain. When you've chosen a name, enter it in the **Blog Address (URL)** box and click on the **Availability** button—this will tell you if that name has already been taken. Now click on the **Continue** button.

• Blogger provides you with a number of preset visual templates. Click on any individual screen that you find attractive and then on the **Preview Template** button to see a full-size example of how it will look. Click on the **Continue** button when you have made your choice.

- The next screen confirms that your blog has been set up. To write your first blog, click on the button marked **Start Posting**.

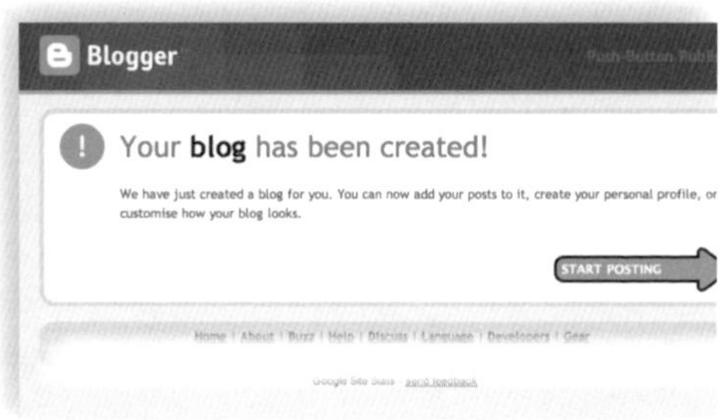
Blogger
Your blog has been created!
We have just created a blog for you. You can now add your posts to it, create your personal profile, or customise how your blog looks.
START POSTING

- Now all you have to do is write your blog. Before you decide to publish, you can click on the **Preview** button to see how it will look. If you don't get the opportunity to finish, you can click on **Save As Draft** and go back to it another time. When you're happy with your work, click on the **Publish** button.

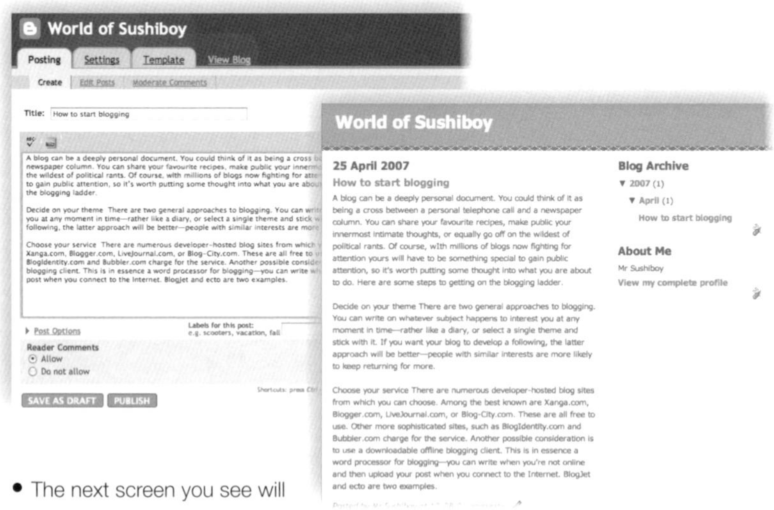
World of Sushiboy
Posting
Settings
Template
View Blog
Create
Edit Posts
Moderate Comments
Title: How to start blogging
Post Options
Reader Comments
Allow
Do not allow
SAVE AS DRAFT
PUBLISH
World of Sushiboy
25 April 2007
How to start blogging
A blog can be a deeply personal document. You could think of it as being a cross between a personal telephone call and a newspaper column. You can share your favourite recipes, make public your innermost intimate thoughts, or equally go off on the wildest of political rants. Of course, with millions of blogs now fighting for attention yours will have to be something special to gain public attention, so it's worth putting some thought into what you are about to do. Here are some steps to getting on the blogging ladder.
Decide on your theme There are two general approaches to blogging. You can write on whatever subject happens to interest you at any moment in time—rather like a diary, or select a single theme and stick with it. If you want your blog to develop a following, the latter approach will be better—people with similar interests are more likely to keep returning for more.
Choose your service There are numerous developer-hosted blog sites from which you can choose. Among the best known are Xanga.com, Blogger.com, LiveJournal.com, or Blog-City.com. These are all free to use. Other more sophisticated sites, such as BlogIdentity.com and Bubbler.com charge for the service. Another possible consideration is to use a downloadable offline blogging client. This is in essence a word processor for blogging—you can write when you're not online and then upload your post when you connect to the Internet. BlogJet and ecto are two examples.
Blog Archive
2007 (1)
April (1)
How to start blogging
About Me
Mr Sushiboy
View my complete profile

- The next screen you see will be your finalized blog.

If you return to your main page—referred to as the "dashboard," you will find plenty of other options for managing your blog, including adding your own profile and any preferred lists.

Other Blogging Sites

The more you encounter Web 2.0-style applications, you'll see that there is vast crossover in many of their features. For example, many of the best-known social networking sites, such as MySpace, have blogging facilities of their own. The list shown below concentrates on those sites that are primarily aimed at writing or editing blogs. They are all what is termed "developer-hosted" sites, meaning that they are all web-based applications.

BattleBlog	http://www.battleblog.com	Blurb	http://www.blurb.com
Bitty	http://bitty.com	Cocomment	http://www.cocomment.com
Blip	http://www.blip.tv	Feedblitz	http://www.feedblitz.com
Blog.com	http://www.blog.com	Freevlog	http://www.freevlog.org
Blogburst	http://www.blogburst.com	LifeType	http://www.lifetype.com
BlogCity	http://www.bogcity.com	LiveJournal	http://www.livejournal.com
Blogcode	http://blocode.com	Measuremap	http://measuremap.com
Bloggersnap	http://www.bloggersnap.com	Qumana	http://www.qumana.com
Bloggoggle	http://www.bloggoggle.com	Textamerica	http://www.textamerica.com
Blogladder	http://www.blogladder.com	Talkr	http://www.talkr.com
Bloglet	http://www.bloglet.com	Vox	http://www.vox.com
Blogniscient	http://www.blogniscient.com	WordPress	http://www.wordpress.com
Blogs	http://blo.gs	Xanco	http://www.xanco.com
Bloxor	http://www.bloxor.com	Xanga	http://www.xanga.com

Offline blogging software

Here is a list of some of the most useful offline blogging software. They all have their own websites where they can be downloaded for free. Type the name of the software into any search engine and you should be able to find them easily.

Apache Roller	http://rollerweblogger.org	LiveJournal	http://www.livejournal.com
B2evolution	http://b2evolution.net	Mephisto	http://mephistoblog.com
BBlog	http://www.bblog.com	Nucleus	http://www.nucleuscsm.com
Beta-Blogger	http://www.umsu.de/beta-blogger/	Pivotlog	http://www.pivotlog.net
Blosxom	http://www.blosxom.com	Serendipity	http://www.s9y.org
DotClear	http://www.dotclear.net	SimplePHP	http://www.simplephpblog.com
Drupal	http://www.drupal.org	Slash	http://www.slashcode.com
Geeklog	http://www.geeklog.net	Subtext	http://subtextproject.com
Horizon	http://www.edgedrive.com	Textpattern	http://textpattern.com
LifeType	http://www.lifetype.net	WordPress	http://www.wordpress.com

Bookmarks and Tagging

Just as we are able to place markers in a real book to remind of us of the page we've reached, or as a pointer to a piece of information we want to revisit in the future, so we can do the same on the Internet. Of course, this is not a radically new idea: almost every browser developed since the birth of the World Wide Web has had some kind of facility for storing and organizing URLs of favorite websites, allowing the user to return there at the click of a button. More recently, web-based applications have emerged, creating more sophisticated approaches to bookmarking or "tagging."

Multiple Tags

So what *are* these new developments? And do they *really* offer anything fundamentally different from the features included within our good old traditional web browsers? To begin with—as with most of the applications we're discussing in this book—storage is migrated from the desktop to the web, so when you bookmark a URL, it isn't retained by your browser, but on an external web server. This, of course, means you can access your collection of bookmarks on any computer, anywhere in the world.

More significantly, these applications recognize that the most useful information retrieval systems require any piece of information to be stored under a variety of different categories. Traditional browser-based systems, such as Internet Explorer (*shown below*), can have bookmarks stored only within a single suitably named folder—perhaps **news**, **sports**, **music,** or **cinema**. To retrieve a page the user would have to know *exactly* which category folder it had been stored in, or else flick through every single bookmark that had been saved. Dedicated bookmarking applications, on the other hand, allow for the allocation of any number of category "tags" to any stored bookmark. So, for example, a story from the *New York Times* about David Beckham joining the Los Angeles Galaxy soccer team might be tagged under a number of different categories: **New York Times**, **David**

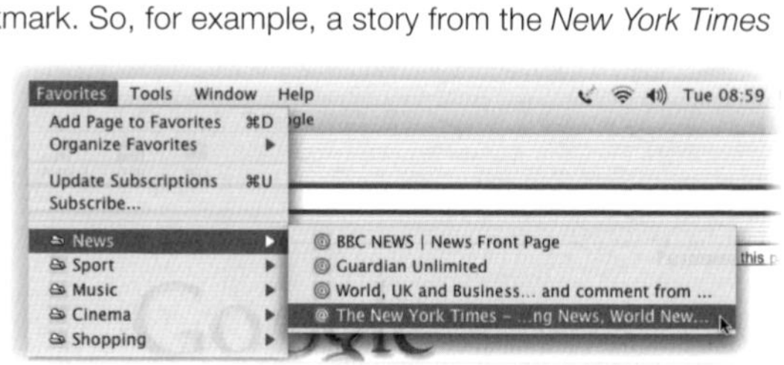

Beckham, **Los Angeles Galaxy**, **Major League Soccer**, or any other tag the user might deem suitable. It then becomes possible to view all of the bookmarks associated with any tag as a single list.

Social Bookmarking

Applying multiple tags would clearly enable us to organize our bookmarks in a much more sophisticated way than was hitherto possible. However, the most interesting aspect of this development is what has been termed "social bookmarking." This means that if you use one of these bookmarking websites, you may also make your stored information available to the rest of the world. This enables ranked lists of universal bookmarks to be created within any category. Furthermore, some websites—such as Del.icio.us—even create the possibility of communication with other users who have similar bookmarks.

In fact, it could be argued that sharing tagged information is a more effective way of finding useful data on the Internet than by using traditional search engines such as Yahoo! or Google. This is based on the premise that tag-based classification is done by *real* people, who *understand* the content of the web page, rather than search engine software "spiders" that algorithmically attempt to figure out whether a piece of data is relevant.

Of course, in true Web 2.0 style, the more people who use the application, the "richer" it becomes—as more and more people bookmark the pages they find useful, those same pages will be allocated a higher ranking. Thus, if you take a look at any single category, the entries at top end of the list will be the pages bookmarked by the most people.

Folksonomy

The idea of a population of end users creating and naming categories according to their own free will is known as a "folksonomy." And this is simultaneously the greatest strength and weakness of the whole idea of social bookmarking. A professionally created taxonomy, or categorization system, will use unambiguous terminology and will generally comprise a sophisticated hierarchy. A folksonomy, on the other hand, is open ended. It can be created quickly, on the fly, and molded entirely to the needs of the individual. Critics of folksonomies as a basis for indexing and retrieving information would argue that the overall effectiveness of the system is heavily defused by polysemy (tags having multiple related meanings), synonyms (tags with the same or similar meanings), or simple inflections or misspellings.

Del.icio.us

http://del.icio.us

The first social bookmarking website we'll take a look at is Del.icio.us. Founded in 2003 by Joshua Schachter, Del.icio.us is siginificantly responsible for the popularity of the whole tagging concept.

Like many modern Internet entrepreneurs, Joshua Schacter is a self-confessed "geeky guy," who created and ran Del.icio.us largely on his own while still holding down a day job as a programmer for Morgan Stanley in New York City. He only turned full time on his project in March 2005, but by the end of that year had sold Del.icio.us to Yahoo! for a figure rumored to be in the region of $30 million.

The Del.icio.us concept is extremely simple: a non-hierarchical keyword indexing system where users can tag their bookmarks with any number of freely chosen category names. Everything posted to Del.icio.us is publicly viewable by default, although users are able to mark specific bookmarks as private if they so wish. A combined universal view of all bookmarks with a given tag is available—for instance, the URL **http://del.icio.us/tag/sports** will display all of the most recent links that have been tagged **sports**. It also features a **hotlist** on its home page, as well as **popular** and **recent** page options. This also makes the website potentially effective in highlighting popular trends at any given moment in time.

Interestingly, Del.icio.us has a URL of **http://del.icio.us**. Although this may look a little odd, lacking the usual "www" prefix, this is an example of what is known as a "domain hack"—an unconventional domain name created by combining domain labels to spell out a "real" name.

How Does Del.icio.us Work?

As a website, Del.icio.us is very simple to use. Once you've created an account, with a user ID and password, you are asked to drag two buttons into your web browser menu: **post to del.icio.us** and **my del.icio.us**. Clicking on the former will bookmark the website you are currently viewing; clicking the latter will enable you to view all of your bookmarks and tags in a variety of different ways. (By the way, for those who are nervous about the idea of storing personal data on a remote server, Del.icio.us bookmarks can also be exported into most of the popular browsers.)

So let's take a more detailed look at some of the features you can expect to use in Del.icio.us, beginning with the account creation process.

Registration

Let's begin by creating a Del.icio.us account and setting up some posting buttons in your browser.

• Enter the URL **http://del.icio.us** in your web browser. You'll be directed to the Del.icio.us home page. Take a look at this page—it gives a pretty succinct rundown of what this application is all about. To get started, click on the **Register** button.

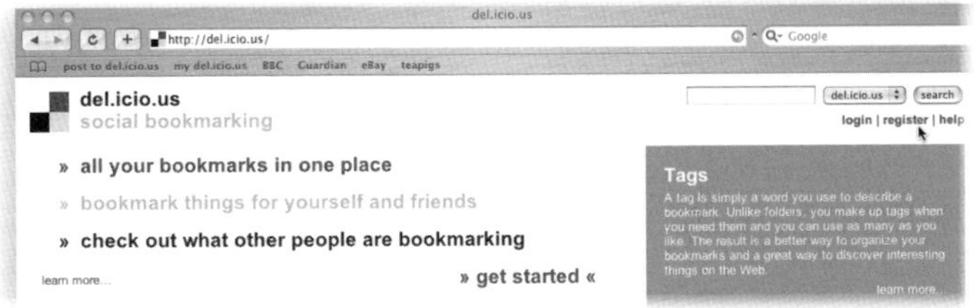
del.icio.us
http://del.icio.us/
del.icio.us
social bookmarking
login | register | help
» all your bookmarks in one place
» bookmark things for yourself and friends
» check out what other people are bookmarking
learn more...
» get started «
Tags
A tag is simply a word you use to describe a bookmark. Unlike folders, you make up tags when you need them and you can use as many as you like. The result is a better way to organize your bookmarks and a great way to discover interesting things on the Web.
learn more...

• This takes you to the first part of the registration page. Enter a **user name** (the name you want to known as to other Del.icio.us users), your **full name**, a **password**, repeat the password, enter your **e-mail** address, type in the visual code—the letters shown in the box—and then click on the button marked **register**.

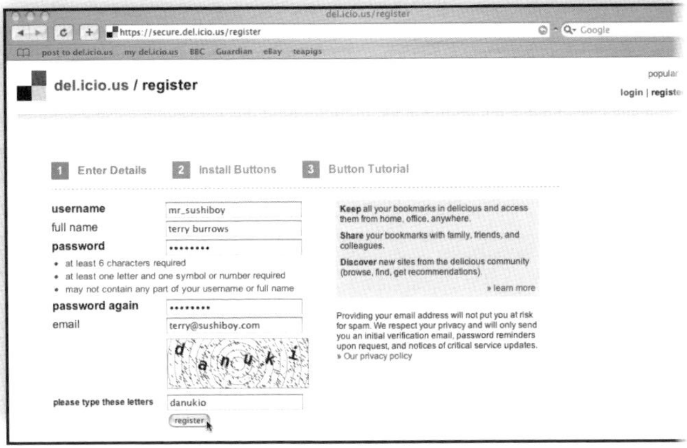
del.icio.us/register
https://secure.del.icio.us/register
del.icio.us / register
1 Enter Details
2 Install Buttons
3 Button Tutorial
username
mr_sushiboy
full name
terry burrows
password
at least 6 characters required
at least one letter and one symbol or number required
may not contain any part of your username or full name
password again
email
terry@sushiboy.com
please type these letters
danukio
register
Keep all your bookmarks in delicious and access them from home, office, anywhere.
Share your bookmarks with family, friends, and colleagues.
Discover new sites from the delicious community (browse, find, get recommendations).
» learn more
Providing your email address will not put you at risk for spam. We respect your privacy and will only send you an initial verification email, password reminders upon request, and notices of critical service updates.
» Our privacy policy

Note: Ensure that that the e-mail address you give is a valid one—at the end of the registration process you will be sent an e-mail that contains a validation link.

• The second part of the registation process enables you to install your Del.icio.us buttons. Click on the arrow marked **post to del.icio.us** and drag it into the menu bar of your web browser. Do the same for the button marked **my del.icio.us**.

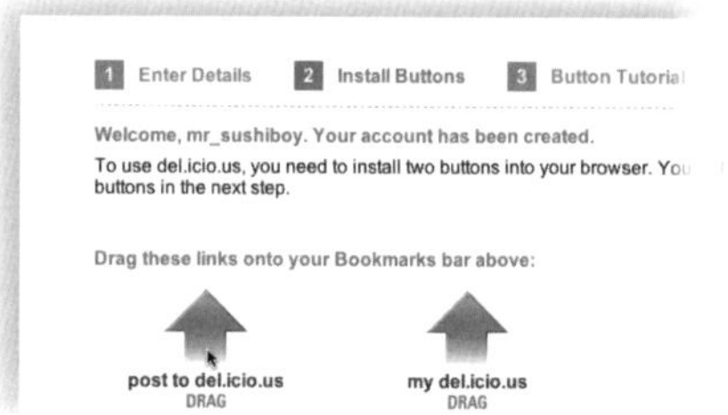

• The menu bar in your browser should now look something like the one shown above. (Different browsers may look slightly different from one another.) Now click on the button marked **proceed to step 3**.

• After you've read the button tutorial, click on the button marked **view your saved pages now**. This will take you to your personal Del.icio.us page. After you have answered the validation e-mail we mentioned on the previous page, your screen will look like this. You will now be able to access this page on any computer armed with a web browser by entering the URL **http://del.icio.us/your username**—in this example, that would be **http://del.icio.us/mr_sushiboy**.

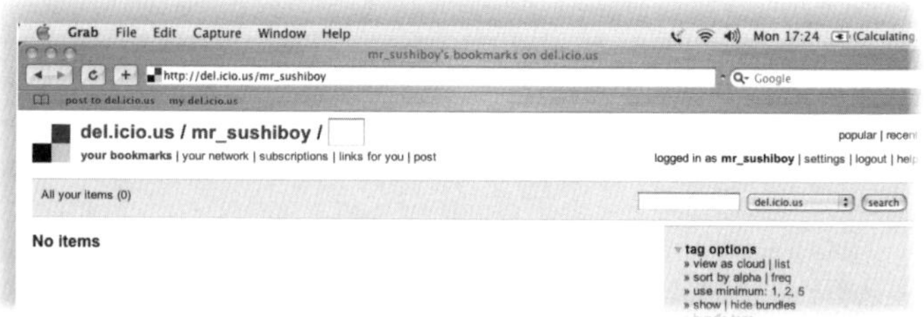

At this moment, of course, the page is marked **no items**, because no bookmarks have yet been created. So let's move on to that subject right now.

Bookmarking and Viewing

Once you've set up the menu bar buttons, bookmarking and viewing pages is a very simple process.

- Begin by opening your browser and typing in the URL for the *New York Times*—that's **http:///www.nytimes.com**. To bookmark this website, click on the button marked **post to del.icio.us** on your web menu bar.

- This will open your own Del.icio.us page.You will see that there are four text areas that relate to the web page: **Url** takes the web address of the site being bookmarked; **Description** takes the header information from the web page; **Notes** appears as an empty box—here you can enter any descriptive data you choose. The box marked **Tags** is where you select a category—we'll look at this in more detail on page 34. When you have finished, click on **save**, and you'll be returned to the web page you have just bookmarked. When you next open your Del.icio.us page, the bookmark you've just listed will be visible.

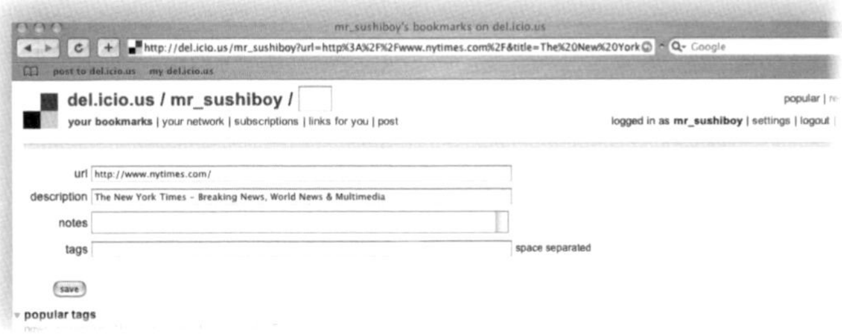

Tagging with Del.icio.us

It would, of course, be quite possible to view your bookmarks as a single list, scrolling through until you find exactly what you're looking for. That's fine if you only have a few bookmarks stored, but a dull, time-consuming process if you have several thousand. So Del.icio.us makes life a little easier by enabling you to apply tags to any bookmark you've saved. A tag is simply a category that enables you to store bookmarks into meaningful groups of your own choosing. So for the home page for the *New York Times*, you could apply a tag called **newspapers** to your bookmark. If you were then to look at your list of tags (which can be found on the right of your Del.icio.us screen) and click on **newspapers**, ONLY bookmarks for those sites that have been similarly tagged will appear on the screen. Let's see how to do that right now.

Adding Tags

Re-open the Del.icio.us page that we just created. As you can see, there is just one entry bookmarked. Click on the **edit** button alongside the name of the website. The screen that appears will show a number of edit options for this bookmark.

- The box marked **tags** enables you to assign a variety of different categories to any bookmark. You can either type your tags in by hand, leaving a space between each one, or select them from one of the lists at the bottom of the page. If you look at the list marked **popular tags**, this shows how other Del.icio.us users have tagged this same website. If you click on the tag **newspapers**, you will see that it appears immediately in the box. Click on **save** to finish. This will take you back to the bookmarked website.

Multiple Tags

So is this *really* so different from keeping bookmarks in categorized folders within your web browser? It is: the power of

Del.icio.us is in that it allows you to apply *multiple* tags to any bookmark.

If you look again at the entry we just created, and click on the **edit** button once again, you can create additional tags. In this example, choosing more from the **popular tags** list, you might add a further tag called **news** and another called **nyc**.

Clearly Del.icio.us enables users to create a very powerful indexing and cross-referencing system that no web browser could match. If you were to bookmark cocktail recipes, you could create tags for their ingredients—if, say, you clicked on a tag marked "rum," you could expect to get a list of all the cocktails in your list that featured rum as one of its ingredients.

Filtering with Tags

When you first go into your Del.icio.us page, on the left of the screen you will see a simple list of bookmarks, with the most recent entry showing first. If you now take a look on the opposite side of the screen you'll see information about your tags. As you can see, there are entries for the three tags that you have so far set up—**news**, **newspapers**, and **nyc**.

Let's now suppose that many new additional bookmarks had been set up for this account, using many different types of tag. On the left-hand side of the screen

you'll see a scrolling list of ALL of your stored bookmarks; on the right there is a list of all the different tags you've set up. If you click on the **news** tag you'll see that your list of bookmarks has now been reduced to ONLY those that have had the same tag applied.

Social Bookmarking in Action

Now let's take a practical look at some of the *social* aspects of Del.icio.us.

Popular Tags

On the top right-hand side of the Del.icio.us screen (above the login information) you'll see a button marked **popular**. Click on this button.

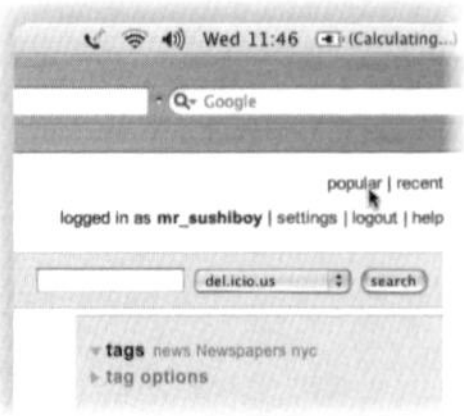

• The screen that follows shows two distinct types of information. On the left of the screen you'll see a list of the most recently popular sites to have been bookmarked. On the opposite side of the screen you'll find a list of the most popular tags created and used within Del.icio.us. Now click on the button marked **see more tags**.

• On display here is what is known as a "cloud" of tags. They are shown by default in an alphabetical sequence—the size of the typeface used indicates its relative popularity. Each tag is also a "live" button. So let's click on the one marked **games** to see what happens.

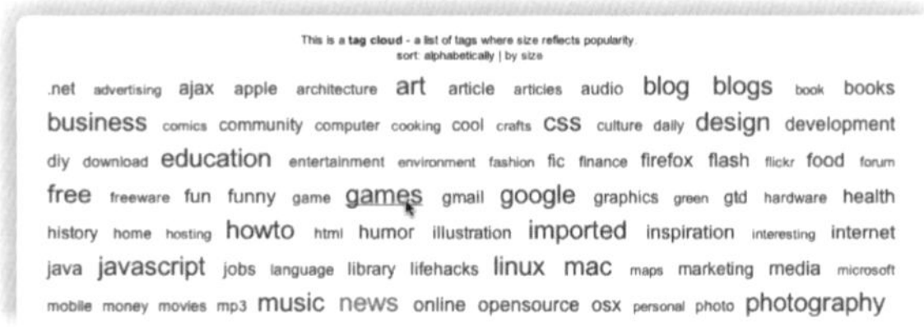

• The resulting screen presents a list of the most recently bookmarked websites. Beneath the description of each website you'll find the user name of the person who created the bookmark, and the category tags that were applied. Now let's click on one of the user names in the list.

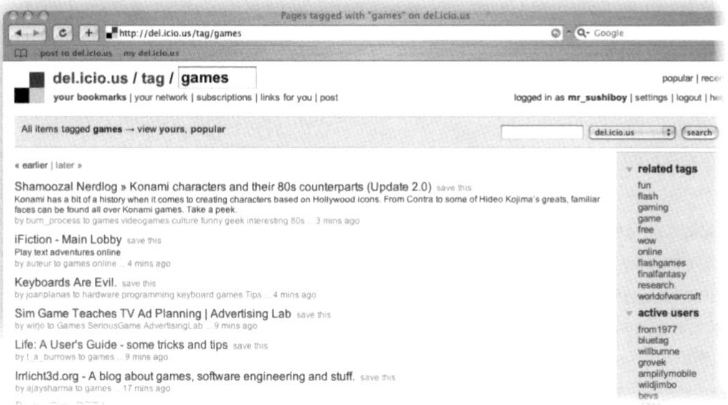

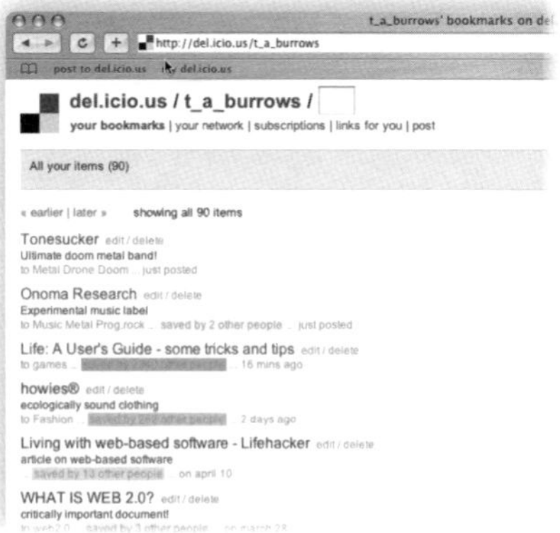

• You're now able to look at that individual's personal Del.icio.us screen—or at least all of the items that have been made public. Any of the bookmarks you see in the list you can click on to view the linked website.

Tag Stars

As has sometimes happened with the blogging phenomenon of the past five years, some "taggers" have been so successful in building up online reputations based on the quality of their links that they have been pursued by website owners who believe that inclusion in a specific bookmark list may have commercial benefits.

Digg

http://www.digg.com

Digg is a news website that combines social bookmarking and blogging with democratic editorial control. Stories are chosen for the site not by an editor, but by community members.

News stories and websites are submitted by Digg users, and appear in an **Upcoming Stories** list on the main page. These can then be ranked by other users by clicking a "digg it" symbol. Entries with the highest number of "diggs" will appear in the **Popular Stories** list. Each one may be tagged and searched under a number of different categories. All stories fall under one of the main headings of **Technology**, **Science**, **World & Business**, **Sports**, **Entertainment,** and **Gaming**. There is a separate area in which videos and podcasts can also be "dugg."

On the surface, Digg would appear to be democratic in its aim of highlighting the most popular stories on the Internet. However, critics have claimed that self-censorship enables sensationalism or misinformation to thrive. Furthermore, Digg also has a facility to "bury" stories—if a sufficient number of "buries" are received, the story is dropped from the website. This feature is intended to allow users to filter out spam, but there's some suspicion that it may have been used by groups of people to remove stories containing opinions countering their own.

Digg was created by Californian Internet celebrity Kevin Rose and launched at the end of 2004. It is now ranked among the 100 most heavily used websites online.

Digg in Action

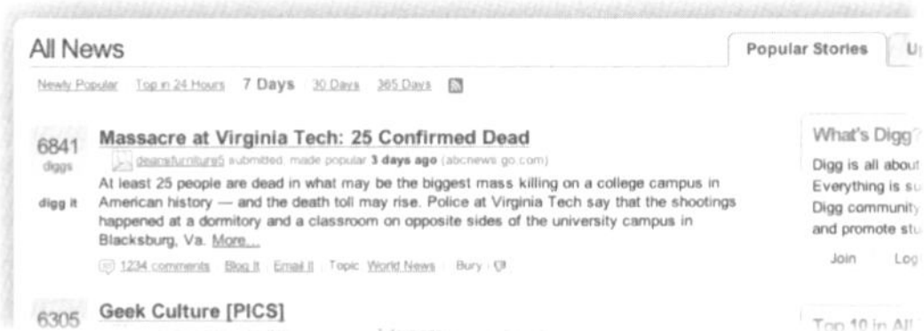

To try out Digg, type **http://www.digg.com** into your web browser. When the main screen appears, click on the tab marked **7 Days**. What follows is a list of the stories to have been submitted over the past week with the most "diggs." Other options exist for similarly popular stories over the last day, month, and year. To view a story from the list, all you have to do is click on the title, which opens the URL in a new browser window. To "digg" a story, click the **digg it** button to the left of the URL.

Submitting an Article

Find the story you wish to add to Digg and make a note of its URL. Click on the button marked **Submit a New Story**.

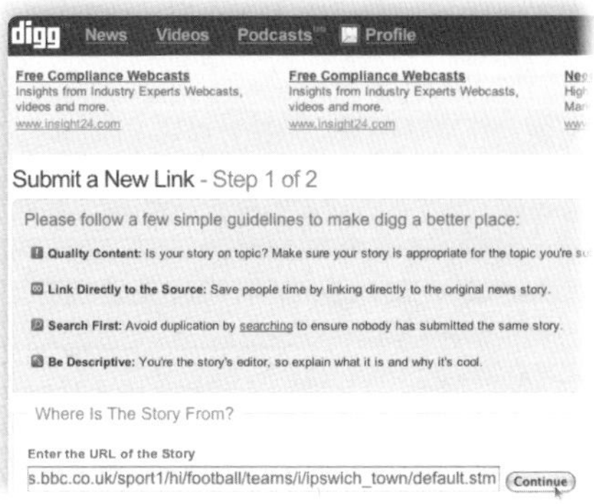
digg
News
Videos
Podcasts
Profile
Free Compliance Webcasts
Insights from Industry Experts Webcasts, videos and more.
www.insight24.com
Free Compliance Webcasts
Insights from Industry Experts Webcasts, videos and more.
www.insight24.com
Submit a New Link - Step 1 of 2
Please follow a few simple guidelines to make digg a better place:
Quality Content: Is your story on topic? Make sure your story is appropriate for the topic you're
Link Directly to the Source: Save people time by linking directly to the original news story.
Search First: Avoid duplication by searching to ensure nobody has submitted the same story.
Be Descriptive: You're the story's editor, so explain what it is and why it's cool.
Where Is The Story From?
Enter the URL of the Story
s.bbc.co.uk/sport1/hi/football/teams/i/ipswich_town/default.stm
Continue

• On the screen that follows, read Digg's editorial guidelines and satisfy yourself that your choice fulfills its quality-control criteria. Enter the story's URL and click on the button marked **Continue**.

• Step 2 of the submission process allows you to check the URL, give the story a title, description, and category, and preview it before publication. If everything is fine, click on the **Submit Story** button.

Submit a New Link - Step 2 of 2
Story Details
URL of the News Story:
http://news.bbc.co.uk/sport1/hi/football/teams/i/ipswich_town/default.stm
Story Title
BBC Sport - Ipswich Town
Story Description
What's happening at Ipswich Town FC as reported by the BBC.

• When you submit a story, Digg will do some automated checks to see if the same story, or a similar one, has already been submitted. A list of any likely candidates will be shown. If you are happy that you are not duplicating, click on the button marked **Continue, Submit**.

• The confirmation screen tells you that your submission is now queued up and is due to join the **upcoming stories** list.

• Now the story has been set up, and registered users can begin adding further information, such as comments and blogs.

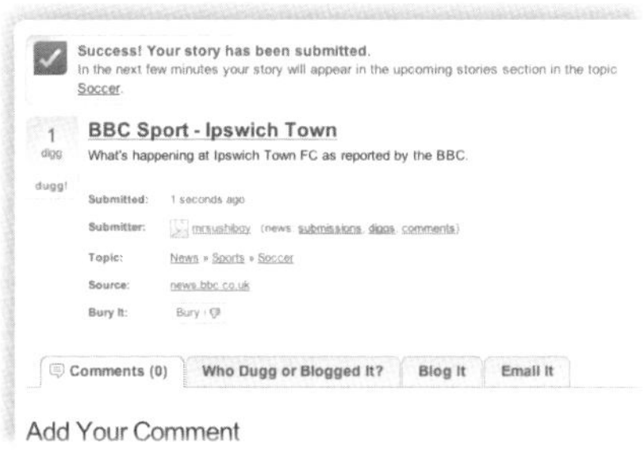
Success! Your story has been submitted.
In the next few minutes your story will appear in the upcoming stories section in the topic Soccer.
1
digg
dugg!
BBC Sport - Ipswich Town
What's happening at Ipswich Town FC as reported by the BBC.
Submitted: 1 seconds ago
Submitter:
Topic: News » Sports » Soccer
Source: news.bbc.co.uk
Bury It: Bury
Comments (0)
Who Dugg or Blogged It?
Blog It
Email It
Add Your Comment

StumbleUpon

http://www.stumbleupon.com

Another approach to bookmarking websites is the "recommendation" system used by StumbleUpon. Not a stand-alone website as such, StumbleUpon is a web browser plug-in that enables its users to discover and rate webpages, photos, videos, and news articles and recommend them to other like-minded users. Navigation is performed by downloading a plug-in toolbar and filling out a form detailing interests by category. Relevant web pages appear when the user clicks the **Stumble** button on the browser's toolbar—StumbleUpon decides which new web page to display based on the user's ratings of previous pages, ratings by friends, and the ratings of users with similar interests. The new web page can be rated using the **thumbs up** or **thumbs down** buttons.

StumbleUpon uses what is known as "collaborative filtering," a combination of human opinion and automated interpretation of a user's personal preference, to create a social network. Users thus "stumble upon" pages explicitly recommended by friends, peers, and like-minded people.

Using the StumbleUpon Toolbar

Enter **http://www.stumbleupon.com** in your web browser, and click on the button marked **Join StumbleUpon Today**. Once you've worked through the registration process you will be given the option of downloading the toolbar. As this is a plug-in, you'll need to quit and restart your browser for it to appear.

When you first click on the **Stumble** button, a category screen will appear. Tick the check boxes for any subjects that interest you. Next time you click on the Stumble button, a recommended web page will appear. You can rate it one way or another using the **thumb** buttons. The **Send to** button enables you to send recommendations to friends. The rest of the toolbar enables you to bookmark your chosen websites.

On the surface, this may seem like a slightly random form of web surfing. And yet, as with other social bookmarking applications, it is based on the recommendations of "real" people.

More Bookmarking and Tagging Sites

There are a great number of other social bookmarking sites that are worth investigating. A small selection is shown below. Like other applications and websites that appear throughout this book, many of the sites listed below would likely appear in a number of other categories. In the previous pages, we chose to highlight Del.icio.us not because it's necessarily the best product out there but because it is one of the most popular, and so its social content is increasingly enriched by the greater number of people who use it.

9rules	**http://www.9rules.com**
30 Day Tags	**http://www.30daytags.com**
AllYourWorlds	**http://www.allyourworlds.com**
Blinklist	**http://www.blinklist.com**
Blogmarks	**http://www.blogmarks.net**
Blummy	**http://www.blummy.com**
Bmaccess	**http://www.bmaccess.com**
Buddymarks	**http://www.buddymarks.com**
Butterfly	**http://www.butterflyproject.nl**
Chuquet	**http://www.chuquet.com**
Clipmarks	**http://www.clipmarks.com**
Connotea	**http://www.conotea.org**
Diigo	**http://www.diigo.com**
Dogear	**http://www.elgology.com/dogear**
Feedmarker	**http://www.feedmarker.com**
Furl	**http://www.furl.net**
Jeteye	**http://www.jeteye.com**
Listible	**http://www.listible.com**
ListMixer	**http://listmixer.com**
LiveMarks	**http://sandbox.sourcelabs.com**
LookLater	**http://www.looklater.com**
Magnolia	**http://ma.gnolia.com**
Mylinkvault	**http://www.mylinkvault.com**
Onlywire	**http://www.onlywire.com**
Philoi	**http://www.philoi.com**
Qoosa	**http://www.qoosa.com**
Searchfox	**http://www.searchfox.com**
Shadows	**http://shadows.com**
Simpy	**http://www.simpy.com**
Socialmarks	**http://www.socialmarks.com**
Spinspy	**http://www.spinspy.com**
Spurl	**http://www.spurl.net**
Startaid	**http://www.startaid.com**
Surftail	**http://www.surftail.com**
Taggle	**http://www.taggle.de**
Tagtooga	**http://www.tagtooga.com**
Tendango	**http://www.tendango.com**
Thumblicio.us	**http://thumblicio.us**
YahooMyweb2	**http://myweb2.search.yahoo.com**
Yoono	**http://www.yoono.com**
ZoomClouds	**http://www.zoomclouds.com**

Communications

What is the Internet all about if it isn't communication? Indeed, much of the thrust of the Web 2.0 debate has been about whether social networking has less to do with communicating with others and is *really* about creating a platform where lone voices can be heard—regardless of there necessarily being an audience for what they were saying. Well, in this section, we will be looking at developments in two-way communication. E-mail, of course, was one of the applications that initially created such a popular buzz in the early days of the Internet. However, two-way online communication can now also include telephone systems, voicemail, links to cell phones, and the bulk transfer of hefty volumes of data. And much of this can be done without paying a cent.

The E-mail Revolution

Since the middle of the 1990s, the widespread use of e-mail has had a truly radical impact on our daily lives. How many of us now even think about communicating by writing hard-copy letters? Why would we do that when we know we can send an e-mail that will arrived at its destination anywhere in the world within a few moments? While a lot of people still use specific e-mail software such as Mail, Outlook, Entourage, Windows Mail, or Eudora, a growing number are now dealing with their e-mails in a different way, by switching to "webmail."

What Is Webmail?

Webmail is not a new concept—Hotmail, one of the first popular webmail systems, is well over a decade old. At its most basic, webmail is simply a way of reading and writing e-mails via the Web. This approach does have some significant advantages over using dedicated software. First, your mail is stored remotely on a server, which means that it is accessible on any computer with an Internet connection and a web browser. Second, web applications, backups, upgrades and security are the responsibility of the host. On the downside, the user has to stay online to read and write mail.

The prime mover in the world of webmail is, once again, Google. The introduction of the seemingly all-encompassing GMail has led an ever-growing army of users to abandon their existing e-mail software.

GMail (Google Mail)

http://www.gmail.com

GMail—or Google Mail as it is officially known in some parts of the world—is a free AJAX-based webmail and POP3 e-mail service. It was first released as an invitation-only beta application in 2004. The fully functional version was made public in February 2007. As well as offering its own e-mail service, it can also gather mail from up to five other e-mail accounts. GMail also offers free storage space, so many users will never have to delete archived mails. Every GMail homepage also has a standard Google search capability.

Setting Up an Account

To create a GMail account, enter the URL: **http://www.gmail.com**. Click on the hot text labeled **SIgn Up for Google Mail**.

- In the account creation page, complete your personal details, including the GMail login name that will form part of your new e-mail address. When you're happy with this information, click on the button marked: **I Accept, Create My Account**.

- You'll then see your GMail homepage. This looks and works much like any other e-mail software. For example, if you click on the button marked **Compose Mail** a blank e-mail page will open up.

GMail Settings

One of GMail's most powerful assets is its ability to integrate other e-mail accounts. If, for example, you have several different e-mail addresses for different purposes, you can still access them via your GMail homepage. So let's look at how you can customize GMail.

• In your homepage, click on the text labeled **Settings**. (It can be found in the top right-hand corner of the screen.)

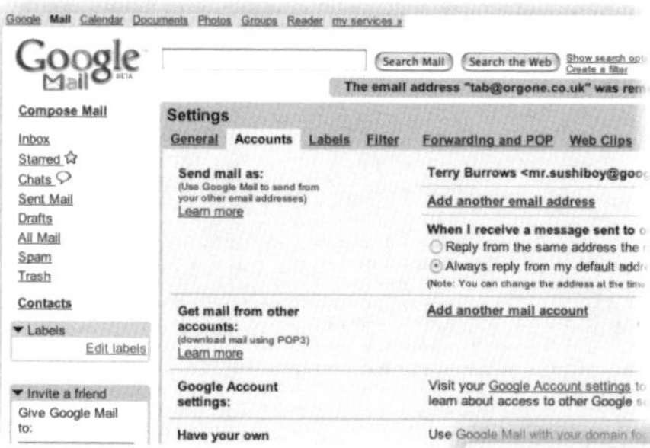

• The **Settings** window contains a number of tabbed pages. These equate broadly to the preferences options found in most e-mail software. If we click on the **Accounts** tab we start adding other e-mail addresses to the system.

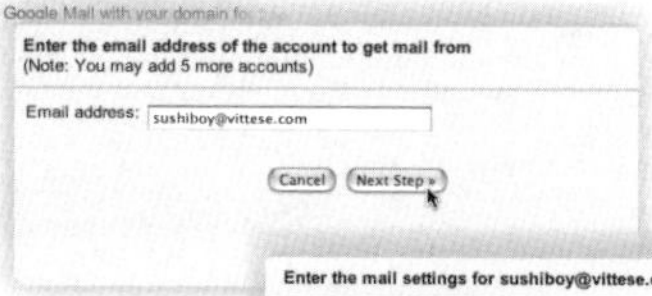

• Click on the text labeled **Add Another Mail Account**. This opens a pop-up window.

• Enter the e-mail address you want to add and then click on the **Next Step button**.

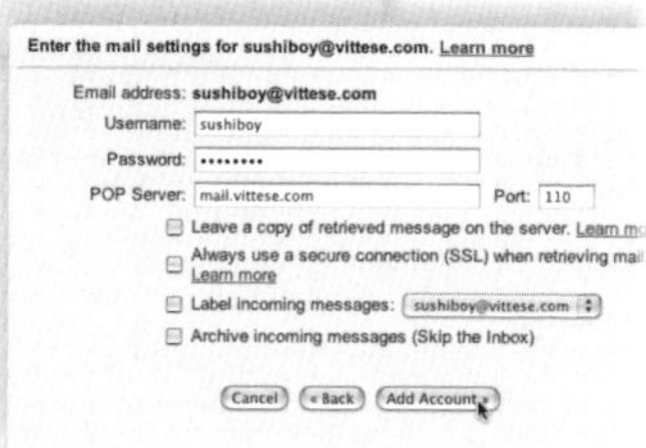

• A second pop-up window opens. Here you must add your POP3 data—typically, username, password, and the name of your POP server.

• Finally, click on the **Add Account** button. When you return to the **Settings/ Accounts** window you'll see that the newly entered e-mail address appears on the page. GMail will now automatically check this account at the same time as checking your GMail account.

Forwarding Mail to a Cell Phone

If you have a suitably equipped cell phone, you can set GMail to forward e-mails to your phone. (Note: this may not be possible in some countries outside the U.S. Your phone must have its own e-mail address, the prefix being a ten-digit number.)

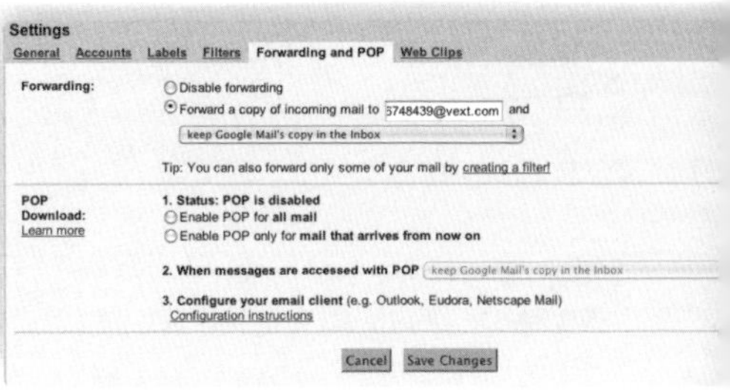

• In the **Settings** window, click on the tab marked **Forwarding and POP**. In the Forwarding section, enter your phone's e-mail address. Click on the **Save Changes** button. GMail will now automatically forward e-mails to your cell phone.

This really does just scratch the surface of what's possible with GMail. You'd be well advised to take a look at the various FAQs that Google has created to this end—**http://mail.google.com/mail/help/about.html**.

The GMail Hoax

Although its founders are among Àmerica's wealthiest entrepreneurs, Google's origins as a university research project occasionally resurface with bursts of geeky humor. In fact, Google usually now makes some kind of announcement to the world on April Fool's Day.

In 2002, Google came up with PigeonRank, a parody of its own PageRank system. The press release claimed that clusters of pigeons could be used to rank web pages faster than human editors or machine-based algorithms, and that PigeonRank provided the basis for all Google's web search tools.

In 2004, job ads were placed for Google's Copernicus Center, a ficticious research facility on the moon. The project was the development of a new operating system called Luna/X—a pun on Linux, and with a logo that looked remarkably like Windows XP.

In 2007, Google changed the GMail login page to announce a new service called Gmail Paper. This offered users of the service the opportunity to add e-mails to a "paper archive," which Google would print and return via traditional postal means.

The company has also announced genuine products on April Fool's Day. This marketing strategy has been used to make people think that a product is a hoax, spread the word virally, and then create publicity when it becomes clear that it is real. GMail itself was announced in this way. Since at that time (2004) a free e-mail service that featured one gigabyte of free storage space was unheard of, it looked quite like a feasible hoax.

Telephone and Messaging

One of the reasons for the growing popularity of Internet-based live communications systems is that they are cheap—or even free—to use. It's true that peer-to-peer voice and video systems have existed in the past, but they have now migrated from a technical user base toward those for whom computers have traditionally offered little in the way of allure. So let's take a look at some of the most popular of these applications.

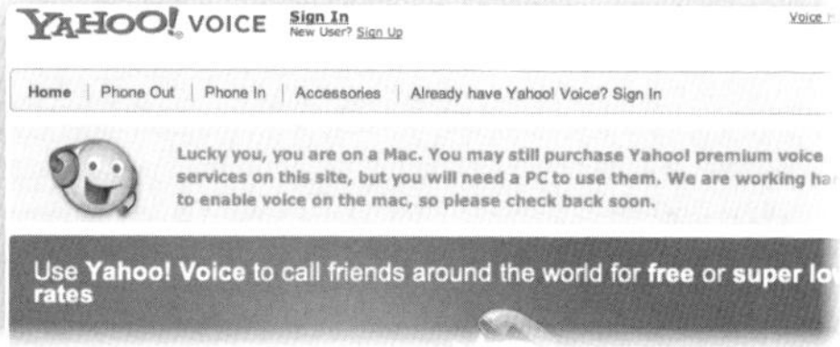
YAHOO! VOICE
Sign In
New User? Sign Up
Home | Phone Out | Phone In | Accessories | Already have Yahoo! Voice? Sign In
Lucky you, you are on a Mac. You may still purchase Yahoo! premium voice services on this site, but you will need a PC to use them. We are working
to enable voice on the mac, so please check back soon.
Use Yahoo! Voice to call friends around the world for free or
rates

Skype

http://www.skype.com

Skype is a peer-to-peer telephone network system developed by Niklas Zennström and Janus Friis—the duo that were also behind the file-sharing application Kazaa. The beta version of Skype was made available in 2003, and within two years its success was such that it was acquired by the eBay company. Skype's first wave of popularity came from the fact that any two suitably equipped individuals, anywhere in the world, could talk across the Internet for no cost at all. Users were required to have a computer fitted with a microphone and speaker, and a broadband Internet connection. Later, Skype evolved to incorporate moving images, so users with webcam-equipped computers could use it as a videophone system. As a business model, unlike many others operating in the field of technology, Skype has been able to evolve successfully with the introduction of a number of paid services, for example, calls from computers to landline phones. As of March 2007 there were 171 million users registered worldwide.

Installing Skype

Unlike most of the applications in this book, Skype is a piece of stand-alone software that runs on your computer. So the first stage is to download and install Skype on your computer.

• Enter the URL **http://www.skype.com** in the menu bar at the top of the screen and click on the button marked **Download**.

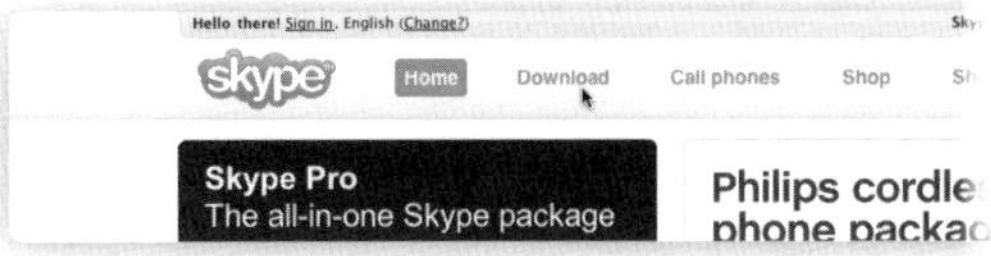

• The Skype download window will be loaded. From the menu list on the left of the screen, select your computer's operating system—Skype offers compatibility with Microsoft Windows and Apple Macintosh OSX. Click on the button marked **Download Now**.

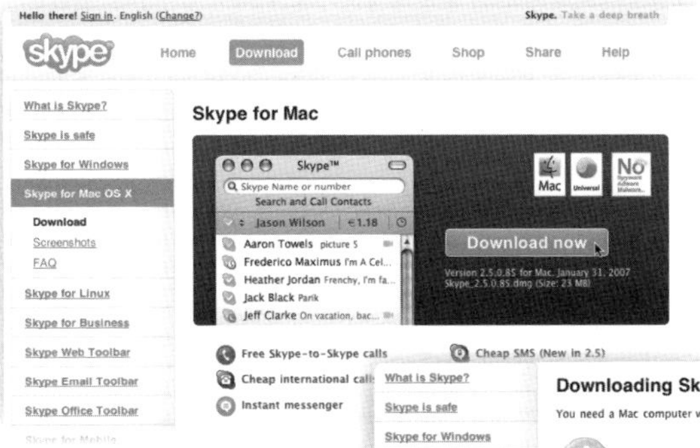

• A step-by-step instruction window will now appear. This will differ depending on the operating system you have selected.

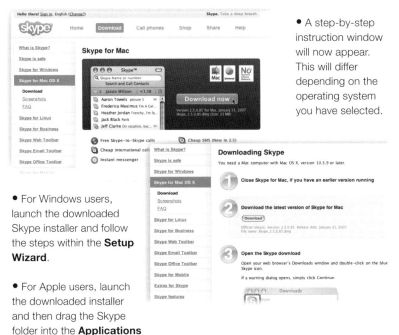

• For Windows users, launch the downloaded Skype installer and follow the steps within the **Setup Wizard**.

• For Apple users, launch the downloaded installer and then drag the Skype folder into the **Applications** folder.

You are now ready to launch Skype on either platform.

Making a Call with Skype

Here are the simple steps you need to follow to make telephone calls using Skype. Regular Skype calls—those made to other computers—are free of charge, even if you are at opposite ends of the world. Additionally, you can make SkypeOut calls from your computer to a regular telephone. These, however, are charged.

- Launch the Skype application. In the welcome screen you are asked to enter your **Skype Name** and **Password**. If you don't have one set up, click on the text labeled **Don't Have a Skype Name?**

- In the **Create a New Account** window, enter the name you want to use as your Skype identity, a password, and an e-mail address. Finally, click on the **Create** button. This will take you back to the welcome screen, but now your details will automatically appear in the correct boxes. Click on the **Sign In** button. Skype will open.

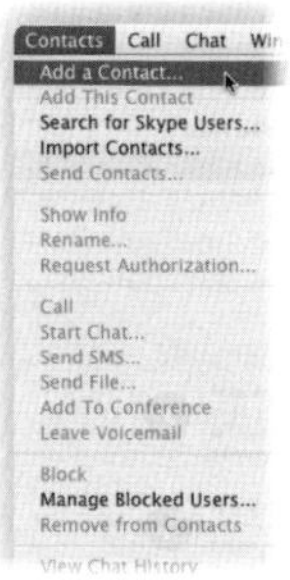

- From the **Contacts** menu, choose **Add a Contact**.

- The **Add a Skype Contact** window appears. Enter the name of the contact you wish to add, and then click on the **Search** button.

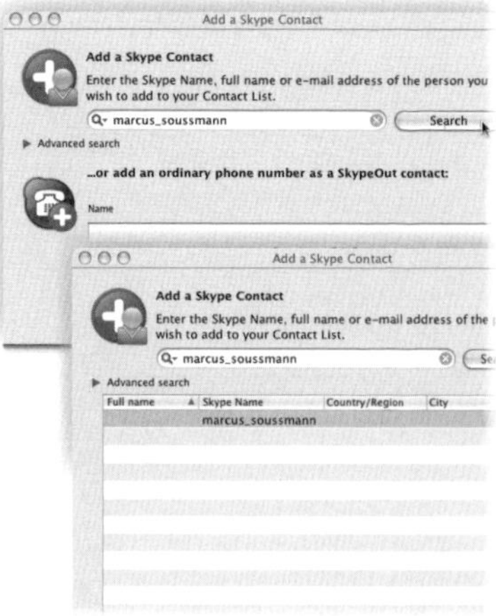

- Skype will now create a list of people of the name you entered. Highlight the correct entry in the list and click on the **Add Contact** button.

- A new window will pop up. This sends an immediate online notice to the person in

question, asking them if they would be happy for you to see when they are online. If they agree, you will receive a confirmation notice, and their name will appear in your list of contacts on the left of the main Skype screen.

• To begin making a call, highlight the Skype Name on your main screen. It will open out to include any profile information that your contact has set up. To make the call, click on the green telephone symbol on the right of the window.

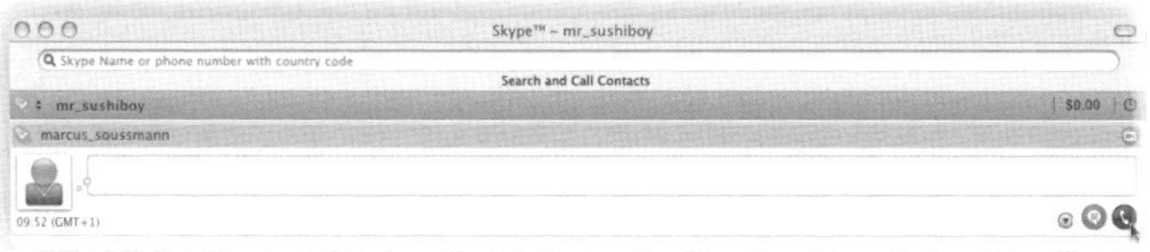

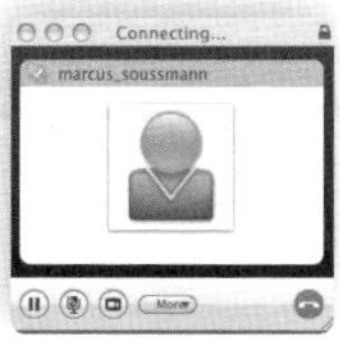

• A window headed **Connecting . . .** will pop up. If your contact has set up a profile, including an image, it will appear in this window.

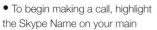

• When your contact answers, a new pop-up window will appear. If he or she has a webcam attached, you will be able to see that person while they are talking. If you both have webcams, your own video image will appear in a small box in the corner of the window. To end the call, click on the red telephone button in the corner of the window.

Avoiding Feedback

When making internet phone calls you can easily experience unpleasant "feedback" or echo effects when the sound from the loudspeaker is picked up by the microphone and then retransmitted. The easiest way to avoid this happening is to use a headset or a pair of earphones.

Instant Messaging with Skype

In addition to making Internet telephone calls, Skype also allows for online text messaging. It works in much the same way as making a telephone call.

- Highlight the name of your chosen contact, and click on the "word bubble" on the far right of the window.

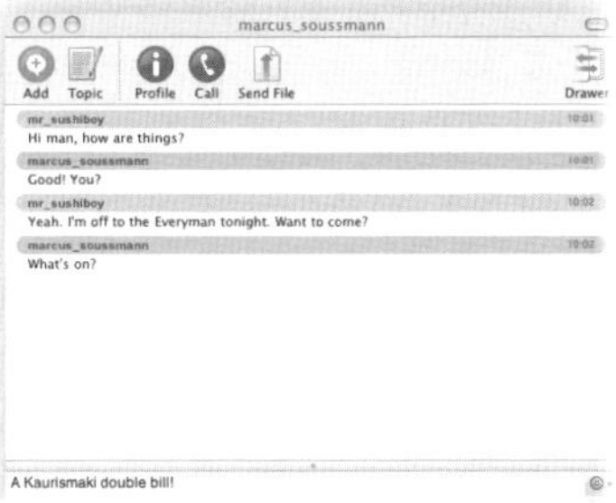
marcus_soussmann
Add
Topic
Profile
Call
Send File
Drawer
mr_sushiboy
10:01
Hi man, how are things?
marcus_soussmann
10:01
Good! You?
mr_sushiboy
10:02
Yeah. I'm off to the Everyman tonight. Want to come?
marcus_soussmann
10:02
What's on?
A Kaurismaki double bill!

- The chat window will now pop up. To send a text message, type in the panel at the bottom of the window and press the Enter key to transmit the message. It will then be moved to the window above.

- Any replies to your message will appear in the window, each message appearing on a separate line.

Meebo

http://www.meebo.com

The true value of any communications system comes down to one basic question. Are enough of the people you want to talk to using the same system? And if not, are the different systems compatible? This is where Meebo comes in. Through the main Meebo website you can access all of the major instant messaging systems—AIM, Yahoo!, Google Talk, MSN, ICQ, and Jabber—from a single portal. Individual chats take place in pop-up windows that you can then move around the screen. Meebo is a very neat system if you have a number of different online lives on different online chat networks.

- Enter the URL: **http://www.meebo.com**. Begin by setting up a Meebo account and password. Once you've done that, simply enter the ID and passwords for all of your instant messaging accounts, and then click on the **Sign On** button at the foot of the screen.

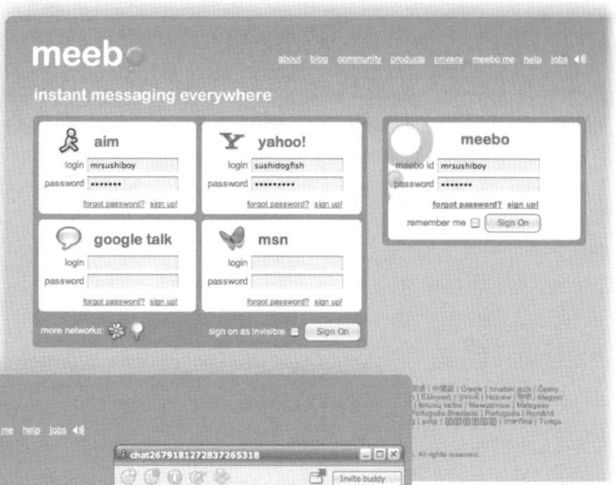

• In this example, accounts have been set up for the AOL Instant Messenger (AIM) and Yahoo! Messenger. The main page can also accommodate Google Talk and MSN.

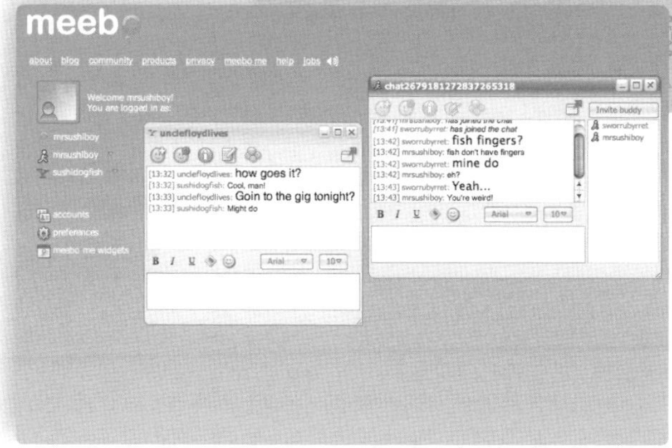

• Your Meebo homepage lists the active messengers on the left of the screen. Whenever a new IM comes your way, a new box will pop up in the window. Meebo uses a generic chat window regardless of which messenger is being used—you type your message at the foot of the screen and then press the **Enter** key to transmit—the running conversation will appear in the top half of the window.

Meebo Widget

Meebo also has a feature known as Meebo Me. This is a small chat window that can be inserted into any web page—such as MySpace—enabling visitors to chat with you. To set it up, click on **Meebo Me** on the menu bar. Name your window, add your ID and password, and Meebo will automatically generate the html code, which you can then copy and paste into your chosen website.

Sending Data

In the past, if we wanted to transfer data files via the Internet, we would simply send an e-mail with an attachment. And for small files this is still probably the simplest solution. However, most ISPs place some kind of upper limit on file sizes, and even if they don't, many company firewalls will prevent e-mails with large attachments from reaching their destinations. One solution is to use an FTP (File Transfer Protocol) system. However, most nonbusiness users don't have easy access to such facilities. A recent solution has come through the emergence of a number of web-based solutions. Let's look at one of the most widely used data transmission websites—YouSendIt.

YouSendIt

http://www.yousendit.com

Founded in 2003, YouSendIt is a temporary file-hosting website. The user uploads data files to the site along with the e-mail addresses of the proposed recipients. YouSendIt then forwards an e-mail to those addresses with a download link back to the file. Files are deleted after a week or a specific number of downloads. It markets itself as an alternative to sending large e-mail attachments. The company offers a number of different levels of service—simple transfers of files up to 100 MB in size are free, but monthly charges are levied for greater sizes or quantities.

- Enter the URL: **http://www.yousendit.com**.

- To send a file, enter the e-mail addresses of the recipients, your own e-mail address, and an optional message, and then select the file you want to transfer. Click on the **Send It** button.

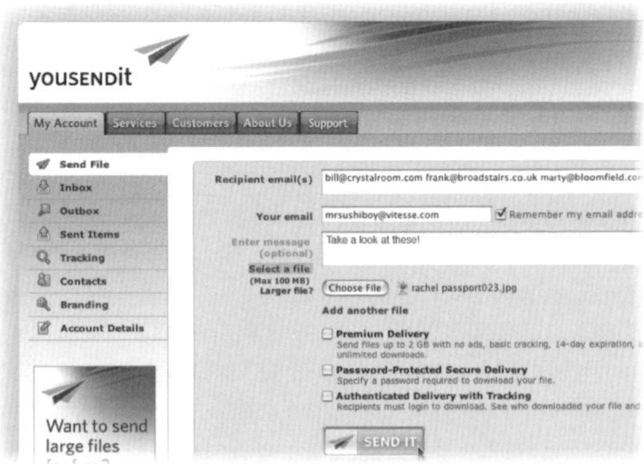

Other E-mail Applications

Many of the larger domain-hosting organizations also offer their own free webmail services. Since these are linked directly to the domain servers, it could be argued that they are likely to be faster and more reliable than a third party.

BigString	**http://www.bigstring.com**	**InBox**	**http://www.inbox.com**
FastMail	**http://www.fastmail.fm**	**MSN Hotmail**	**http://www.hotmail.com**
Goowy	**http://www.goowy.com**	**MyWay**	**http://www.myway.com**
HotPop	**http://www.hotpop.com**	**Yahoo! Mail**	**http://www.yahoo.com**

Other Telephone Applications

There's a growing market for Internet phones that operate without a computer but still communicate through a broadband connection. A number of the companies below operate in this field. They are worth looking into since they generally represent a far better financial deal than those offered by the traditional telecommunications organizations. The downside is that quality of sound and reliability of connection may not always match up to those of conventional landlines.

BroadVoice	**http://www.broadvoice.com**	**Packet 8**	**http://www.packet8.net**
FWD	**http://www.freeworlddialup.com**	**SunRocket**	**http://www.sunrocket.com**
Lingo	**http://www.lingo.com**	**VoiceWIng**	**http://www.verizon.com**
Mediacom	**http://www.mediacomcc.com**	**Vonage**	**http://www.vonage.com**

Other Instant Messaging Applications

These are all dedicated instant messaging websites.

Aim	**https://www.aim.com**	**Jabber**	**http://www.jabber.com**
EBuddy	**http://www.ebuddy.com**	**MSN**	**http://www.msn.com**
Google Talk	**http://www.google.com**	**Xfire**	**http://www.xfire.com**
ICQ	**http://www.icq.com**	**Yahoo! Messenger**	**http://www.messenger.yahoo.com**

Other File-Transfer Applications

All of the applications shown below offer a basic free service—the sort that would satisfy most nonbusiness users. But for larger files or more frequent transmissions or recipients there will be charges.

Dropsend	**http://www.dropsend.com**	**Tempinbox**	**http://www.tempinbox.com**
Myemail	**http://myemail.com**	**Trustmymail**	**http://www.trustmymail.com**
NewsLetterArchive	**http://www.newsletterarchive.org**		
Sendspace	**http://www.sendspace.com**		

Design

This segment of the book is all about applications that aim to aid the design process—that could entail tools to help web designers or just graphics sites that are fun to use and that might at some point be of use.

Buttonator

http://www.buttonator.com

Ask anyone who has ever attempted to design a professional website what the toughest part of that process was, and many would tell you that it is the sheer detailed tedium of creating buttons. It isn't difficult work, but if you have a large number of them to prepare, especially if there are "rollover" images required—meaning that each button may require three different graphics—it can be very time-consuming. This is where websites such as Buttonator are so useful, in that they enable the designer to enter the wording for the button, select a style and a color, and then create the graphic.

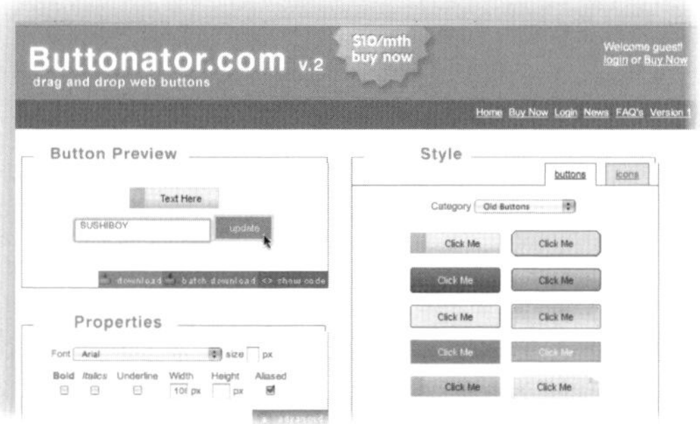

The basic Buttonator service is free. However, a small fee gains access to a much wider variety of designs.

- Begin by entering URL: **http://www.buttonator.com**. Enter your text and select the font and any other design properties. Click on the **Update** buttons.

- Double-click on your selected button. The change will be reflected in the **Button Preview** box on the left of the page.

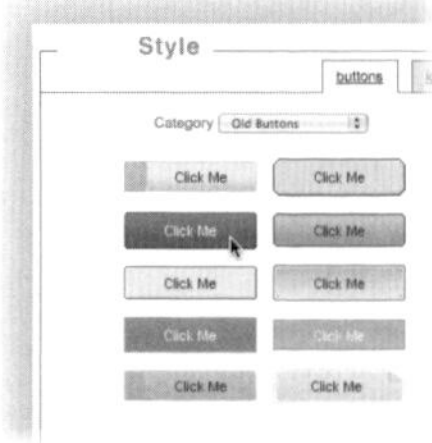

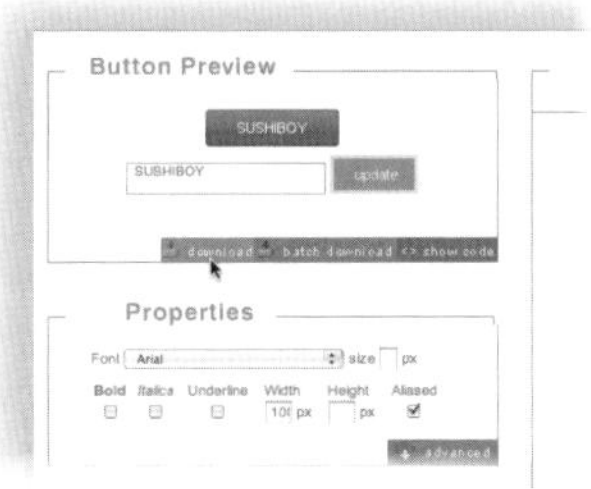

- If you're happy with the preview of your button, click on **Download**. The graphic will be transferred to your hard drive.

Clickdensity

http://www.clickdensity.com

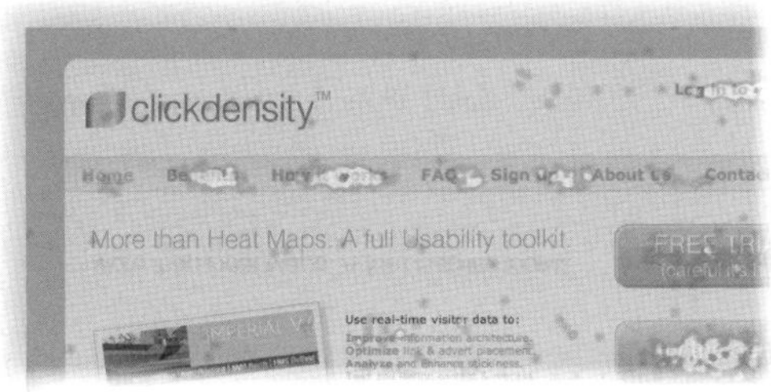

As websites become increasingly important to business, and greater numbers compete with one another for user attention, design efficiency becomes more and more significant. Clickdensity is an analytical tool that enables web administrators to get a greater feel for how their sites are being used. In essence, Clickdensity provides a "heat map," showing concentration of mouse movements on your website. This can be based on mouse clicks or simply where the mouse has been rolled. So not only do you gain an understanding of where your audience's attention is being focused, but also where it is *not*. Hence "dead" space can be identified.

The visual nature of the Clickdensity display makes it particularly good for presentations to nontechnical audiences, such as marketing executives.

Flickrlogomakr

http://flickr.nosv.org

This website produces a Flickr-style logo. Simply type in the text and click on the **Make** button. The graphic can then be downloaded.

LogoSauce

http://www.logosauce.com

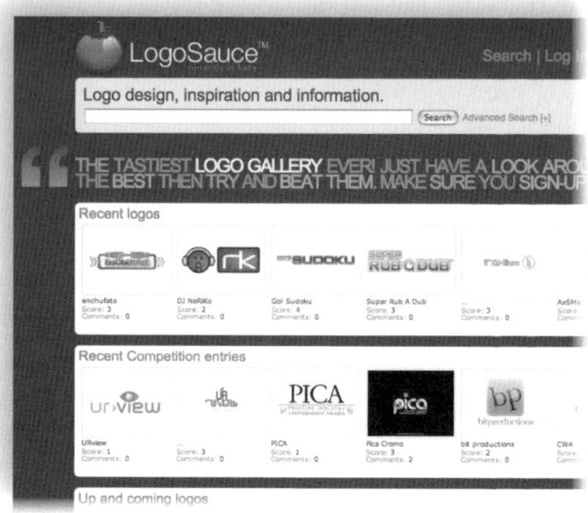

For amateur web designers and owners of small businesses, the subject of a logo can be a troublesome one. Coming up with the right design and suitable typography takes skill—and if you get it wrong your business identity can be affected. LogoSauce is an online catalog of cutting-edge logo design. It allows anyone to see at a glance what the prevailing fashions are within the industry. Users are also able to make comments on designs.

Netcocktail

http://www.netcocktail.com

Just as LogoSauce provides a gallery of cutting-edge logo design, Netcocktail attempts the same for websites, tagging those submitted by its users, and categorizing them according to their color schemes. It's a good source of inspiration for those about to embark upon a web design project.

The Web Award

http://www.thewebaward.com

This interesting site, The Web Award, takes a social networking approach to assessing web design. It describes itself as: "The web design awards where you are the judge." Any user can submit a website design that takes his or her fancy, and allow others to comment. Designs are also tagged, and so can be categorized and searched for in a variety of different ways, such as by rating or using a tag cloud.

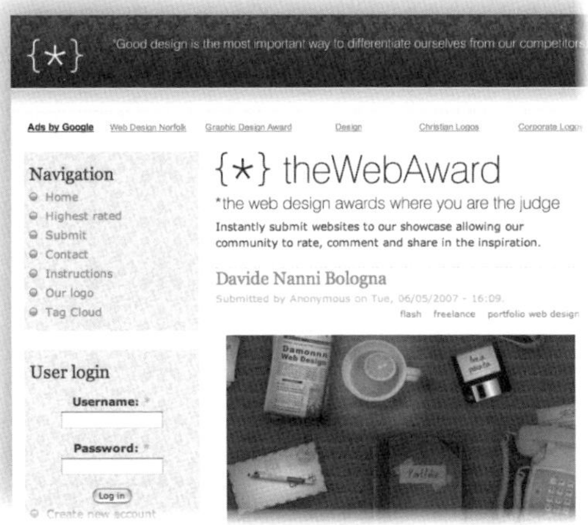

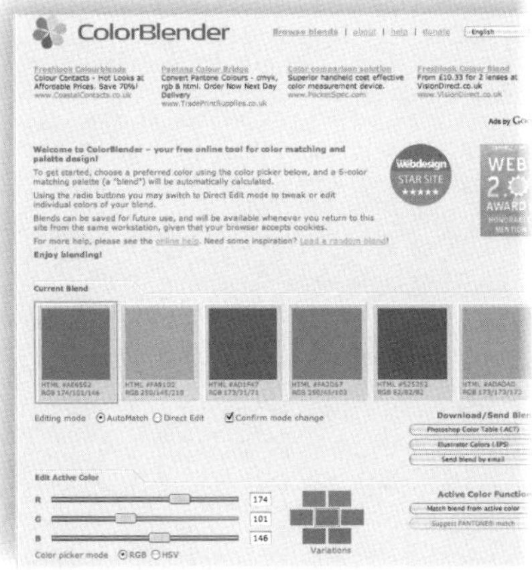

ColorBlender

http://www.colorblender.com

Color matching is obviously a critical skill for most designers. ColorBlender is a web-based tool used for creating palettes in web design. By chosing a single base color, a complementary blend of six matching colors are shown, each with its own HTML and RGB blends. Thus, a complete color scheme can be chosen simply.

Typetester

http://www.typetester.maratz.com

The skill of the typographer is often overlooked in design. However, selecting a font that is both attractive and readable is a critical aspect of any kind of book, magazine, or website design.

Typetester is an extremely useful web-based application that allows users to test out different styles and combinations of text, with the results being immediately visible.

It's very simple to use: you select a typeface (called a "font") from one of the drop-down menus. Directly beneath that are a number of other variables that can be manipulated, such the size of the print, the leading (the space between each line), tracking (the space between each letter), and alignment, as well as foreground and background colors. You can see immediately your changes reflected in the dummy "lorem ipsum" text beneath each column. Typetester allows three different settings to be shown on the screen at the same time, thus allowing direct comparisons to be made between each one.

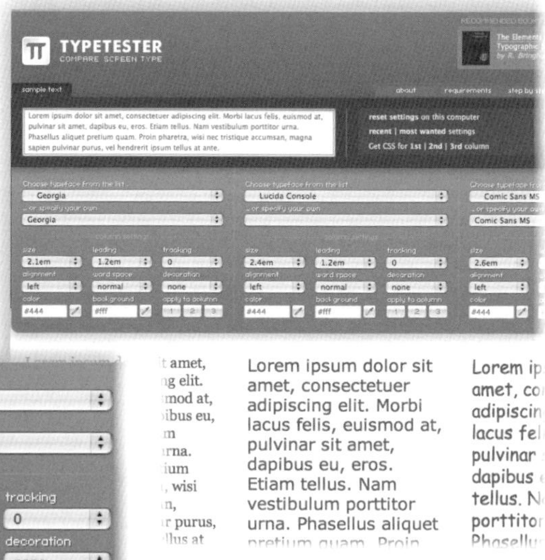

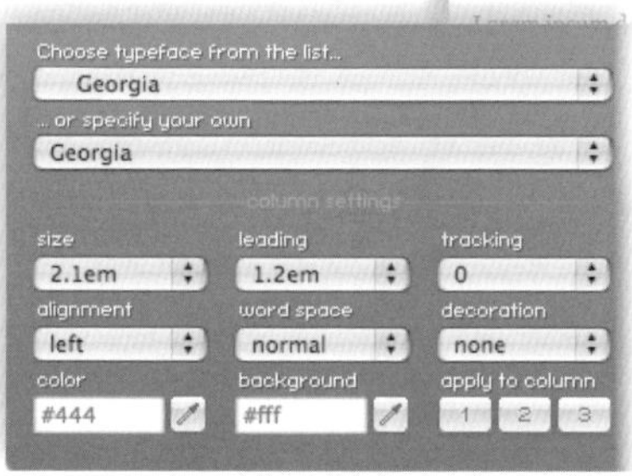

Flower Maker

http://www.zefrank.com/flowers

This application is enjoyable for wasting a few idle moments. The sole purpose of Flower Maker is, as its name suggests, to create images of flowers. On the left of the screen you'll see a variety of petal shapes and a color palette: click on your chosen color and petal, and drag the mouse in the whiteboard area. You will see that it creates a pleasant kaleidoscopic effect. Continue to add more petals as required.

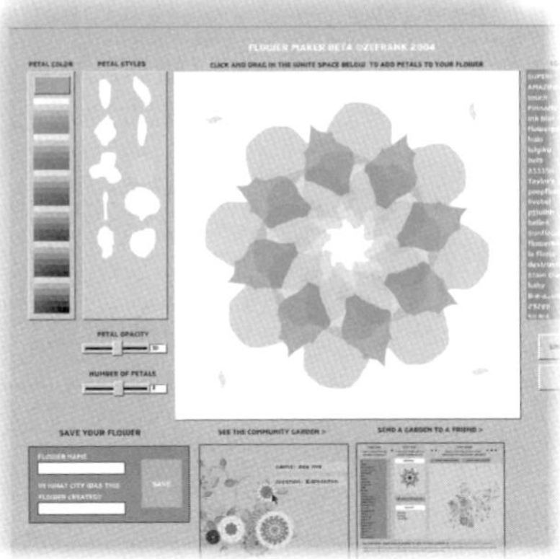

Pixenate

http://www.pixenate.com

Having seen already that there are passable web-based alternatives to the big guns of office software, it comes as no surprise to find that there are also plenty of free-to-use image manipulation applications to be found.

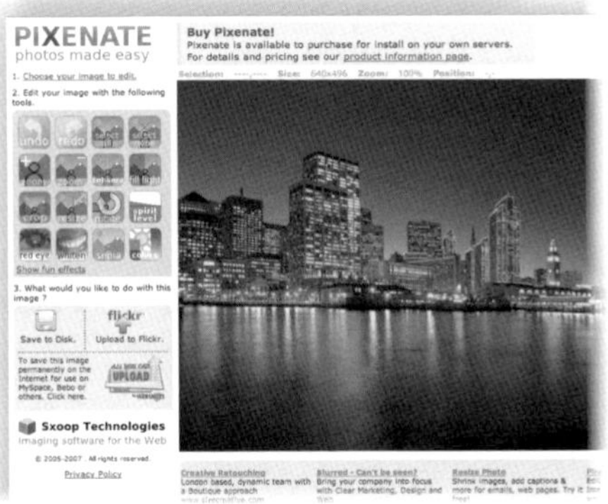

Pixenate is capable of performing some of the basic functions of popular (and costly) desktop applications such as Adobe Photoshop. After you have uploaded an image you can zoom in and out, crop, rotate, or perform simple color alterations, such as altering contrast and brightness or fixing "red-eye." Finished photographs can then be uploaded to Flickr.

e-Commerce

Whether buying or selling, the Internet, and in particular the World Wide Web, has altered the way many of us do business. In some areas—notably CDs, books, and DVDs—online sales make up a very significant proportion of the total. And to help our sales transactions go through more safely and smoothly, Internet-based currencies such as PayPal have now become universally accepted.

eBay

http://www.ebay.com

One of the global commercial successes of the past decade, the online auction website eBay was founded in 1995 in San Jose, California, by computer programmer Pierre Omidyar. The first item purportedly sold on eBay was a broken laser pointer for $14.83. (The oft-repeated story that eBay was founded to help his fiancée trade PEZ dispensers was fabricated by a PR company to generate media interest.) The website flourished at an astonishing speed, and when eBay went public in September 1997, Omidyar became an overnight billionaire.

Although eBay first came to prominence as a means for auctioning used goods, its focus has slowly shifted to the point where a significant proportion of items on sale are now brand-new. Thus, for many, eBay is viewed less as a place to go to find a second-hand bargain than simply as the world's biggest online store.

Finding Products on eBay

Almost anything you care to imagine—and we mean *anything*—is likely to be available in some shape or form somewhere on eBay.

• Enter URL: **http://www.ebay.com**. In this example, we'll see if anyone is selling a Ford Mustang car. Enter **Mustang** in the box at the top of the page and click on the **Search** button.

Notable eBay Sales

- In May 2005, a Volkswagen Golf that had previously been owned by Cardinal Ratzinger (who had just been elected Pope Benedict XVI) was sold on eBay's German site for 188,938.88 Euros.
- A man from Arizona sold an air guitar on eBay.com for $5.50.
- Disney sold a decommissioned monorail for $20,000.
- The German Language Association auctioned the German language to call attention to the growing influence of Pidgin-English in modern German.
- In November 2005, the original Hollywood sign was sold on eBay for $450,400.
- A student from Coventry, UK, sold a single corn flake for just over $2.
- Producers on the TV show *Ally McBeal* once used eBay to auction a walk-on part.
- An old lunch box containing a decade-old cheese sandwich, on which mold had formed in the shape of the face of Virgin Mary, was sold for $28,000.

• The list that follows covers any item that has the word "Mustang" in its title. If we look at the column headed **Matching Categories** and then click on **Cars & Trucks** the list will be filtered.

• The list then reduces to only items in the **Cars & Trucks** category. If you want to find detailed information on one of the items, click on the title of the auction.

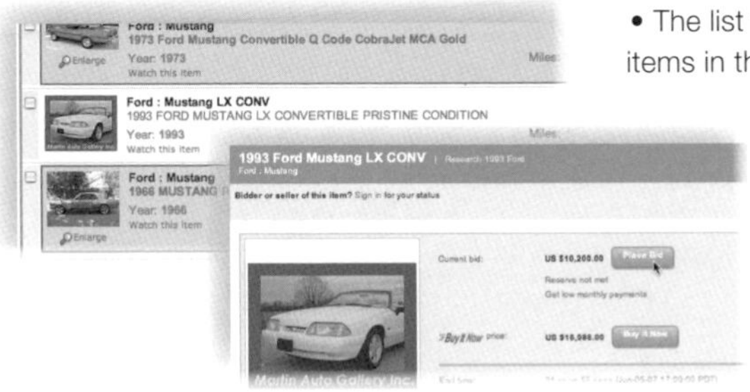

• If you want to bid for the item, click on the button marked **Place Bid**. (Note: you have be signed in to bid for an item.) Enter your maximum bid and click on the **Continue** button.

Selling Items on eBay

To sell an item on eBay you first must be registered and signed in.

• On the main page, click on the **Sell** button in the top right corner of the screen (*see above*).

• There are several different ways you can set up your auction. One of the easiest methods is to use the search feature, which identifies automatically the sales categories that might be relevant. This is much faster than working it out manually.

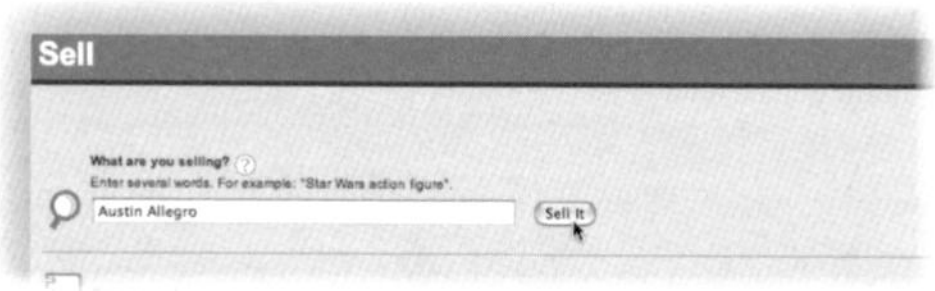

In the **Sell** window, type in some key words that describe the item in question. In this case we'll try to sell a car—enter **Austin Allegro** and click on the **Sell It** button.

• Based on your search, eBay will come up with some possible categories. These will be based on what others have used for similar items. In this example, in the checkbox click on **Cars, Vans & Vehicles > Classic Cars > Austin**. Click on the button marked **Save and Continue**.

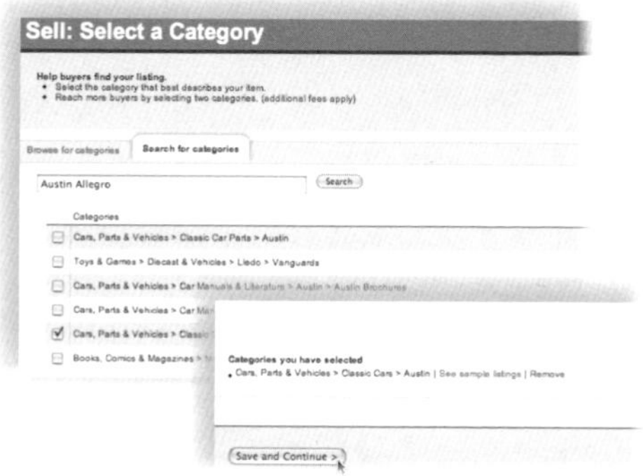

• Now that eBay understands that it's a car you're selling it presents you with a specific template. Complete the details, write your sales blurb, upload a photograph, and then review your listing. When you're ready, click on the **List Your Item** button.

Tips for Selling on eBay

Good image People like to see things before they buy them. Make sure any products you list on eBay are accompanied by good quality photographs.

Research Spend some time researching other similar products and following the bidding process.

Shipping Make sure that you include the shipping costs on your listing.

Details Prepare a powerful listing. The trick is to combine phrasing that will work for a search engine with concrete details about the product that will entice people to bid.

Payments Offer a full complement of payment options. Many eBayers prefer to use PayPal, so make sure that you set up an account

Act professionally Provide the kind of customer service that will build your reputation. Feedback really matters when you're selling on eBay, so do all you can to get postive responses from your customers. If you have a consistent record of positive feedback, prospective buyers will both bid more often and be willing to pay higher prices.

Your listing is now set up and can be viewed by anyone. You can check out bidding by looking at your **My eBay** page, which lists everything that you are bidding for and selling.

Auction Mapper

http://www.auctionmapper.com

An independent website, Auction Mapper is a more attractive way to find items on eBay. Users enter their search criteria, then Auction Mapper looks at what is currently available on eBay and places the results on a Google map.

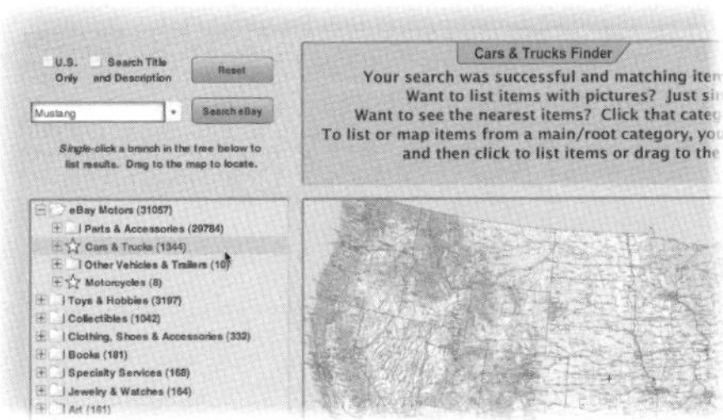

PayPal

http://www.paypal.com

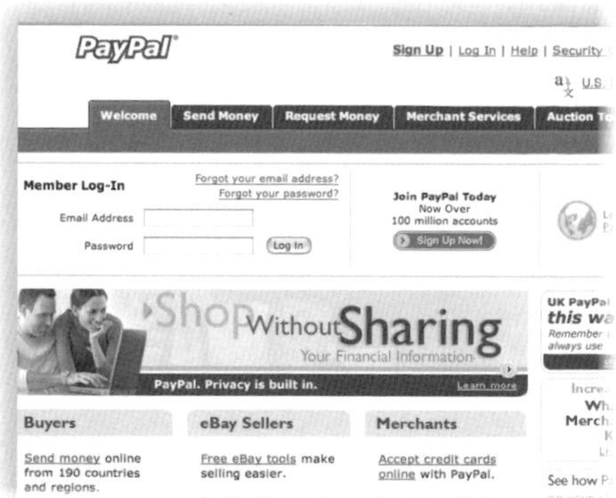

PayPal is the virtual currency at the heart of the Internet. The company came about in 2000, the result of a merger of two smaller online credit organizations. Its success is largely linked to that of eBay, who, two years later, acquired the company. While PayPal had a number of competitors, most have since conceded defeat and closed down.

Registered users place funds in a PayPal account, or provide credit card details against which funds can be drawn. This enables small businesses or those selling items on eBay (or other auction sites) to accept credit card payments without undergoing the punitive costs associated with creating an account with a credit organization. Accounts are free to create, but charges take place on individual transactions. For regular eBay sellers, having a PayPal account is now seen as a basic necessity.

Amazon

http://www.amazon.com

Amazon is probably the world's best-known online retailer. It started out in 1994 selling just books, then gradually spread into other areas, such as CDs, DVDs, toys, and electrical goods.

Although the company itself predates the idea of Web 2.0 by many years, it is often considered to fall under this umbrella because of its early social networking/ blogging features. Amazon quickly saw the value of enabling its customers to

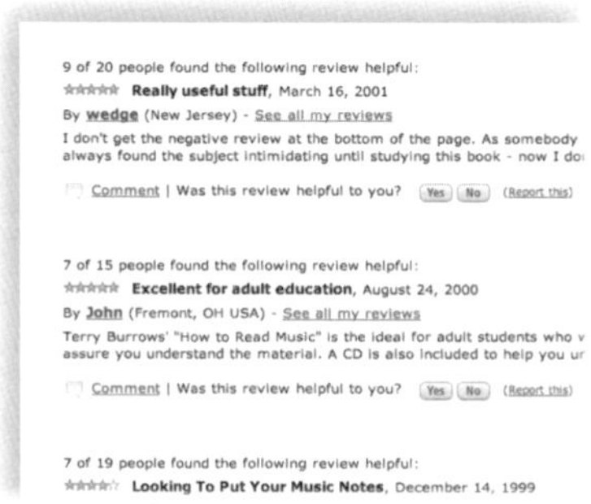

make comments on the things they'd bought. For example, a good set of reviews for a book by a little-known author has been seen to have an impact in terms of sales. So much so, in fact, that there have been a number of well-publicized stories where comments purporting to be independent reviews have been exposed as coming from book publishers, agents, or the authors themselves.

9 of 20 people found the following review helpful:
Really useful stuff, March 16, 2001
By wedge (New Jersey) - See all my reviews
I don't get the negative review at the bottom of the page. As somebody
always found the subject intimidating until studying this book - now I do
Comment | Was this review helpful to you?
Yes
No
(Report this)
7 of 15 people found the following review helpful:
Excellent for adult education, August 24, 2000
By John (Fremont, OH USA) - See all my reviews
Terry Burrows' "How to Read Music" is the ideal for adult students who
assure you understand the material. A CD is also included to help you
Comment | Was this review helpful to you?
Yes
No
(Report this)
7 of 19 people found the following review helpful:
Looking To Put Your Music Notes, December 14, 1999

More e-Commerce Sites

43deals	http://www.43deals.com	Judysbook	http://www.judysbook.com
Adgenta	http://www.adgenta.com	Listsomething	http://www.listsomething.com
Aidpage	http://www.aidpage.com	Lopico	http://www.lopico.com
Bigcartel	http://bigcartel.com	Oolsi	http://www.oolsi.com
Billmonk	https://www.billmonk.com	Peerflix	http://www.peerflix.com
Blish	http://www.blish.com	Prosper	http://www.prosper.com
Castingwords	http://castingwords.com	Qoop	http://www.qoop.com
Cafépress	http://www.cafepress.com	Smarkets	http://www.smarkets.net
Carbonmade	http://www.carbonmade.com	Souki	http://www.souki.com
Clipfire	http://www.clipfire.com	Spymedia	http://www.spymedia.com
Closo	http://www.closo.com	Stuffopolis	http://www.stuffopolis.com
Cooqy	http://www.cooqy.com	Stylehive	http://www.shopify.com
Coverpop	http://www.coverpop.com	Swabba	http://www.swabba.de
Darmik	http://www.darmik.com	Tnook	http://www.tnook.com
Donorschoose	http://www.donorschoose.org	Wazima	http://www.wazima.com
Wuraweb	http://www.wuraweb.com	Wists	http://www.wists.com
Etsy	http://www.etsy.com	Yelp	http://www.yelp.com
Givezilla	http://www.givezilla.com	Yub	http://www.yub.com/mall
Flyspy	http://www.flyspy.com	Zopa	http://www.zopa.com
Fundable	http://www.fundable.com		
Gumshoo	http://www.gumshoo.com		
Hawkee	http://www.hawkee.com		
Inods	http://inods.com		

Education and Knowledge

There has been much written and discussed about the nature of democracy on the Internet—no more so than in access to, and the sharing of, knowledge and information. In fact, this interchange goes back the earliest days of the Internet when specialist "Usernet" newsgroups were used as forums for answering questions. While newsgroups still have many users, the most interesting developments have long shifted the Web, where new technologies like AJAX have allowed for the creation of slick, easy-to-use interfaces. Here is a selection of knowledge-based, user-enriched websites.

7 Tips On

http://www.7tipson.com

7 Tips lists simple, single-sentence hints and tips posted by its users. Tips can be tagged and searched for in a variety of ways—the main screen features a cloud of the most popular tags; alternatively a conventional text search can be used.

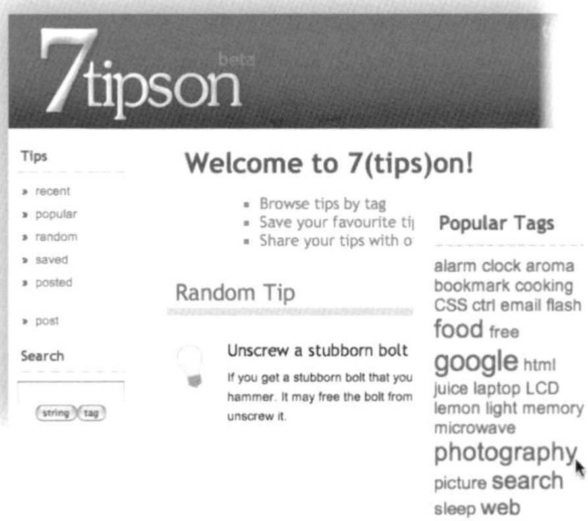

Answers.com

http://www.answers.com

Launched in 1999, Answers.com is a well-established information site, drawing on a variety of different sources on the Internet, although primarily Wikipedia.

MetaGlossary

http://www.metaglossary.com

MetaGlossary is a neat dictionary of user-defined terms, phrases, and acronyms. Enter a phrase in the main window and click on the button marked **Define**. A new window opens containing any definitions posted by other users.

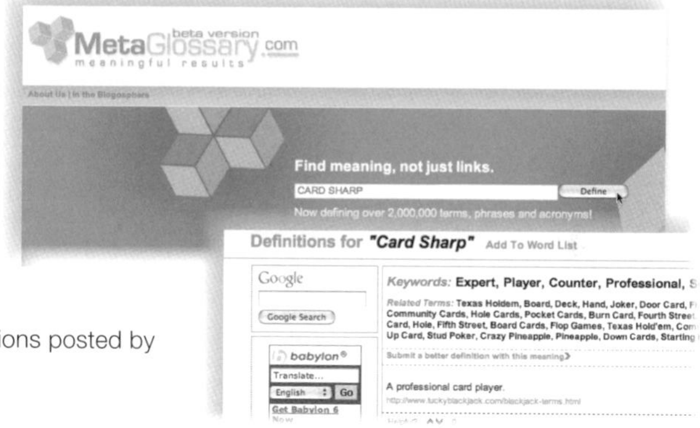
MetaGlossary.com
beta version
meaningful results
Find meaning, not just links.
CARD SHARP
Define
Now defining over 2,000,000 terms, phrases and acronyms!
Definitions for "Card Sharp"
Add To Word List
Google
Google Search
babylon
Translate...
English
Go
Get Babylon 6
Keywords: Expert, Player, Counter, Professional,
A professional card player.

ObjectGraph

http://www.objectgraph.com

ObjectGraph could be described as a "scrolling" dictionary—as the user types, the dictionary comes up with a list of suggestions based on the letters already entered. The data is drawn from a freely available online dictionary—the public domain portion of The Project Gutenberg Etext of Webster's Unabridged Dictionary.

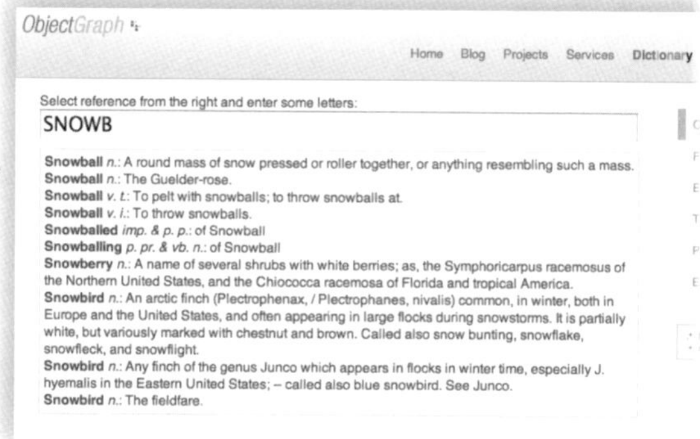
ObjectGraph
Home Blog Projects Services Dictionary
Select reference from the right and enter some letters:
SNOWB
Snowball n.: A round mass of snow pressed or roller together, or anything resembling such a mass.
Snowball n.: The Guelder-rose.
Snowball v. t.: To pelt with snowballs; to throw snowballs at.
Snowball v. i.: To throw snowballs.
Snowballed imp. & p. p.: of Snowball
Snowballing p. pr. & vb. n.: of Snowball
Snowberry n.: A name of several shrubs with white berries; as, the Symphoricarpus racemosus of the Northern United States, and the Chiococca racemosa of Florida and tropical America.
Snowbird n.: An arctic finch (Plectrophenax, / Plectrophanes, nivalis) common, in winter, both in Europe and the United States, and often appearing in large flocks during snowstorms. It is partially white, but variously marked with chestnut and brown. Called also snow bunting, snowflake, snowfleck, and snowflight.
Snowbird n.: Any finch of the genus Junco which appears in flocks in winter time, especially J. hyemalis in the Eastern United States; – called also blue snowbird. See Junco.
Snowbird n.: The fieldfare.

Oyogi

http://www.oyogi.com

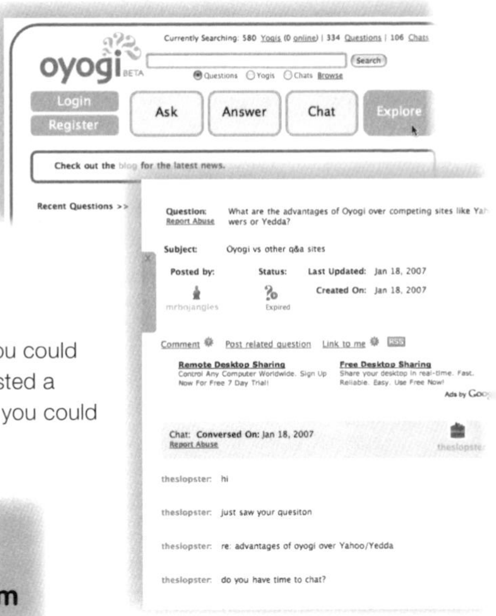

Oyogi is quite unusual in that, although on the surface it seems to be a basic, searchable question-and-answer database, it allows people to interact with one another using its own instant messaging system. For example, you could post a question and if someone posted a response while you were still online you could discuss things further via IM.

Postgenomic

http://www.postgenomic.com

One of the most popular modern science websites, Postgenomic draws articles and collects posts from a wide variety of science blogs across the globe. It's a very useful source for newly published papers, conference reports, and breaking news stories. It's also increasingly popular among science bloggers in search of a larger audience.

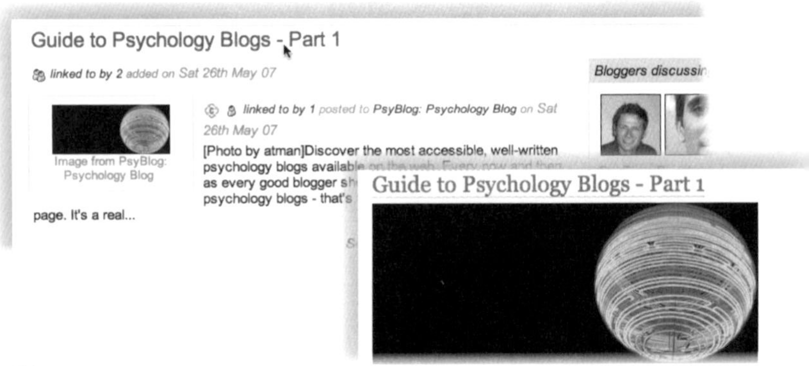

Quotiki

http://www.quotiki.com

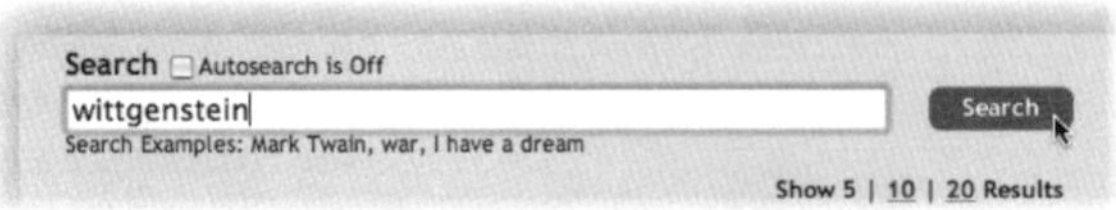

If you've ever tried to remember a quotation, who was responsible for it, or the precise wording, Quotiki could be just the website for you. It's very simple to use: in the single search box near the top of the window, you can enter either a word, name, or an extract from a phrase and click on the **Search** button. The results appear in a new window.

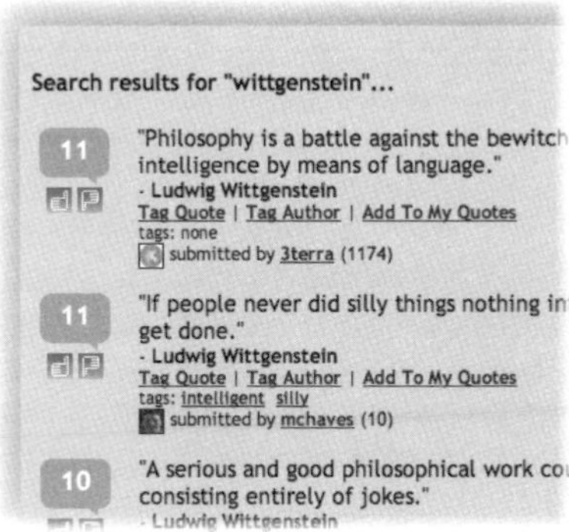

Squidoo

http://www.squidoo.com

Launched in 2005, Squidoo is a network of user-generated "lenses." These are single pages that can be written by anyone on any subject. Squidoo is, in part at least, a charitable enterprise, donating large amounts of its advertising revenue to 45 featured charities.

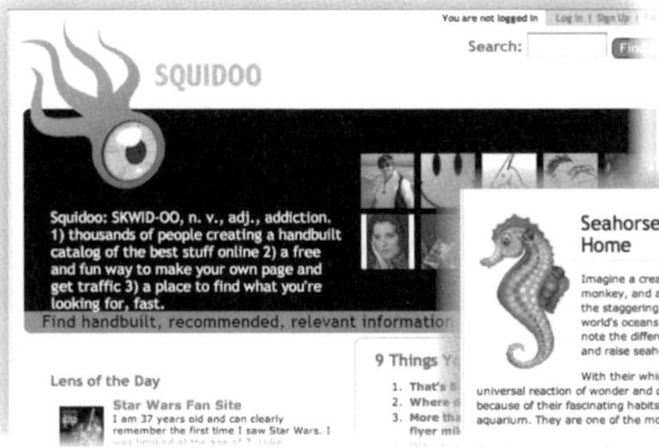

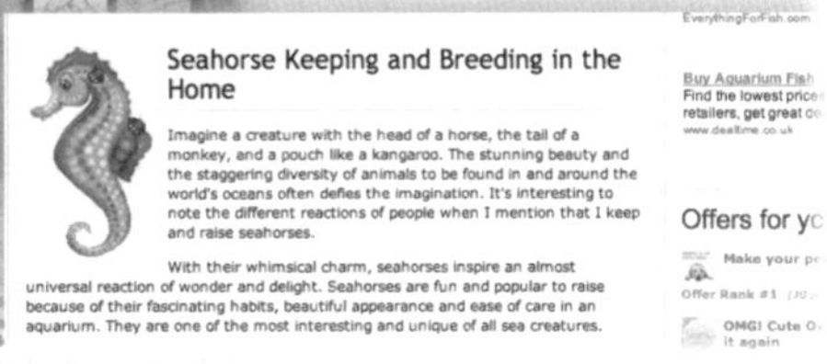

Seahorse Keeping and Breeding in the Home
Imagine a creature with the head of a horse, the tail of a monkey, and a pouch like a kangaroo. The stunning beauty and the staggering diversity of animals to be found in and around the world's oceans often defies the imagination. It's interesting to note the different reactions of people when I mention that I keep and raise seahorses.
With their whimsical charm, seahorses inspire an almost universal reaction of wonder and delight. Seahorses are fun and popular to raise because of their fascinating habits, beautiful appearance and ease of care in an aquarium. They are one of the most interesting and unique of all sea creatures.

TutorLinker

http://www.tutorlinker.com

An idea with great potential, TutorLinker aims to bring together students and tutors in specific locations. Let's look at this application in a little more detail.

- Begin by entering the URL: **http://www.tutorlinker.com**. In the main page enter your address. This can be as detailed as you wish. Choose a country from the drop-down menu, and click on the **Search** button.

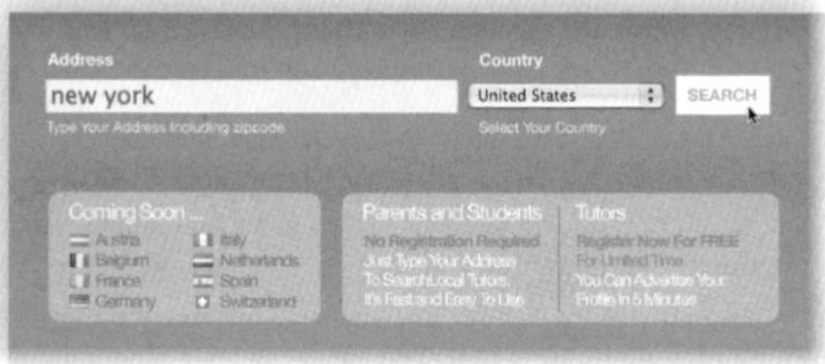

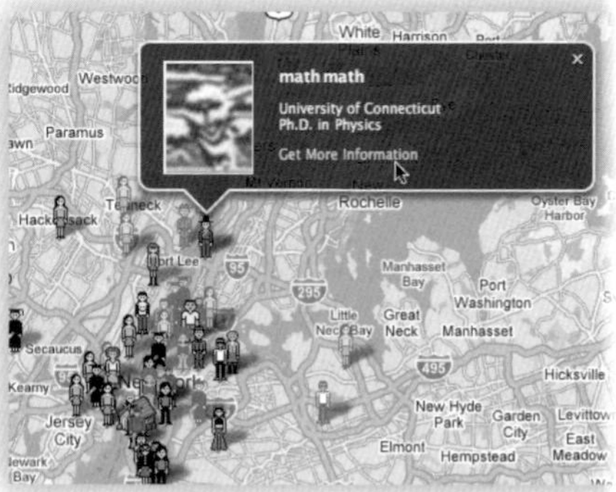

- A Google Map of the requested area will appear. Any registered tutors in that location will appear as avatars on the map. Moving the mouse over any figure will result in a pop-up thumbnail profle. This will provide a name, academic credentials, and specialist subject. If you need additional details, click on the text **Get More Information**.

- You now have access to the tutor's personal page. Here you'll find a resume, timetable of availability, hourly rate, and an e-mail form enabling you to make direct contact.

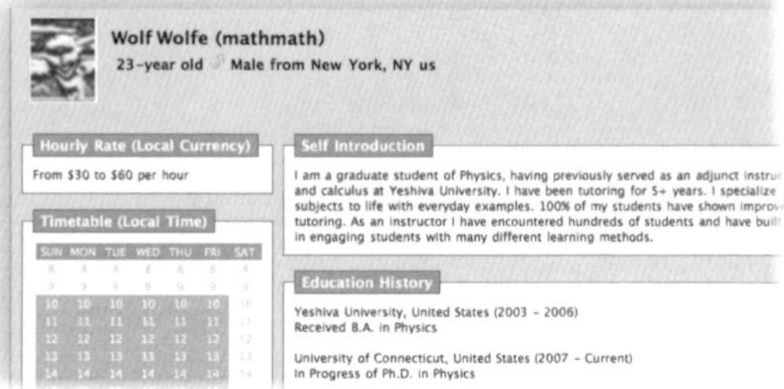

Wolf Wolfe (mathmath)
23-year old Male from New York, NY us
Hourly Rate (Local Currency)
From $30 to $60 per hour
Timetable (Local Time)
SUN MON TUE WED THU FRI SAT
Self Introduction
I am a graduate student of Physics, having previously served as an adjunct
and calculus at Yeshiva University. I have been tutoring for 5+ years. I specialize
subjects to life with everyday examples. 100% of my students have shown
tutoring. As an instructor I have encountered hundreds of students and have
in engaging students with many different learning methods.
Education History
Yeshiva University, United States (2003 - 2006)
Received B.A. in Physics
University of Connecticut, United States (2007 - Current)
In Progress of Ph.D. in Physics

Yahoo! Answers

http://answers.yahoo.com

By far the largest website of its kind, Yahoo! Answers describes itself as "a community-driven knowledge market." It was launched at the end of 2005, and within a year was able to boast over 65 million answers and more than 7 million questions. Although based in the U.S., there are international sites devoted to most major countries and languages.

More Education and Knowledge Sites

3Form	http://3form.org	ProProfs	http://www.proprofs.com
Askeet	http://www.askeet.com	Pubsub	http://www.pubsub.com
Blinkbits	http://www.blinkbits.com	Questionize	http://www.questionize.com
BrainJams	http://www.brainjams.com	Quomon	http://quomon.com
Brainreactions	http://www.brainreactions.net	Root/vaults	http://www.root.net/vaults
Bubbl.us	http://bubbl.us	Sparkhive	http://www.sparkhive.com
Copyscape	http://www.copyscape.com	Study Stickies	http://www.studystickies.com
Echosign	http://www.echosign.com/public/compose		
Findory	http://www.findory.com	Tractis	http://www.tractis.com
Gibeo	http://www.gibeo.net	TTeach	http://yedda.com
Grokker	http://www.grokker.com	WisdonDB	http://www.wisdomdb.net
GuruLib	http://www.gurulib.com	Wondir	http://www.wondir.com
Hanzoweb	http://hanzoweb.com	Yedda	http://yedda.com
Helium	http://www.helium.com		
Jots	http://www.jots.com		
Kaboodle	http://www.kaboodle.com		
Manage My Ideas	http://www.managemyideas.com		
Mouse Brains	http://www.kennieting.com/mousebrains		
Nuvvo	http://www.nuvvo.com		

Games and Virtual Worlds

During the first half of the 1980s, when personal computers first became affordable to domestic users, many people bought them expecting to be able to do useful things, such as managing their accounts; most ended up using them for one thing, and one thing only—playing games. Unsurprisingly, perhaps, computer gaming of some sort has been in existence almost since the birth of the computer. Much of this activity took place within the confines of university research labs, and it wasn't until the development of the microprocessor, which would in turn make possible the invention of the personal computer, that computer gaming reached the public. As computers and their graphics capabilities have become more powerful, so have the games become more sophisticated, enabling the creation of "virtual worlds" with a potential limited only by the imagination of the players. In this section, we'll take a brief look at the history of the computer game, and a selection of those available either via the Web or as free downloaded software.

Background to Computer Gaming

There seems to be no unequivocal agreement as to when the first computer game appeared. One of the most commonly cited candidates is Spacewar!, developed by students at MIT in 1961. The game consisted of two player-controlled spaceships maneuvering around a central star, each attempting to destroy the other. It was designed for use on a PDP-1 computer, a machine intended for number-crunching statistical calculations.

The first generation of personal computers saw the evolution of text-based interactive adventure gaming, in which the player controlled characters by entering commands through a keyboard. The first such popular title, Adventure, was developed in 1972. During the explosion of growth in the 1980s, adventure games were still among the most popular, but, as CPU power began to increase dramatically, graphics started to take a more prominent role. Furthermore, as the mouse became an increasingly standard piece of hardware on personal computers, its use was gradually adopted in more and more games.

In 1991, the first first-person "shooter" game appeared—Hovertank 3D also represented the first use of real-time 3D graphics. The same producer went on to develop Wolfenstein 3D a year later, which is widely viewed as having kick-started the biggest-selling genre of modern times. The PC release of Doom in 1993 represented a major breakthrough in computer gaming, providing players with a 3D experience of unprecedented realism. Since then, in terms of content, the games themselves have not changed massively: what continues to evolve at a startling rate is the quality of the 3D graphics.

To a large degree, developments over the last decade have taken place away from the pesonal computer and have shifted to dedicated gaming units, such as the PlayStation series, X Box, and various Nintendo products. One exception has been the growth of virtual world games, which take place either via a web browser or dedicated software linked to a network of players via a fast Internet connection. The most famous example of this is Second Life, a world where it's possible to buy virtual property, build houses, and buy products—"real" or otherwise—from virtual stores.

Web 2.0 Games

http://www.ajaxgames.blogspot.com

This is as good a place to start as any—Web 2.0 Games is a directory site/ blog that enables users to make links and comment on games that have been designed using what could be described as "Web 2.0 technology." (This is, of course, a fairly meaningless term, since there really is no such thing!) More broadly, the intention here is to highlight games that have been created using AJAX or similar technologies.

The main page consists of two elements. On the right of the screen is a scrolling list of games—you click on the name of the game to link to its website. On the left of the screen is blog information about such games entered by users. Let's try an example.

Weewar
Saturday, June 02, 2007
Weewar is a round based strategy game featuring real action on real maps. Up to 6 players command pixel armies against each other on a player chosen map.
This game is currently in private beta and you can apply for an invite here.The game starts when a player chooses from a number of terrains and then invites other players. Players then take over factories and set them to produce more armies and tanks and/or attack their opponents.
Although without an invit eyou can't play Weewar at the moment you can view the games in progress on their site.
My Mini Life
Monday, May 21, 2007
Linez
Kdice
Wings
Pictaps

• Enter the URL: **http://www.ajaxgames.blogspot.com**. From the list of games on the right click on **Kdice**.

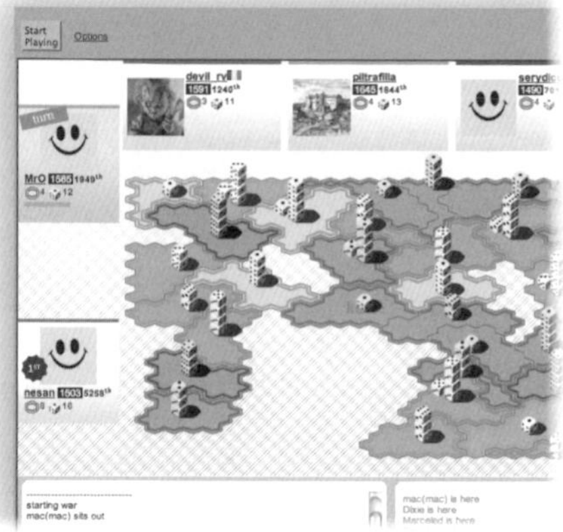

- The AJAX game Kdice opens up. This is a multiplayer interactive strategy game based on the popular online Dice Wars—itself a variation on the board game Risk, where players seek to control all of the territories on the map. The other players currently online can be seen dotted around the edges of the board.

- To begin, click on the button marked **Start Playing**.

Game Snips

http://www.gamesnips.com

You could think of this as Digg for gamers. (*See page 38.*) Users submit game-oriented links, which can be links to game sites or related news items. Each game is voted on by the community, and lists can be sorted according to their popularity.

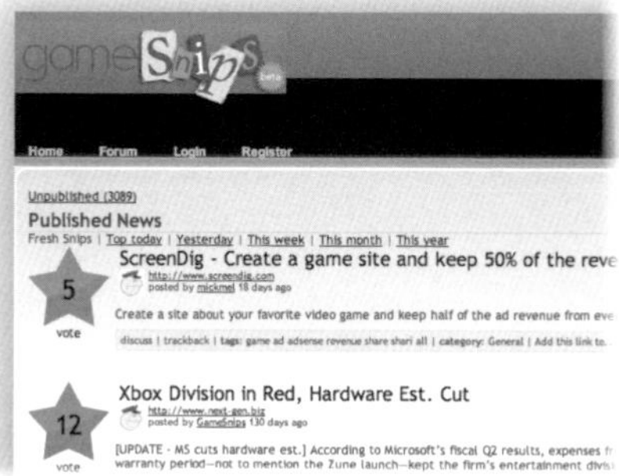

Pictaps

http://roxik.com/pictaps

Here's a fabulous piece of weirdness from Japan. Pictaps allows you to draw and paint a character on the screen and then see it perform an animated dance routine! Begin by entering the URL: **http://roxik.com/pictaps**. Click on the button marked **Paint**.

• Use the paint box to create your figure. The basic outline of the body is already sketched—your job is to fill in the details. You can paint freehand in different colors, draw boxes or polygons, or use the erase tool to delete parts that you don't like. When you've finished your figure, click on the **OK** button.

• Pictaps will now ask you to name your figure by clicking the letters on the keyboard. We'll call our character **FRED**. Click on the **Submit** button. This saves the figure on the Pictaps server for all to see.

• Now all that's left to do is sit back and watch Fred—and his lookalike back-up dancers—strut his funky stuff.

Trendio

http://www.trendio.com

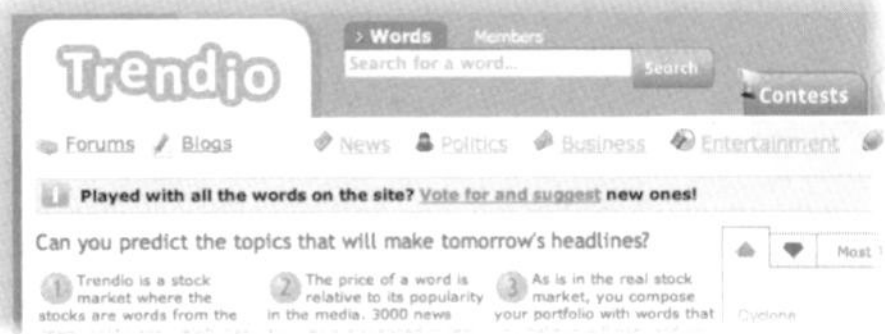

Trendio is a prediction market, where players buy stock in news stories. Key words are chosen from the worlds of politics, sports, and entertainment. The more the word appears in the news, the higher the value of the stock.

Second Life

http://www.secondlife.com

Second Life is quite simply the phenomenon of the online virtual world. Founded in 2003 by Linden Research, Inc., it uses a downloadable client program to create a network where users (often termed "Residents" or "Lifers") are able to interact with one another in a surreal, three-dimensional world. Each participant has a graphic representation, or avatar, within Second Life. Initially, he or she chooses from a number of human likenesses and dress styles. These can later be altered dramatically, or new looks purchased from virtual stores.

Second Life (or "SL," as it is commonly known) was by no means the first virtual world, and not even the most widely inhabited—that would arguably be the online version of The Sims. SL is noteworthy for having created such an advanced level of social networking. Residents can explore, meet others, socialize, participate in individual and group activities, and even create and trade items (virtual property) and services from one another. There are over six million registered users, although many of these are thought to be inactive.

Second Life was inspired by the cyberpunk literary movement of the 1980s, particularly the novels of William Gibson and Neal Stephenson. Indeed, the stated goal of Linden was to create a place like the Metaverse described in Stephenson's novel *Snow Crash*—a user-defined world of general use in which people interacted, played, and conducted business.

To this end, SL developed a virtual currency, the Linden Dollar (L$), which is exchangeable in the "real" world for U.S. Dollars—this rate fluctuates like any other currency market, but is usually somewhere between L$270–300 to a single U.S. dollar. But business is no joke in Second Life: there are known to be a handful of Lifers earning in excess of U.S. $200,000 a year purely from trading activities within Second Life.

What's the Point in Second Life?

SL is not a computer game as such, since there is no scoring system, nobody gets killed, and hence there are no winners or losers—indeed, Lifers tend to resent their universe being described in such a way. Perhaps it's best thought of as a game in the sense more traditionally played by small children, where activities are played out with little more in mind than enjoyment in its own right.

Getting Started

Second Life has such depth than we can only really scratch the surface within a few pages. So let's take a look at how to get started.

• Begin by entering the URL: **http://www.secondlife.com**. To set up your account, click on the **Join Now** button.

• In the registration page, enter a **First Name** of your own choice and then click on the drop-down menu to choose a **Last Name** from the options provided. Enter your **Birthdate** and an **E-mail Address**. Click on the button marked **Continue**.

• Now select your basic avatar. Choose one of the options—you'll see a full-size image alongside when you click on any button. When you're ready, click on **Choose This Avatar**.

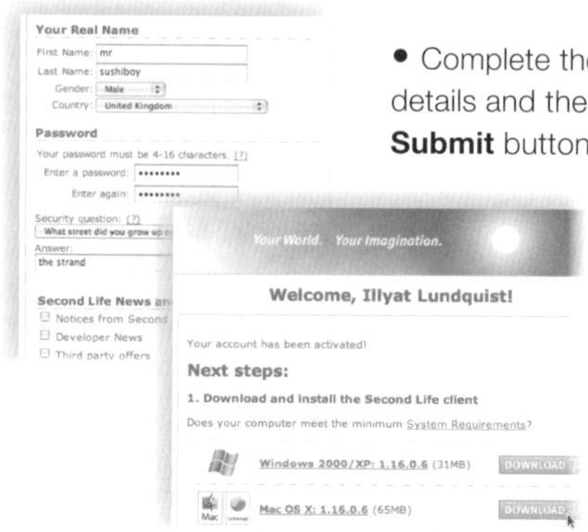

- Complete the registration by adding more personal details and then a password. Finally, click on the **Submit** button.

- You are now ready to download the Second Life client software. Choose the appropriate version for your computer's operating system and then click on the **Download** button. Finally, follow the specific installation instructions for your operating system.

Running Second Life

To join the Second Life network, launch the client program on your computer. Enter your registered **First Name**, **Last Name**, and **Password** and click on the **Connect** button. Now wait to be hooked up—this can take a few minutes the first time you try.

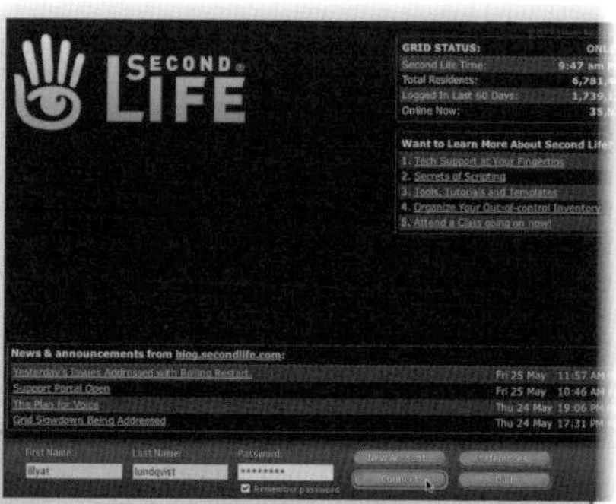

Shopping in Second Life

Second Life is a world where there are limitless possibilities for changing personal appearance, so if you stick to the basic defaults you'll quickly be identified as "tourist." A few moments spent playing with the **Appearance** tools in the **Edit** menu will enable you to alter your look drastically—you can stretch or squash anything from your shirt to your head! Of course, Second Life features numerous stores where you can go to buy new clothes—and even the odd new body part. Midnight City, for example, is one of the oldest shopping centers in Second Life, and is strewn with boutiques featuring creations from top designers, all of which can be procured by handing over your Linden dollars. Similarly, if you care to head off for the Lusk area you'll come across Luskwood Creatures—here you can get yourself some cool animal outfits, such as bats, skunk, foxes, wolves, or dragons.

You're now a part of a new virtual world! Your avatar will appear in the center of your screen with your name above your head. To begin with, all new members must attend Orientation Island. Here you will learn the basics of Second Life.

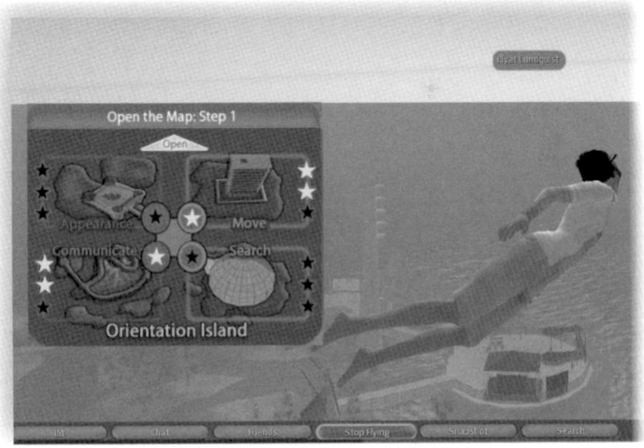

• To fly, click on the button at the foot of the screen marked **Fly,** and maneuver using the arrow keys on your keyboard. You can fly up or down using the **E** or **C** keys (or the **Page Up/Page Down** keys if you have them).

- To chat with another Lifer, go up to them, click on the **Chat** button, type in your text, and press the **Enter** key. Everyone in the close vicinity will be able to "hear" what you've said—the text will appear on their screen. If you want to talk with someone privately, then you can use the instant messenging facility—click on the **IM** button.

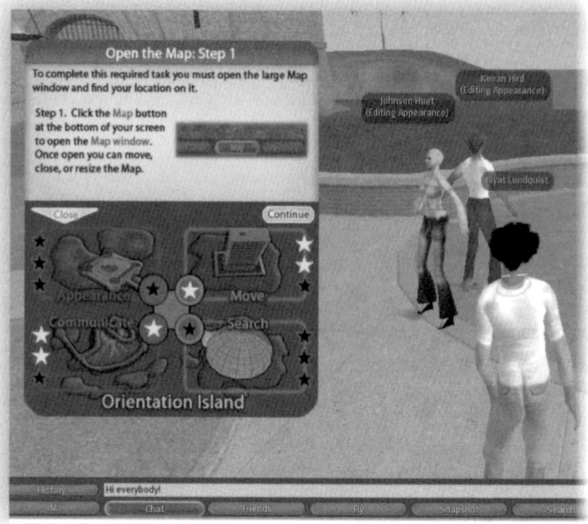
Open the Map: Step 1
To complete this required task you must open the large Map window and find your location on it.
Step 1. Click the Map button at the bottom of your screen to open the Map window. Once open you can move, close, or resize the Map.
Close
Continue
Appearance
Move
Communicate
Search
Orientation Island
Keiran Hird (Editing Appearance)
Johnson Huet (Editing Appearance)
Hi everybody!
History
IM
Chat
Friends
Fly
Snapshot
Search

Games Within Second Life

If there's one thing guaranteed to rile a "Lifer," it's referring to their universe as a "game." However, there are plenty of places you can go on Second Life to play games created by residents.

Samurai Island Visually spectacular, magic-enhanced combat where hundreds of players brawl individually or in "clans." The game was created by a former dancer who now makes a better living from Second Life than she ever did on stage!

Darklife Old-school dungeon-crawler. Strap on armor and begin battling monsters, exploring foreboding chambers, and earning your way to higher levels.

Slictionary A kind of 3D version of the popular board game Pictionary—players get a secret word and then use Second Life's building tools to create sculptures as clues for the other players. This can yield seriously weird results!

Tringo One of the most popular types of game in Second Life, Tringo is a mash-up of Tetris and Bingo. So successful, it's been exported to the real world for play on Game Boy Advance.

Pikipimp

http://www.pikipimp.com

Not exactly a game, but it is a bit of fun, Pikipimp allows you to upload a photograph and "pimp" your image by dragging and dropping items from the menu. For example, if you want to add a mustache to your picture, select Mustaches from the drop-down menu, and choose one of the options and drag it into place. It's as simple as that. Other possibilities include adding funny hats, hair, lips, noses, and scars.

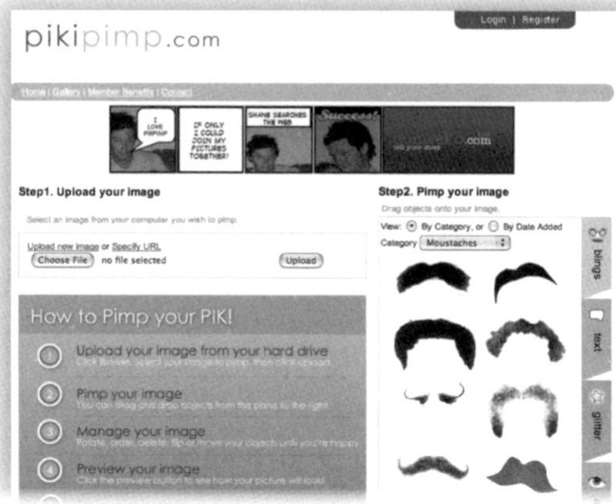

My Mini Life

http://www.myminilife.com

Whereas Second Life requires a client program to work, there's a tiny, web-based alternative in the form of My Mini Life. Here you can create a miniaturized version of yourself, design and decorate your own house, and interact with your neighbors—you can even pick a fight with them!

Arcaplay

http://www.arcaplay.com

Arcaplay is another well-sourced games directory. In particular, it benefits from its games being located in a series of well-organized categories. Many of the games within were produced using AJAX technologies. Unsurprisingly, given its name, Arcaplay is particularly stong on arcade-style games. Highlights include Fleabag Vs Mutt, a "shoot-em-up" cat and dog caper, and Spooky Hoops, a basketball game where the player has to score without being caught by a skeleton.

Chihuahua

http://chi.lexigame.com

Chihuahua is a Boggle-style game in which the object is to create as many possible words of four letters or more from a nine-letter selection. Click on the letters to make up the words. Players can match themselves against others in real time.

Sink My Ship

http://www.sinkmyship.com

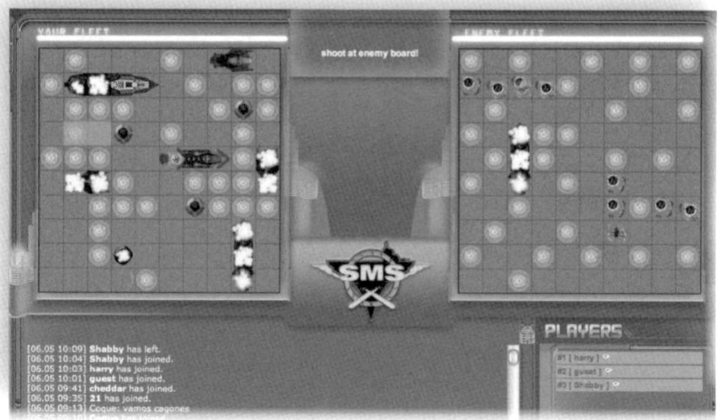

Another online interactive version of a "classic," Sink My Ship is a nice take on Battleship. The interface is slick, with excellent sound effects and some nice visual animated touches—for example, the crew of sunken vessels floating on the water in life boats. To set up, drag your boats onto the grid; to fire missiles, click on your enemy's cells.

More Games Sites

Alexadex	http://alexadex.com/ad	Trade Over	http://tradeover.net
Averageshoveler	http://www.zanni.org	We Boggle	http://weboggle.shackworks.com
Bunchball	http://www.bunchball.com	Weewar	http://weewar.com
Bunny Hunt	http://www.themaninblue.com/experiment/BunnyHunt		
Fastr	http://randomchaos.com/games		
Linez	http://linez.varten.net		
Llor	http://www.llor.nu		
Might & Magic	http://www.heroesmini.com		
Millionsofgames	http://www.millionsofgames.com		
Morkik Chess	http://chess.labs.morfik.com		
Multitap	http://multitap.net		
Phrasr	http://www.pimpampum.net/phrasr		
Spell with Flickr	http://metaatem.net/words		
Tag Man	http://www.apogee-web-consulting.com/tagman		

Hosting

Just as software has begun a slow migration process from desktop to web server, the concept of backing up important data has also shifted in a similar direction. Although it *is* pretty mundane, and certainly at the unglamorous end of the Web 2.0 rainbow, data hosting is an area of development certain to experience massive growth over the coming years. The idea is extremely simple: instead of storing your data on your own media—be it hard drive, CD-R/DVD-R, or memory stick—you upload it to an external server.

Do You Need a Server?

So why, when computer memory seems to be getting cheaper by the day, would you want to back up your data onto someone else's server? The first reason is safety. We've all read the horrible stories about unfortunate people having laptops stolen, and losing irreplaceable family photographs that hadn't been backed up. In truth, anyone owning digital content deemed to be of such importance would be advised to keep copies *somewhere* off-site, even it means a stack of DVD-Rs in a drawer at your parents' house. Which brings us to a second reason—reliability. Any professional hosting operation will have its own remote backup server. By using such a service, you *should* be guaranteed that your data is safe.

Depending on how much data you have to store, external hosting can also be a very economical solution. The business model used by most hosting websites entails offering a free service for storing small amounts of data (1–5 gigabytes), and then charging for larger amounts of space or additional services. Many digital image collections will easily fit within these free hosting criteria. If not, with sufficient organizational skill, it would be possible to split a collection over a number of different free hosting services. Musicians or filmmakers, on the other hand, would certainly need to use a paid subscription service to make copies of large audio or video files.

Finally, one increasingly significant reason for using a hosting service is that you can, if desired, share your digital content with others. This is better suited for files that are to be used for collaborative purposes, rather than simply, say, sharing photographs, which can be done more elegantly on a dedicated website like Flickr (*see page 132*). We'll look at the interesting issue of digital collaboration later in the book (*see page 210*).

Box

http://www.box.net

Let's now look at a typical example of a host service. Like most others, Box offers a free service for storing small quantites and charges for using larger amounts of space.

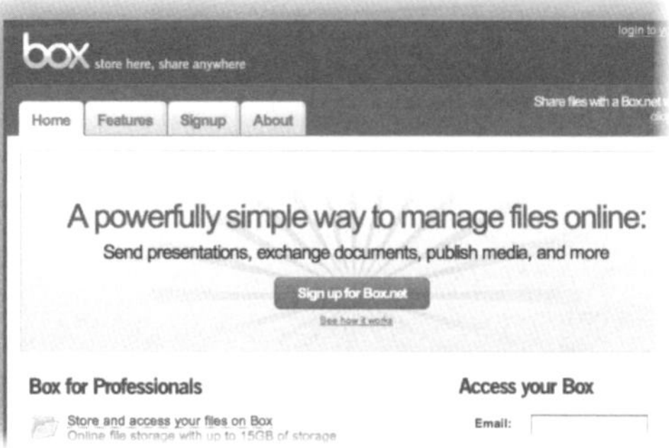

• Begin by entering the URL: **http://www.box.net**. To open a new account, click on the button marked **Sign Up for Box.net** in the middle of the main page.

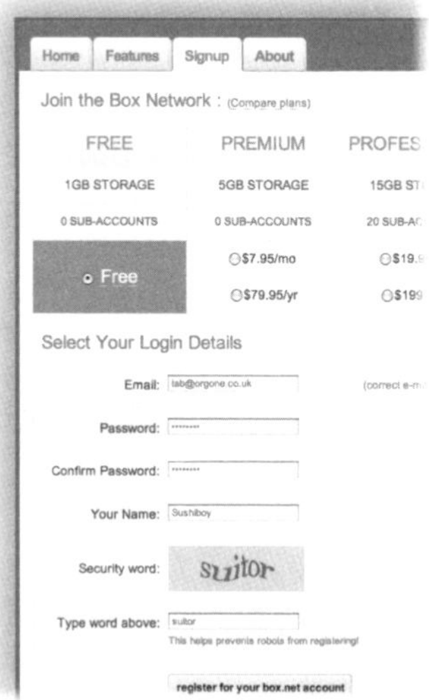

• In the **Signup** window (*see left*), first select the service plan you wish to use. In this case, we'll select the **Free** service, which allows us to store up to a gigabyte of data.

• Now enter your login details. Enter your e-mail address, a user name, password, and the security word. Click on the button marked **Register for Your Box.net Account**.

• When your registration has been confirmed, log in using your name and password. This will take you to your **My Files** page.

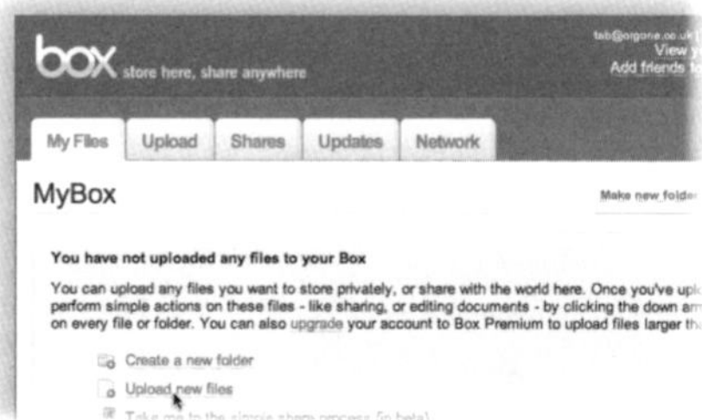

• Now let's upload a file to your Box account. Click on the text marked **Upload Files Now** (*see right*).

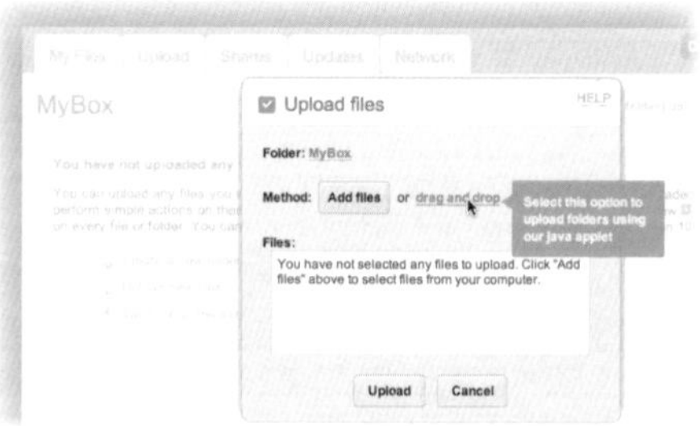

• The **Upload Files** pop-up window appears in front of your **MyBox** screen. There are two ways in which you can transfer files to the Box server. If you click on the **Add Files** button you can browse through your hard drive and choose the file to copy. Alternatively, you can "drag and drop" using a built-in Java applet. We'll use the latter method: click on the button marked **Drag and Drop**. (Before you do this, have a copy of the file you intend to upload on your desktop.)

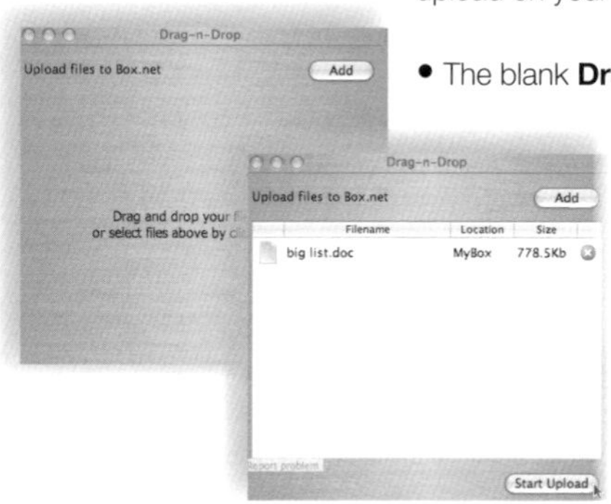

• The blank **Drag-n-Drop** pop-up window appears. Drag the icon of your chosen file from your desktop until it is in the window. Now "drop" the file.

• To start the file transfer, click on the button marked **Start Upload**. A progress window will appear while the transfer is taking place. You will now see the document in your **MyBox** window.

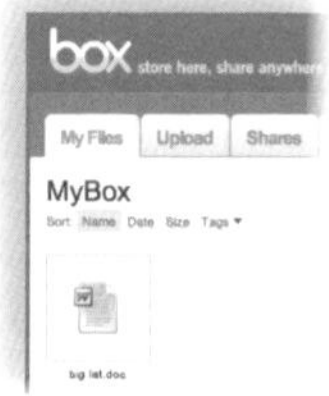

Tagging Your Data

Like many other data hosting services, Box enables its users to apply category tags to their own files. Here's how we can do that.

• Highlight your chosen icon. A box will appear around the icon (*see above*). Click inside the top right-hand corner of the box to reveal the down-pointing arrow.

- If you click on the arrow a drop-down menu will appear containing a number of possible options. Slide down the list and select **Tags**.

- The **Tags** window will now open. Enter any category tags that you wish to add. Multiple tags should be separated by a comma and a space. If you previously set up categories they will appear in the box below—they can be selected by clicking on the tag name. Click the **OK** button to add your tags.

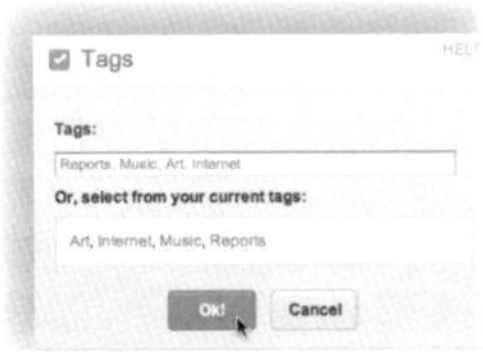

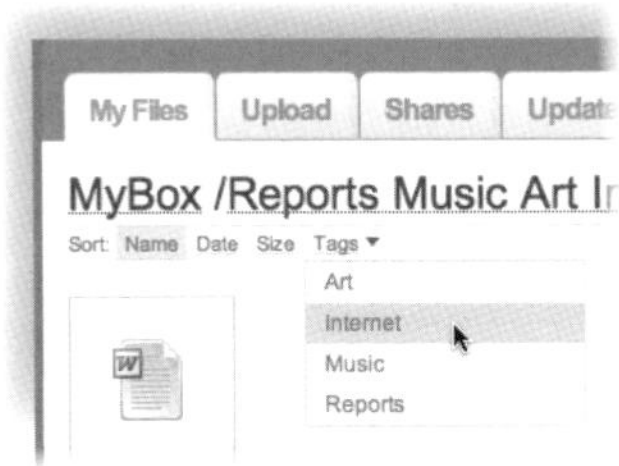

- Back at your **MyBox**, you can sort your documents by **Name**, **Date**, **Size**, and **Tags**. If you click on the **Tags** button, a drop-down menu will appear showing all of your category tags. You can choose a tag from the list as a basis for your sort.

Making Your Files Public

Box enables you to take your data into the public domain in two different ways. You can share your files with other Box users and take advantage of features such as social bookmarking tags, or you can simply make them available to anyone with a web browser. Both can be achieved using the drop-down menu found in the icon box. To make a document public, choose the option **Get Public Link**. This will open the **Public Link** window.

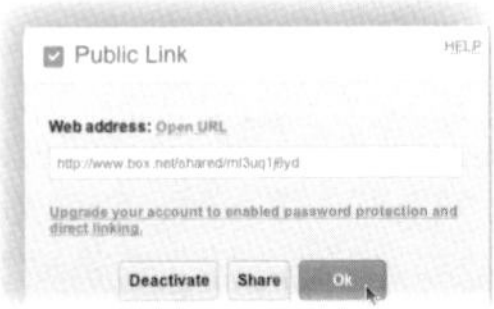

Make a note of the URL—this is the web address at which your document will be available. When you are ready, click on the **OK** button.

Carbonite

http://www.carbonite.com

Online backup systems represent another recent growth area, of which Carbonite is a fairly typical example. This is not a web-based solution—Carbonite is a piece of software that runs in the background on your computer, automatically copying or updating specified files or file types to a remote server. The moment you modify or create a new file, the server is updated. Consequently, if you accidentally erase a file or you have a drive failure, you can use the software to restore the originals from the server. If you're concerned about security, it isn't possible for your files to be viewed by other users as they are encrypted prior to leaving your computer.

Omnidrive

http://www.omnidrive.com

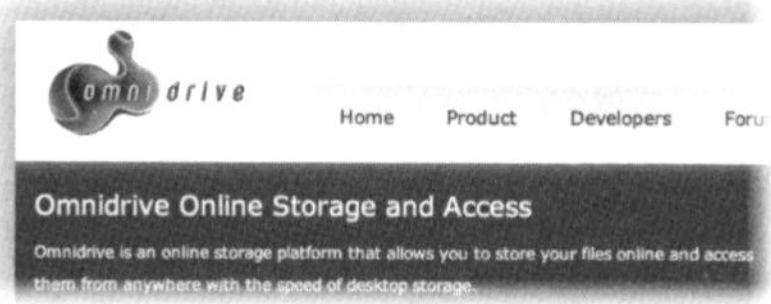

Omnidrive is another data hosting server. It works in much the same way as most others, although there is an emphasis on not only storing data, but on accessing it online. So, for example, if you have a text file uploaded, you can open and work on your document from within your web browser. To do this it uses the Zoho suite of web applications (*see page 208*), which has many different applications and is capable of reading many popular file formats, such as all of those used by Microsoft Office.

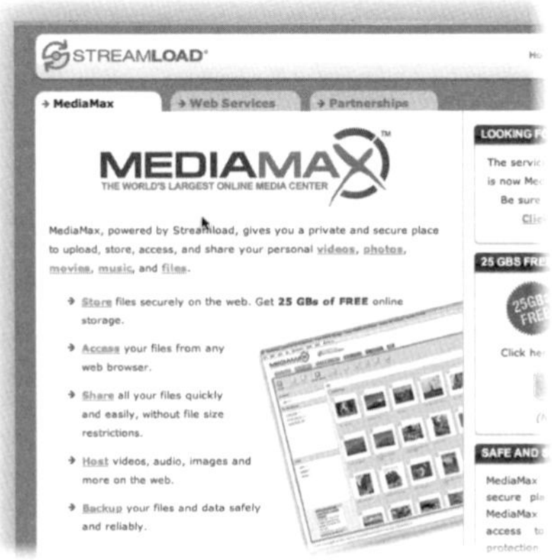
STREAMLOAD
MediaMax
Web Services
Partnerships
MEDIAMAX
THE WORLD'S LARGEST ONLINE MEDIA CENTER
MediaMax, powered by Streamload, gives you a private and secure place to upload, store, access, and share your personal videos, photos, movies, music, and files.
Store files securely on the web. Get 25 GBs of FREE online storage.
Access your files from any web browser.
Share all your files quickly and easily, without file size restrictions.
Host videos, audio, images and more on the web.
Backup your files and data safely and reliably.

StreamLoad

http://www.mediamax.com

The MediaMax/Streamload site offers not only secure data hosting and access to stored documents, but it can also be used as a host for music and video files. MediaMax claims to be the world's largest online media center, and can cater the storage of up to 1,000 gigabytes of data.

More Data Hosting Sites

4shared	http://4shared.com	TextDrive	http://www.textdrive.com
Allmydata	http://www.allmydata.com	Xdrive	http://www.xdrive.com
Bolt	http://www.bolt.com	Xmail	http://www.xmailharddrive.com
Bryght	http://www.bryght.com	Zingee	http://www.zingee.com
Gdisk	http://gdisk.sourceforge.net		
Grokthis	http://www.grokthis.net		
Hula	http://www.hula-project.org		
Iron Mountain	http://www.ironmountain.com		
Mailbigfile	http://www.mailbigfile.com		
Mozy	http://www.mozy.com		
Multiply	http://multiply.com		
Openomy	http://www.openomy.com		
Ourmedia	http://www.ourmedia.org		
Pando	http://www.pando.com		
Putfwd	http://www.putfwd.com		
Railsbase	http://railsbase.com		
Smartimagine	http://smartimagine.com		
Sproutit	http://www.sproutit.com		
Strongspace	http://www.strongspace.com		
Swapzies	http://www.swapzies.com		

mozy
online backup
HOME
LEARN MORE
BLOG
SUPPORT
NEWS
mozy
unlimited
automatic
secure
Download and install Mozy to ensure your data is safely backed up at a secure, remote location.
Mozy Unlimited
Got lots of stuff to backup?
Get Started Now!
Unlimited - $4.95/month
"Faster, safer and often less expensive than other storage methods"
— Jessica Vascellaro
How Does Mozy Online Backup Mea

Mapping

In 1962, in his book *The Gutenberg Galaxy: The Making of Typographic Man*, Marshall McLuhan described how electronic mass media had turned the world into a "global village." While he was by no means the originator of the phrase, his prophetic use of the term has been used by successive generations as a metaphor to describe the impact of new technology on the way we live and communicate—since the early 1990s, this has generally referred to developments on the Internet.

Few aspects of the World Wide Web are more awe-inspiring that its ability to reduce the globe to the size of a computer screen. Anyone who has downloaded the satellite software Google Earth (http://www.earth.google.com) could surely never fail to be amazed at how it's possible to shrink an image of the planet taken in space to a single street with a few clicks of a mouse button. Indeed, if you live in a large city in the U.S. or Western Europe you are more than likely to be able to see an aerial photograph of your home using this program.

This section of the book will focus on how you can use web-based maps to find your way around the world. Here, we'll focus unashamedly on some of the great features of the market leader, Google Maps.

Google Maps

http://maps.google.com

With its finger seemingly in all major web-related pies, here Google has provided a comprehensive mapping system that can be navigated by mouse to different levels of detail. Users may enter an area name, specific address, zip code (or its equivalent), or name a prominent location to quickly find it on the map. Google Maps also provides driving instructions between two locations, providing both a mapped diagram and a step-by-step list of how to get to a destination, along with estimates of how long the journey is likely to take. The system uses the same sources as Google Earth to provide high-resolution satellite images of most urban areas in the U.S. and Canada, and many others across the globe, including most of Europe and parts if South America, Australia, and the Far East.

Getting Started with Google Maps

Let's now take a look at Google Maps at work. We'll start off with a simple example of finding a location—in this case, 10 Downing Street, London—the residence of the British prime minister.

• Enter the URL: **http://maps.google.com**. If you have a Google account then sign in. If you don't have an account, now is the time to set one up—click on the text labeled **Sign Up** in the top-right-hand corner of the main screen and work through the registration process. Sign in with your ID and password.

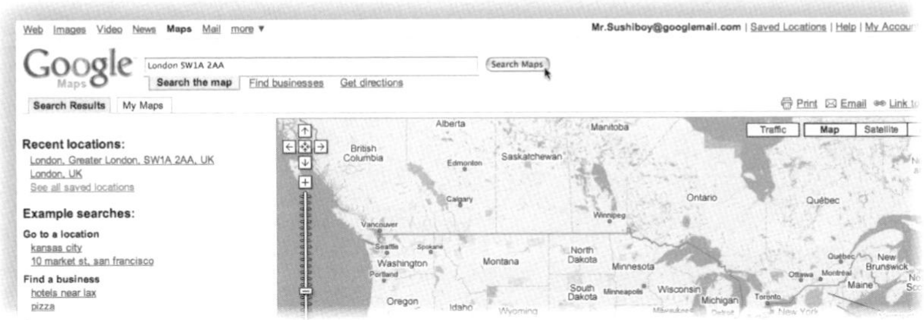

• Google Maps launches with an overview map of the U.S. Before we go any further, let's try out the navigation controls. Click on any of the buttons to maneuver around the map (*see box on right*). If you have a mouse with a scroll wheel, you may be able to use that to zoom in and out.

• To find a new map location, type it into the box near the top of the screen. In this case, we have entered **London SW1A 2AA**. (The latter is the post code of 10 Downing Street.) Click on the button marked **Search Map**.

Navigation Controls

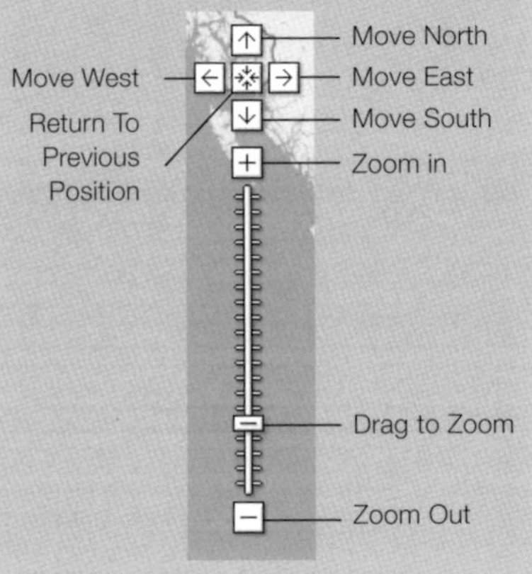

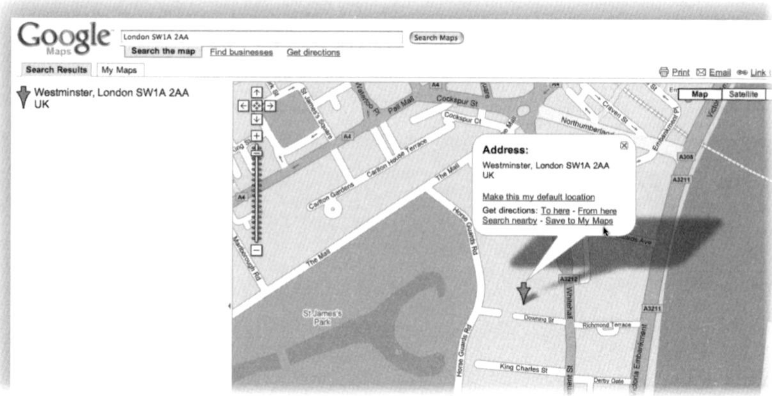

• You will now see a detailed map of the London address you chose (*see above*). This shows the map zoomed in to the maximum level of detail.

• A pop-up balloon will appear that contains the details of the address. It is linked to a marker on the map. You can store this location in your own **My Maps** list—it will remain in place on your map each time you open it up. Click on the button marked **Save in My Maps**.

• Give your location a title, and click on the **OK** button.

• Your My Maps list will open on the left-hand side of the screen. There you'll see the location that you have just entered. Click on the **Save** button to store your information.

Finding a Route Between Two Locations

Google Maps will also provide you with optimum routes between two different points. Let's now try to discover the quickest way to get between 10 Downing Street and the British Museum. (For this example we've already set up the latter location.)

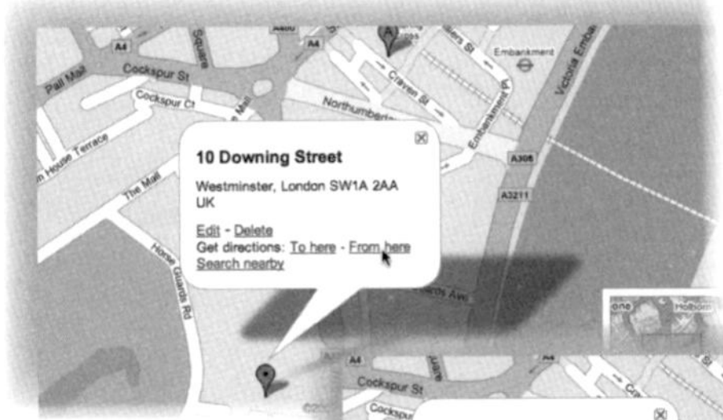

• Click on the **Downing Street** marker. In the pop-up balloon click on the text labeled **From Here**.

• A new pop-up balloon appears. Enter your destination in the box marked **End Address**. Click on the **Go** button.

• The route between the two destinations is shown on the map. To the left of the map there is a list of road directions, distances, and times involved in the journey.

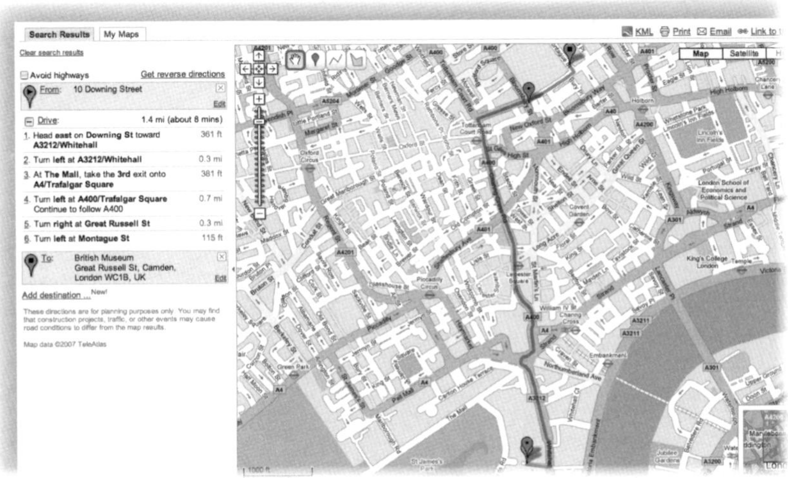

Alternative Views

Google Maps allows you to see a marked road-style map, a satellite photograph, or a hybrid of the two. Let's see how these work.

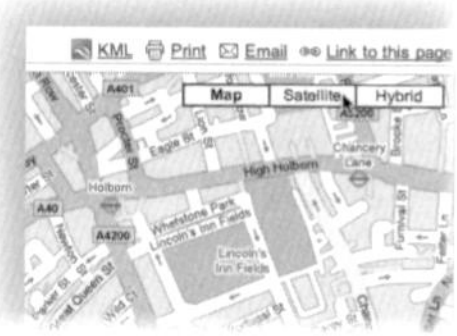

• In the top right-hand corner, click on the button marked **Satellite**.

• Your map has now transformed into a satellite photograph of the same area. These are the same images found when using the Google Earth software.

• Return to the top right-hand corner of the screen and click on the button marked **Hybrid**.

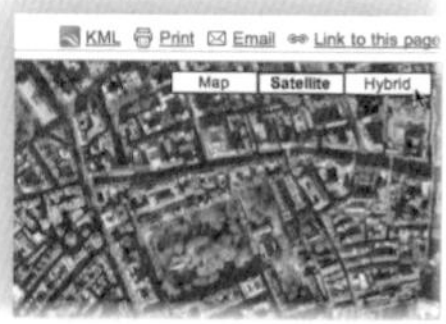

• The street names from the map are now applied to the satellite photograph. (Throughout these changes, the route line between destinations remains visible.)

Close Zoom

We'll now take a look at the highest available photographic resolution of our chosen destination.

- Click on the **Satellite** button. This will remove the street names from your map. In the **Navigation Control**, click on the button marked "**+**" until the photograph reaches its maximum level of magnification.

- This is a satellite aerial view of Number 10 Downing Street, London. As you can see, your location marker remains in place (*see bottom left of the picture*). Such high-resolution images are not available everywhere, but will be possible for most major cities.

Out of This World

Google Maps are not restricted to our own planet. There are NASA maps of some parts of the Moon available (**http://moon.google.com**) as well as an infrared map of the surface of Mars (**http://www.google.com/mars**). *(See right)*. The Moon maps contain location markers for all of NASA's previous moon landings.

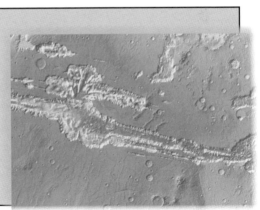

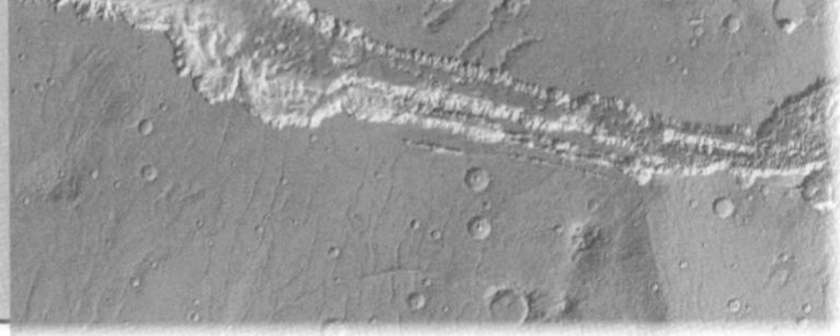

What's Nearby?

When you store locations on your Google Map, you have the option of making them public or private. If they are public, then others may find them in searches. Let's take a look at some potential uses for this idea.

• Returning to our map, click on the **Downing Street** marker. In the pop-up balloon, click on the text labeled **Search Nearby**.

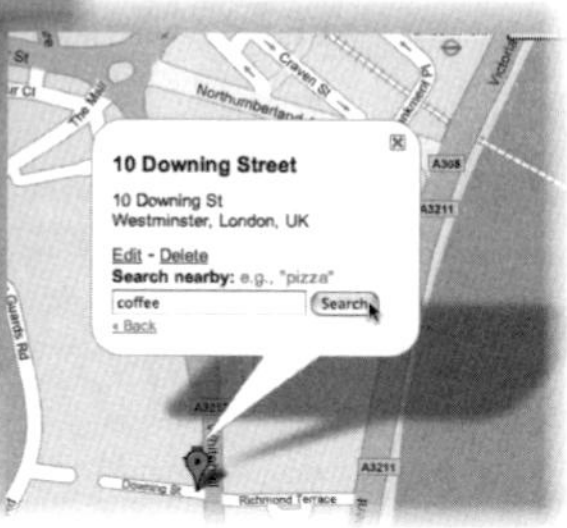

• The pop-up balloon will expand to include a search box. In this example we'll try to find a coffee bar as close as possible to 10 Downing Street. Type **Coffee** in the box and click on the **Search** button.

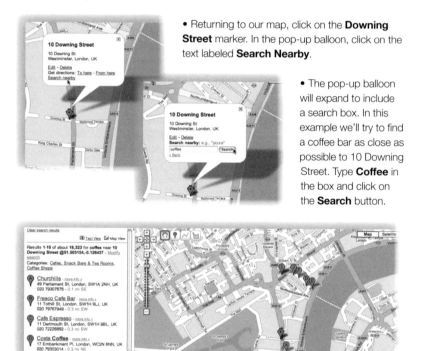

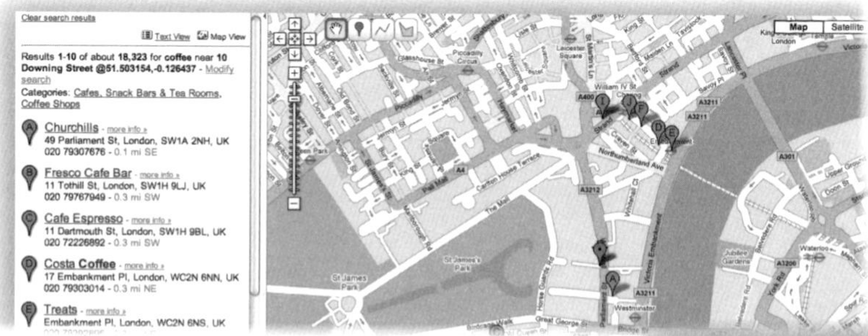

• The map will now show any nearby markers that have been tagged "coffee." The markers are labeled from A to Z, reflecting how close they are to the chosen location. There is a key to this list down the left-hand side of the screen. You can click on any of these markers to find more information.

Map Builder

http://mapbuilder.com

There are a growing number of "mash-up" websites on the Internet that make use of the vast resources of Google Maps, or its Yahoo! equivalents. Map Builder is one such application. It allows you to create maps and embed them into a personal website or other application, such as a MySpace page.

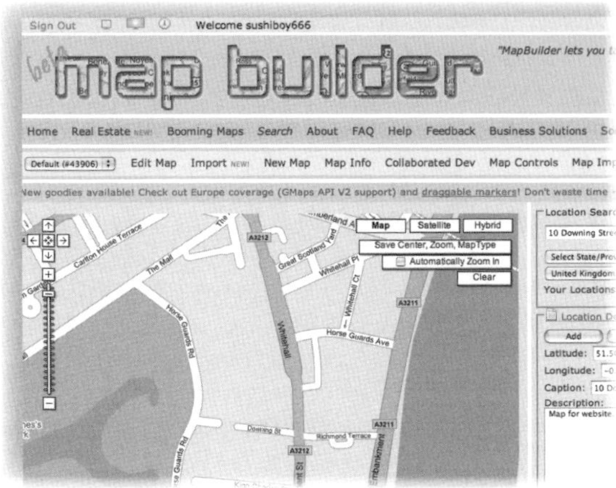
Sign Out
Welcome sushiboy666
map builder
"MapBuilder lets you
Home
Real Estate
Booming Maps
Search
About
FAQ
Help
Feedback
Business Solutions
Default (#43906)
Edit Map
Import
New Map
Map Info
Collaborated Dev
Map Controls
New goodies available! Check out Europe coverage (GMaps API V2 support) and draggable markers! Don't waste time
Map
Satellite
Hybrid
Save Center, Zoom, MapType
Automatically Zoom In
Clear
Location Search
Your Locations
Add
Latitude:
Longitude:
Caption:
Description:
Map for website
Whitehall
Horse Guards Ave
Downing St
Richmond Terrace

• Enter the URL: **http://mapbuilder.com**. Navigate the map space in the same way as you did with Google Maps until you find your chosen location. Add the location details to the panel on the right, including the latitude and longitude data, which can be copied and pasted from beneath the map.

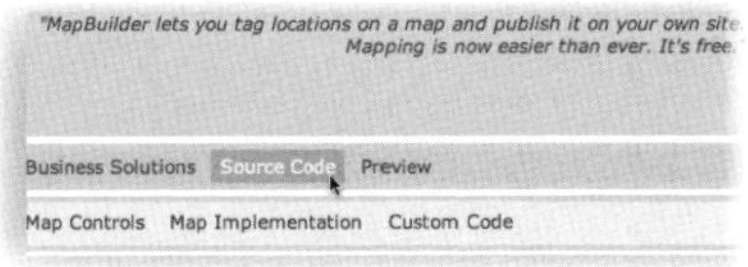
"MapBuilder lets you tag locations on a map and publish it on your own site
Mapping is now easier than ever. It's free
Business Solutions
Source Code
Preview
Map Controls
Map Implementation
Custom Code

• Click on the **Source Code** button.

Niagara Falls
<!DOCTYPE html PUBLIC "-//W3C//DTD XHTML 1.0 Strict//EN" "http://www.w3.org/TR/xhtml1/
<html xmlns="http://www.w3.org/1999/xhtml">
<head>
<meta http-equiv="content-type" content="text/html; charset=utf-8"/>
<title>Default</title>
<meta name="title" content="MapBuilder - GoogleMap API Source Code Generator." />
<meta name="description" content="MapBuilder.net lets you tag locations on a map and publi
<meta name="keywords" content="Google Maps API, PHP, AJAX, XML" />
<meta name="author" content="Andrew Bidochko. http://www.mapbuilder.net" />
<style type="text/css">
/* Generic map, side bar holder styles */
.MapBuilder {font: normal small verdana, arial, helvetica, sans-serif; font-size: 10pt; margin:
.MapBuilder a {text-decoration: none; color: #0066CC; background-color: transparent;}
.MapBuilder a:hover {color: #F60; background-color: transparent;}
.MapBuilder h1 {font-weight: bold; font-size: 16pt; color: #369; border-bottom: 2px solid #3
/* Info Window styles */
.IW { width: 350px;}
.IWContent {height: 120px; overflow:auto;}
.IWCaption {font-weight: bold; font-size: 12pt; color: #369; border-bottom: 2px solid #369;}
.IWFooter {margin-top: 5px; font-size: 8pt; }
.IWFooterZoom {}

• The window that opens shows a scrolling box containing HTML code. Highlight the code, copy it, and paste it into your website or MySpace page.

Planiglobe

http://www.planiglobe.com

A different—and simpler—approach comes from Planiglobe. This website enables users to create digital maps for download in EPS or vector form—which can be imported by such graphics programs as Adobe Illustrator. They can then be used in any digital documents.

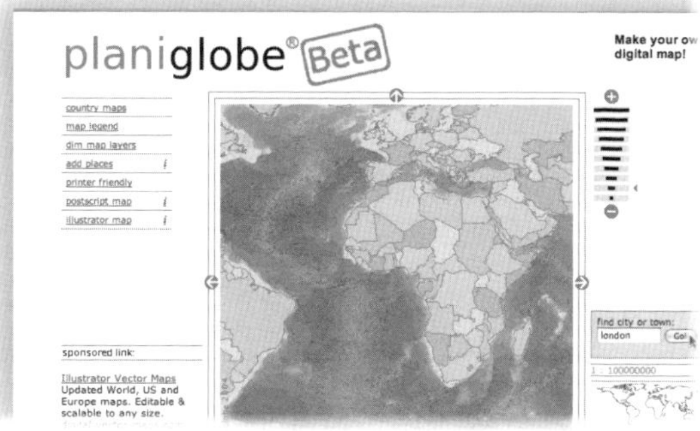

- Enter the URL: **http://www.planiglobe.com**.

- In the box labeled **Find City or Town**, type in your chosen location name—in this example, we'll use **London**.

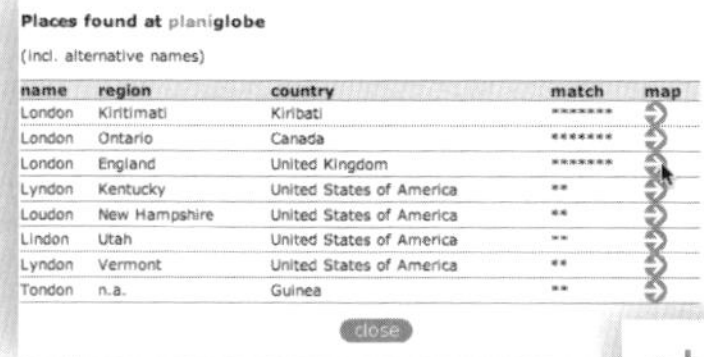

Places found at planiglobe

(incl. alternative names)

name	region	country	match	map
London	Kiritimati	Kiribati	*******	
London	Ontario	Canada	*******	
London	England	United Kingdom	*******	
Lyndon	Kentucky	United States of America	**	
Loudon	New Hampshire	United States of America	**	
Lindon	Utah	United States of America	**	
Lyndon	Vermont	United States of America	**	
Tondon	n.a.	Guinea	**	

close

- If your search yields more than one result, a pop-up window will emerge listing all of the available possibilities. Choose one from the list and click on the arrow button.

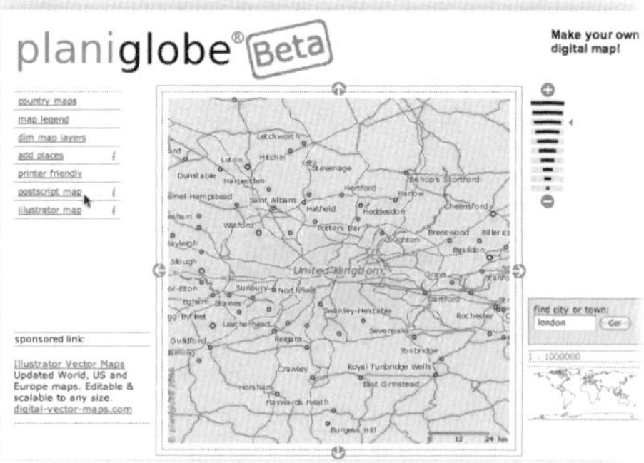

- To create your digital map, click on either the **Postscript Map** or **Illustrator Map** buttons, depending on the format you require. The digital files will then be downloaded to your hard drive.

Tagzania

http://www.tagzania.com

Tagzania is a cross between tagging and mapping. Users may mark any locations they choose and allocate multiple tags to them. If you perform a text search you'll see a Google map with its markers in place.

Other Mapping Sites

Chicagocrime	http://www.chicagocrime.org
Feedmap	http://www.feedmap.net
Flashearth	http://www.flashearth.com
Flickrmap	http://www.flickrmap.com
Gchart	http://www.gchart.com
Gvisit	http://www.gvisit.com
Locallive	http://local.live.com
Map24	http://www.nl.map24.com
Mappr	http://www.mappr.com
Panoramio	http://www.panoramio.com
Placeopedia	http://www.placeopedia.com
Platial	http://platial.com
Plaze	http://www.plazes.com
Powermap	http://hobbiton.thisside.net
Publicloos	http://paul.kedrosky.com/publicloos
Toeat	http://www.toeat.com
Tripmojo	http://www.tripmojo.com
Vlogmap	http://www.vlogmap.org
Wayfaring	http://www.wayfaring.com
Web20map	http://www.fourio.com/web20map
Yahoo! maps	http://maps.yahoo.com/beta

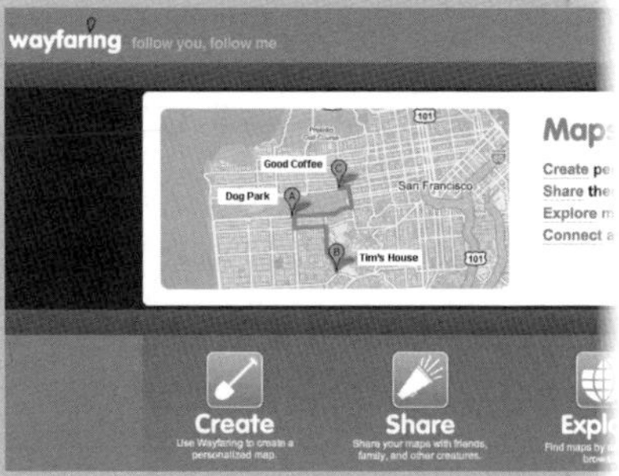

Music

Easy-to-access music content was one of the factors that drove the great demand for faster Internet connections speeds. This in turn largely fueled the whole music download culture, creating a generation of potential consumers who rarely went anywhere near a music store to buy a CD. Much of the well-documented illegal activity takes place on news groups or peer-to-peer file sharing networks (*see page 112*). Here, however, we'll look at legitimate ways in which you can listen to music on the Internet—in particular, some that have successfully integrated aspects of social networking.

Last.fm

http://www.last.fm/dashboard

Last.fm is a UK-based Internet radio station and music community website. It was founded in 2002 and is one of the world's largest social music platforms, with an estimated active user base of over 15 million listeners in more than 232 countries. Last.fm evolved out of the merger of two different applications: Audioscrobbler was a music recommendation system which began as a computer science project by Richard Jones, an undergraduate at the University of Southampton in the UK. Last.fm was founded in Germany as an Internet radio station and music community website, but used similar music profiles to generate playlists, with "love" and "ban" buttons enabling users to customize their profiles. In 2003 the Audioscrobbler and Last.fm teams merged and set up headquarters in London. In summer 2007, the company was acquired by CBS Interactive for $280 million, but its creators remain at the helm.

Last.fm in Use

At the heart of Last.fm remains the "Audioscrobbler" music recommendation system, which enables the creation of a detailed profile of each user's musical tastes based on storing details of all the songs the user plays, either on the streamed radio station or on the user's own computer or mp3 player. This data is then "scrobbled"— transferred to the Last.fm database—via a plug-in. Profile data can be viewed on the user's personal web page. Registration is necessary to set up a profile but is not necessary to view the Last.fm website or listen to radio stations. With over 10 million tracks "scrobbled" each day, the popularity of the site at peak times can cause the databases to overload.

Last.fm also offers numerous social networking features. For example, it can recommend and play artists similar to the user's favorites.

Let's now look at Last.fm in action. Here we'll select a band, see what's available by them, and then see if it can recommend any music in a similar style.

• Begin by entering the URL: **http://www.last.fm/dashboard**. Click on the button marked **Music**.

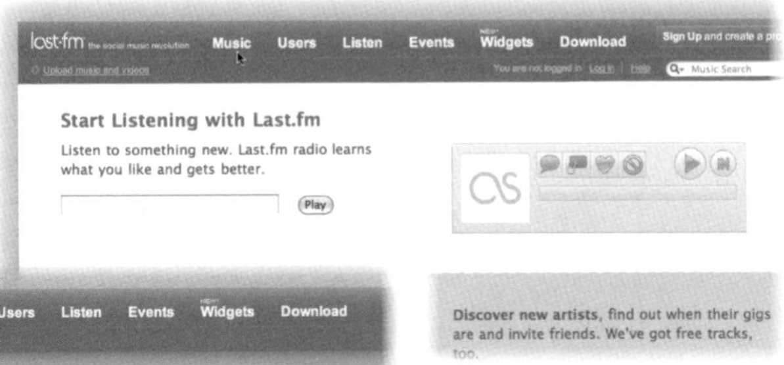

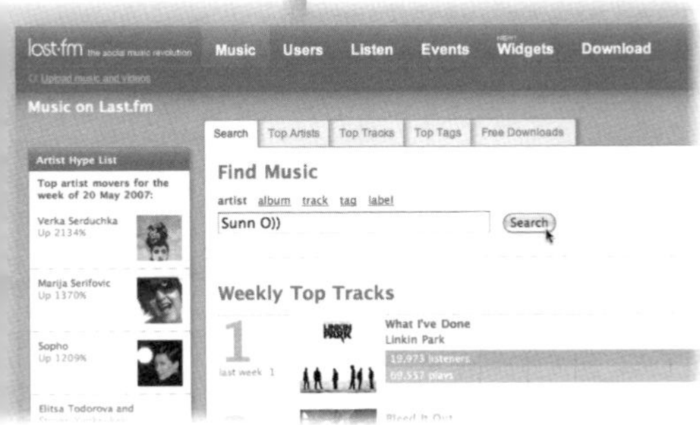

• In the **Music** page (*see left*), click on the tab marked **Search**. In the box beneath the legend **Find Music**, enter the name of the musician or band you wish to seek. In this case we'll use the rock band **Sunn O)))**. Click on the **Search** button.

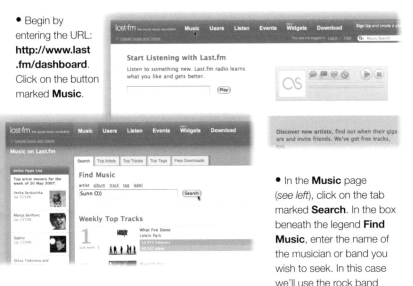

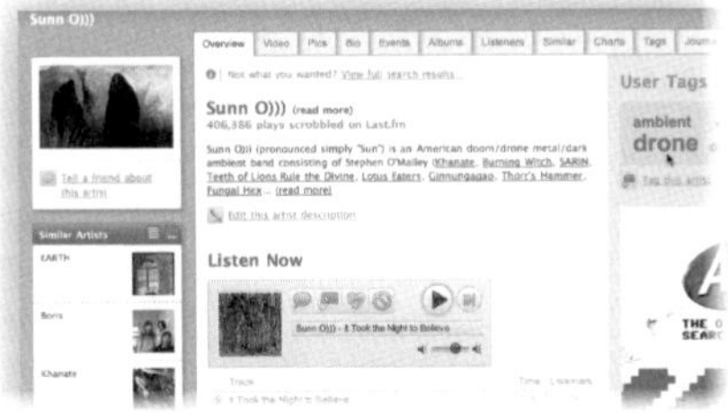

• If the band is known to the website a new set of tabbed pages will appear, opening at the **Overview** tab. In this case, we have a brief biography and can also listen to a track by the band by clicking on the **Play** button.

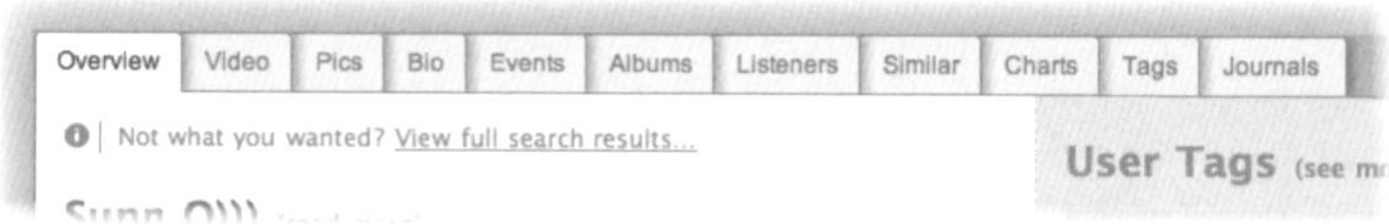

Let's take a brief look at all of the tabs for a moment. As you can see, there is scope for watching videos by the band if they exist, looking at photographs, discographies, biographies, and even latest events in which the band is involved. Significantly, much of this information is provided by Last.fm users. For example, the biography page (click on the **Bio** button), takes the form of a "wiki," and can be written and edited at will by any registered users.

- Now let's look at some of the suggestions that Last.fm can identify. If you click on the **Tags** tab, you will see a "cloud" of categories set up by other users for the artist in question. In this case, click on the tag marked **Drone**.

- You'll now see a list of albums that have also been tagged **Drone**. There are also links to where they can be bought online.

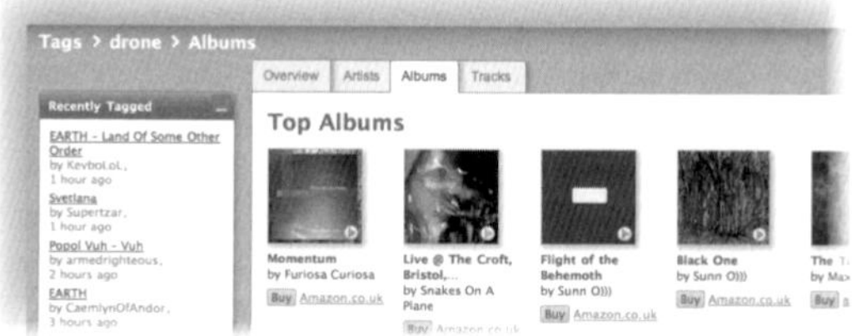

Pandora

http://www.pandora.com

Working on lines that are not altogether dissimilar from Last.fm, Pandora is an automated recommendation and Internet radio service created by the Music Genome Project. Users enter a song or artist and the service responds by playing selections that it believes to be musically similar. Users can then provide feedback on song choices—the system then takes that into account for future selections.

Over 400 different musical attributes (or "genes") are taken into account when suggesting tracks. If we look at a selection beginning with the letter "H," we find: "hand percussion," "hard bop qualities," "hard bop roots," "hard rock roots," "hardcore rap attitude," and "harmonica playing." These 400 attributes are combined into larger groups called "focus traits," of which there are 2,000.

So let's see Pandora in action.

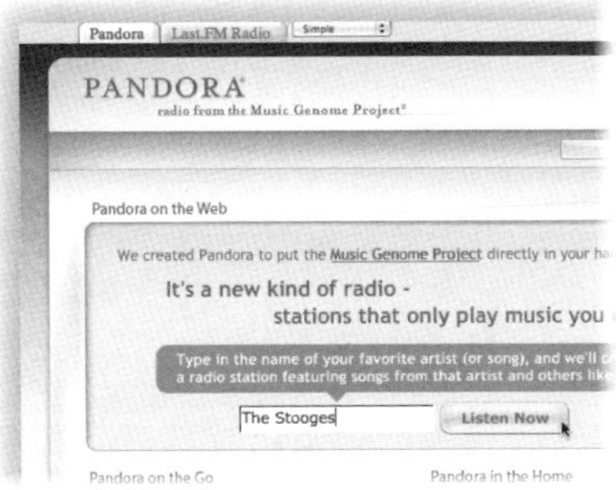

• Begin by entering Pandora's URL: **http://www.pandora.com**. Type in the name of the artist or song that interests you, and Pandora will create a personal streamed radio station based on your request. In this example, we've entered **the Stooges**. Click on the button marked **Listen Now**.

• Pandora will select your first track. If you like the track, click on the **Thumbs-Up** button; if you don't, click on the **Thumbs-Down** button. To find out more information about the track, or where to buy it, click on the **Arrow** button in between. If you want to move the track on, click on the **Fast-Forward** button, on the right of the navigation bar, and Pandora will begin to play your second selection.

Yahoo! Music

http://music.yahoo.com

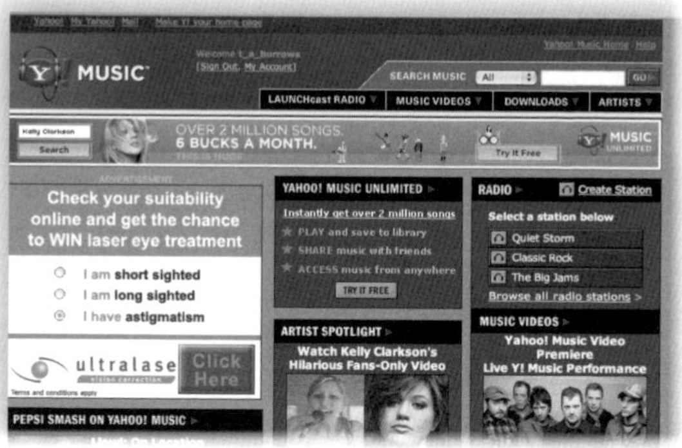

The most popular Internet site of its kind, Yahoo! Music provides of a variety of music services, including Internet radio, music videos, news, artist information, and original programming.

It began life as a magazine called Launch, which was issued in both standard print format and as an interactive CD-ROM. The service was purchased by Yahoo! in 2001 for $12 million and integrated into their website. Unlike Last.fm, which has a large core of "underground" music fans, Yahoo! Music is resolutely mainstream.

eJamming

http://www.ejamming.com

An interesting experiment with huge possibilities for musicians, eJamming has been touted as a kind of Skype for musicians. This is not a web-based product, but downloadable peer-to-peer software that enables musicians to play with one another remotely. The cofounder, Alan Glueckman, conceived eJamming with his his cousin in mind—Aerosmith's drummer

Joey Kramer—so that the band could still rehearse when one or more of its members were away. It's unknown if Aerosmith has tried it out yet, though.

The technology is quite tricky, though. Not only does it require very high quality audio, but there has to be very low audio latency—the microsecond delays that can affect timing when recording and playing music using computers.

There's also a social networking angle to eJamming in that it aims to put like-minded musicians together. However, it isn't a free service—at $15 per month per person that can mount up over an entire band.

Kompoz

http://www.kompoz.com

A slightly different approach to eJamming, Kompoz is aimed at collaborative composition and recording rather than live performance. A musician will kick off a new project by uploading an audio file and other musicians can then add their own parts. As new files are added, previous files are given a version number, so there's a record of the history and progress of the work. Each new project has its own workspace, which includes a forum where ideas, lyrics, chord charts, and the like can be discussed.

The H-Lounge

http://www.h-lounge.com

H-Lounge is a digital music distributor that enables artists, musicians, and labels to sell their music directly to public as mp3s, ringtones, or Skypetones.

Singshot

http://www.singshot.com

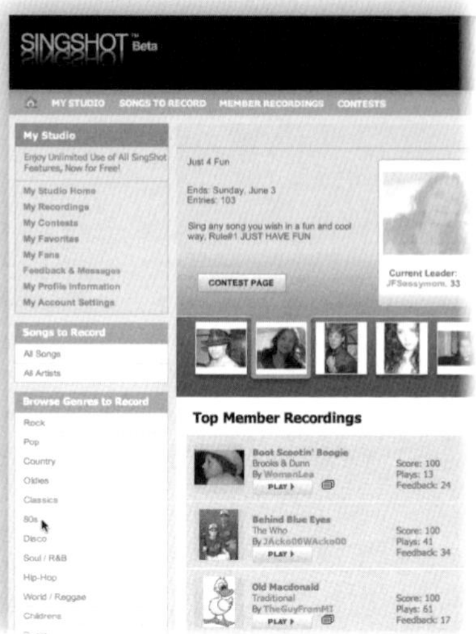

This is a fantastically entertaining website! In essence, it's an online social networking karaoke machine. You can record a vocal track over the top of pre-recorded backings, save it, tag it, and let others hear what you've done.

Let's begin by listening to some of the work that's already there.

- Begin by entering the URL: **http://www.singshot.com**. In the panel headed **Browse Genres to Record**, let's click on **80s**.

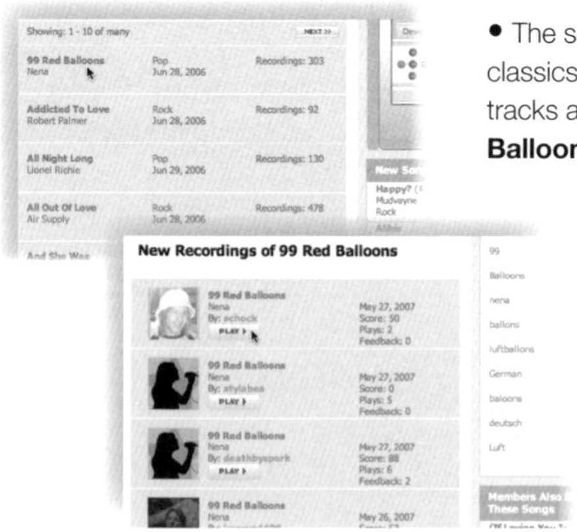

- The screen that follows gives you a list of classics from the 1980s that have backing tracks available. Let's choose **99 Red Balloons** from the list.

- You'll now see a list of the most recent versions of the song stored on Singshot. To hear one of them, click on the **Play** button. Once the track has finished playing, you can give it a star rating or add your own comments. Or record your own version.

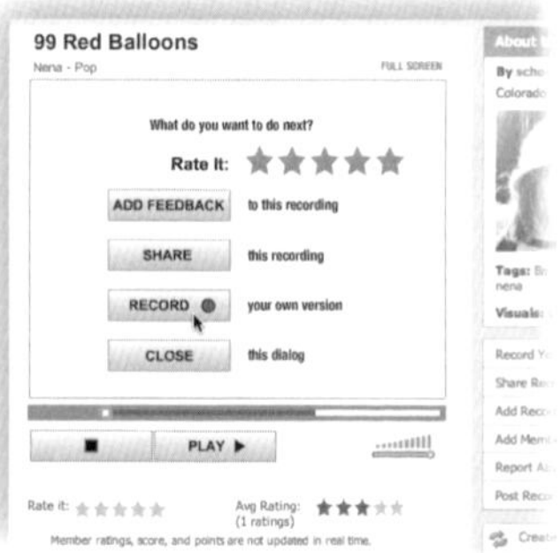

Recording a Song

To record your own version of a song, you first need to connect a microphone to your computer. If you have a built-in microphone you can use that, although it won't sound too great! The best results will be obtained by plugging a reasonable quality microphone into a built-in soundcard or external unit. There are also a number of USB microphones available that simply plug directly into a USB socket. Singshot can also make video recordings if you have a DV recorder or webcam connected. Click on the **Settings** button and work through the options to set up your microphone and (if required) video camera.

To begin recording, simply click on the **Record** button. In true karaoke style the lyrics will pop up on the screen as you sing along. At the end of the song you can see/hear what you've done by clicking on the **Review** button. If you want to save your performance on Singshot, click on the **Store** button. (But only do that if you don't mind people seriously dissing your singing!)

More Music Sites

Dottunes	**http://www.dottunes.net**	**Projectopus**	**http://www.projectopus.com**
FunkPlayer	**http://www.funk-player.com**	**RateYourMusic**	**http://rateyourmusic.com**
Jamendo	**http://www.jamendo.com**	**SideLoad**	**http://www.sideload.com**
Mercora	**http://search.mercora.com**	**Snaptune**	**http://www.snaptune.com**
MusicIP	**http://www.musicip.com**	**Squihr**	**http://www.squishr.com**
Musicmobs	**http://www.musicmobs.com**	**Streampad**	**http://www.streampad.com**
Musipedia	**http://www.musipedia.org**	**Tubes**	**http://www.tubesmusic.com**
Plurn	**http://www.plurn.com/app**	**UpTo11**	**http://upto11.net**
PodBop	**http://podbop.org**	**Webjay**	**http://www.webjay.org**

News

Some of the most successful websites of the past decade—at least in terms of regular and loyal users—have been news broadcast sites. The BBC "ticker" website, for example, is one of the most popular news sites in the world, let alone the UK. Also widely viewed are sites allied to the most popular daily broadsheet newspapers. Some of these sites, while not necessarily at the technical sharp end, were swift off the mark in paving the way for many of the innovations commonly associated with Web 2.0, such as RSS newsfeeds, podcasts, and allowing their readers the opportunity to make comments on news stories. The most innovative of the current crop of news based websites are those that draw their news stories from a wide variety of other sites, or those whose users have acted as news editors in selecting stories.

Bits of News

http://www.bitsofnews.com

A vast scrolling news resource, Bits of News contains items from across the world on a wide range of topics, including politics, culture, economics, science, and technology. Registered users are able to submit news stories they have found elsewhere to the site's editorial staff.

A particularly valuable aspect of the Bits of News site can be found in the sidebars, which contains links to most of the major British and American news sources on the Internet. Stories can also be syndicated via RSS, ATOM, and Del.icio.us.

Clipmarks

http://www.clipmarks.com

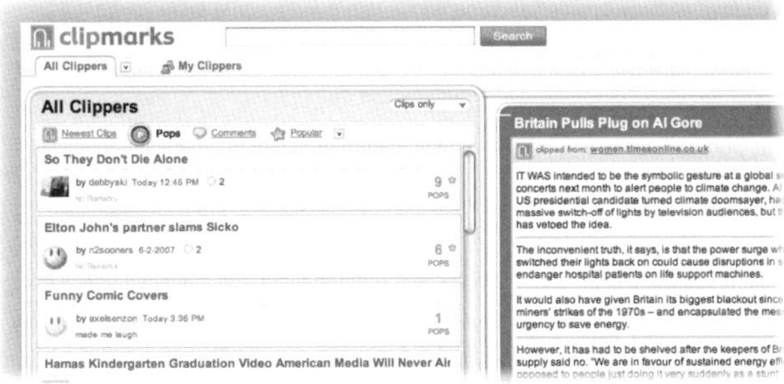

As with many aspects of this book, there is considerable crossover between some of the sections: Clipmarks could equally be termed a social bookmarking site or a blogging tool. It was founded by New York lawyer Eric Goldstein, who claims to have been inspired by cutting and pasting from the Web into a Word file only to create an unreadable mess. It is an application that enables users to clip and save information from the Web. This need not be an entire website or news story, but simply the required part. Clips can be stored privately, tagged and made public, or attached to blogs. Clipmarks uses a browser plug-in that brings up an interactive clipping menu. When you scroll over text, Clipmarks highlights it and allows you to clip it and store it on the Clipmarks server.

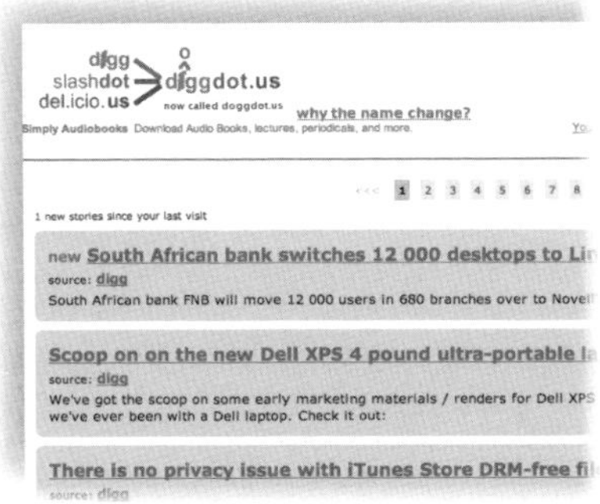

Doggdot.us

http://doggdot.us

Doggdot.us is a news mash-up using Digg, Slashdot, and Del.icio.us. Formerly it was known as Diggdot .us until receiving a cease-and-desist order from Digg's lawyers, forcing them into a change of name.

Findory

http://www.findory.com

Filtering information has been a growing issue since the early days of the Internet. Simply *how* do we process such a vast amount of data and still have time for a life? One way forward is to allow filtering websites to make choices on your behalf.

Findory is a news site that claims to learn from choices you make, and thus, over time, aims to offer information tailored to your own interests. Once you have registered and signed in, Findory keeps a record of the news stories that you read, and those for which you search. The website itself draws its data from the world's major news sites.

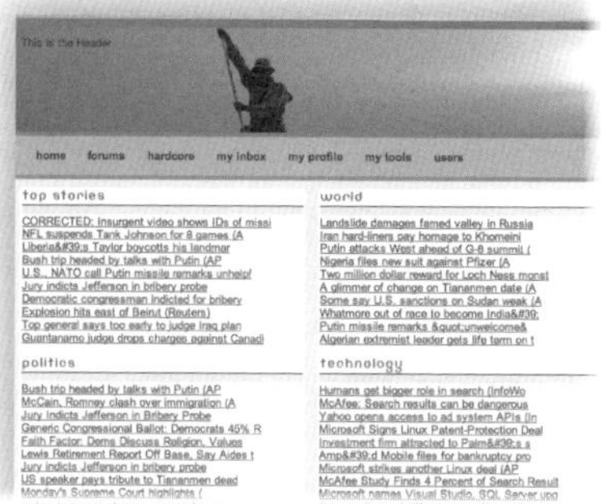

Gabbr

http://www.gabbr.com

Gabbr is a community-based social networking news site that streams and organizes the latest news from such important agencies as CNN, Reuters, Associated Press, and the BBC. Main headlines are updated in real time and are readable through Gabbr's interface. Users can interact with one another and discuss or debate any news story, scoring "karma" points for their contributions. Gabbr also includes online bookmarking features that, rather like Del.icio.us, are stored online and can be accessed from anywhere. There's even a very basic online gaming capability where users can play "Rock, Paper, Scissors" against the computer to earn additional points.

Newsvine

http://www.newsvine.com

Based in Seattle, Washington, Newsvine is a website consisting of community-driven news stories and opinions. Users can write articles and save links to external content, vote, comment, and chat on article pages created by both users and by journalists from the Associated Press, ESPN, and New Scientist.

Wired

http://www.wired.com

One of the Internet's best-loved magazines, the Wired website is a rich source of news stories on technology, science, culture, business, and politics.

More News Sites

Backfence	http://www.backfence.com	Megite	http://www.megite.com
Blogniscient	http://blogniscient.com	Memeorandum	http://www.memeorandum.com
Buzzingo	http://www.buzzingo.com	Newsalloy	http://www.newsalloy.com
Crisscross	http://www.crisscross.com	Newsgarbage	http://www.newsgarbage.com
Dailymashup	http://dailymashup.com	Newzingo	http://newzingo.com
Frankenfeed	http://www.frankenfeed.com	Nowpublic	http://www.nowpublic.com
Hypersuper	http://www.hypersuper.com	Shoutwire	http://www.shoutwire.com
Hypetracker	http://www.hypetracker.com	Slashdigg	http://www.slashdigg.com
Inform	http://www.inform.com	Tailrank	http://www.tailrank.com
Knownow	http://www.knownow.com	Topix	http://www.topix.net

Peer-to-Peer Sharing

One of the most controversial aspects of the Internet over the past decade, peer-to-peer (or "P2P" as it's usually known) is a method of sharing files between two computers. It has been the bane of the world's media industries since it came to prominence in the late 1990s, when increasing numbers of young people started using programs such as Napster to illegally download mp3s of music, and CDs sales began to fall sharply. In turn, this aided the acceptance of the mp3 format, the appeal of which was that it could produce an audio quality not vastly lower than a CD, but at less than a tenth of the size—making download times substantially faster. More recently, BitTorrents have taken P2P file sharing further, enabling much larger files, such as video formats or computer software, to be distributed across the Internet.

A Brief History of File Sharing

In the early days of the Internet, the only effective way of sharing large files was by FTP (File Transfer Protocol). An "anonymous" FTP server would be used to give users access to send or receive files to one another. It was a messy process, very user *un*friendly, and was only understood by those with technical savvy. However, for most people, the principal impediment was more basic—the slow speed of domestic Internet connections meant that large music and video files could take hours (even days!) to download.

In 1999, Napster made its mark on the world as the first popular P2P application, taking advantage of the development and early uptake of the file compression techniques that gave birth to the mp3 format. At its peak in 2001, it was estimated that there were 60 million Napster users across the globe—and that was beginning to bite significantly into the world's commercial CD markets. Unsurprisingly, the major music labels began to flex their muscles, threatening both the P2P software providers and music downloaders with legal action. However, the main problem they faced was that there was nothing intrinsically wrong in allowing people to copy legal files from one computer to another, and how would Napster and other networks be able to tell what was legal and what was not? Furthermore, so many people were now engaged in illegal music copying that it was simply not practical to launch lawsuits against individuals. In the end, Napster in its original form was put out of business by the sheer bulk of filed lawsuits and attempts at reaching out-of-court settlements. The

same fate befell WinMX, the other major P2P application of the early 1990s. However, as soon as one P2P ceased operation, others emerged to fill the hole, and it was clear that chasing downloaders, uploaders, and software developers through the courts was not a long-term solution. Some turned toward other tactics, such as making legal downloads more attractive. But, in truth, the mass acceptance of download culture has forced the industry to reconsider what it considers to be commercial "product" —and recorded music is accepted as no longer being the earner it once was.

P2P applications, whether of the traditional variety or the newer BitTorrent style, continue to increase in popularity.

How Does P2P Work?

The basic concept of P2P is pretty simple: a person with a fast Internet connection runs a dedicated piece of software that links their computer to a network of other users who are hooked up to the same network at that moment in time. Users will make a selection of files on their hard drives available for sharing. Anyone looking for a specific item will use a search feature built into the software to see if it matches anything offered within the network. If they see something they like, they can then download that file directly from the other person's computer. There are a large number of different popular P2P programs—Kazaa, LimeWire, imesh, SoulSeek, and BearShare, for example. All of these can be downloaded free of charge.

More recently, a different approach to P2P has taken over in popularity. "BitTorrents" work by downloading small segments of files from many different websites at the same time. This takes the pressure away from the file sharer, who only has to upload once. This is especially significant for those with monthly bandwidth allowances set by their ISPs, which can easily be eroded if a large number of individuals decide they want to download their files.

BitTorrents are widely used for sharing video material—indeed there have been cases of feature films being pirated and made available in this way before their official release. Not that we are endorsing such practices in this book, of course.

LimeWire

http://limewire.com

Gnutella is one of the world's most popular P2P file sharing networks. It was developed in 2000, and it is thought that up to one million users can be found online at any given time. There are a number of popular software clients for accessing Gnutella; we'll look at a Java-based program called LimeWire.

Loading LimeWire

Start by downloading and installing the LimeWire software. There are two versions available: the basic version is free; the "pro" version contains additional features, but is a commercial product, and so has to purchased.

• Enter the URL: **http://www.limewire.com**. To kick off the download process, click on the button marked **Get It Now!** In the next screen, choose which version of LimeWire you want to download—select **Get Basic**.

• Before the download begins, LimeWire will ask you to state what you intend to do with the software. Click on the button marked **I Will Not Use LineWire for Copyright Infringement**. If you click on the other button—the one indicating that you *might* break the law—you won't be allowed to go any further.

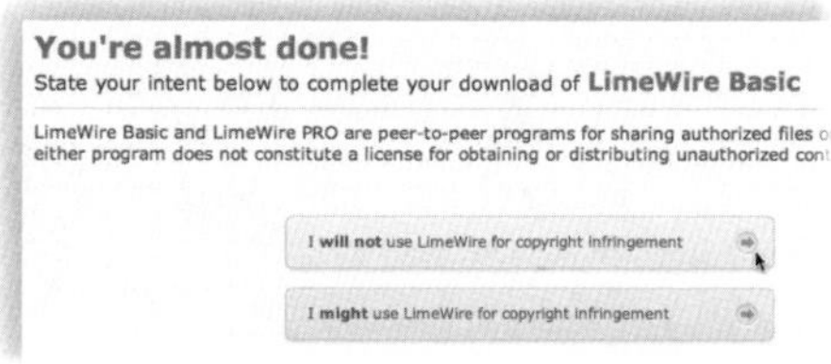

• Choose the version of the software appropriate to your type of computer. Click on the text to start the download.

• To install the software, follow the instructions—these will be specific to your chosen platform. LimeWire is now ready to run.

Running LimeWire

Now let's run the program and try to download something from another user on the Gnutella network.

• Launch the program. From the **File** menu, select **Connect**. You will now be joined up with the network.

• Now let's look for something to download. In the top left of the window you can select what type of item you are looking for: **Images**, **Documents**, **Audio**, **Video**, and **Programs**. Click on the button marked **All Types**.

• In the box headed **Filename** we'll enter our search. Let's see if we can find anything on there relating to everybody's favorite band, the Ramones.

• As we can see from the panel above the list in the window, there are 251 items that fit the bill. The columns to the right of the name are worth looking at: **Type** tells you the file format; **Size** indicates how large it is; **Speed** tells you the kind of connection that the other person has—which will give an indication of how fast the download will be; **Bitrate** indicates the quality of the file—mp3s below 192 kbps will not sound the best.

• Highlight the track that interests you and click on the **Download** button. The file will be copied onto your drive. (Note: we won't *actually* be downloading this track because that would be infringing copyright, which is, of course, illegal.)

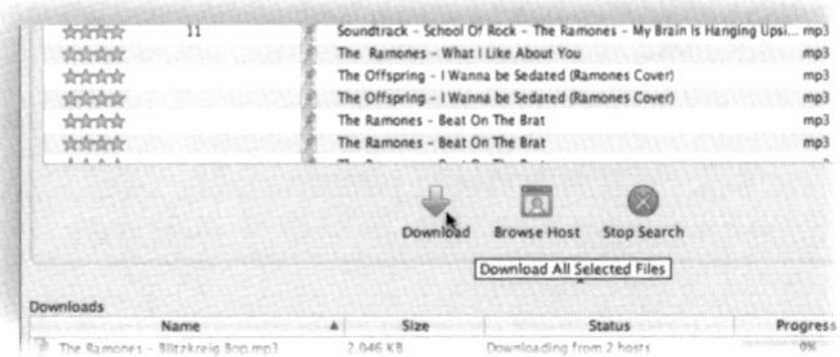

SoulSeek

http://www.slsknet.org

While the LimeWire/Gnutella network is very good for all kinds of content, if you are interested in music—especially of the independent variety—then SoulSeek is seriously worth considering. The work of former Napster programmer Nir Arbel, SoulSeek relies on its own central server. It has one major advantage over most other traditional P2P programs in that it has the capability of selecting and downloading a complete folder of files. This saves time if you want to download a complete album's worth of mp3s—to do the same with LimeWire you would have to figure out which tracks made up the album, and then select and download each file independently.

SoulSeek is very popular with producers and musicians, so there is a good deal of music available legitimately.

Using SoulSeek

To download software for Windows computers, go to the SoulSeek website, which is **http://www.slsknet.org/download.html**. For Mac users, you can download a program called SoulseeX from **http://chris.schleifer.net**.

• Launch your chosen software.

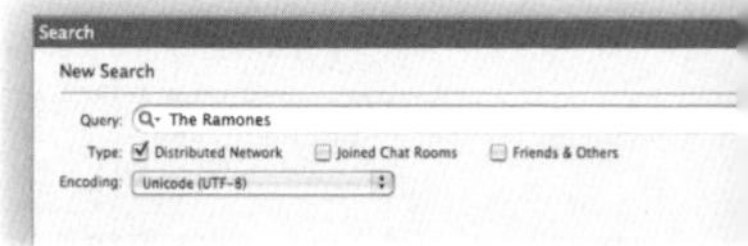

• In the **Query** box at the top of the screen type in your search text. Press the **Enter** key.
• The files available for download appear in staggered folders. The sharer has a top-level folder, which may contain a number of album folders, each of which contain mp3 files. You can download individual files, albums, or *everything* that user has on offer. (Note: SoulSeek users may prevent anyone they choose from downloading their files: taking too much while sharing too little is one of the most common reasons for such "bans" taking place.)

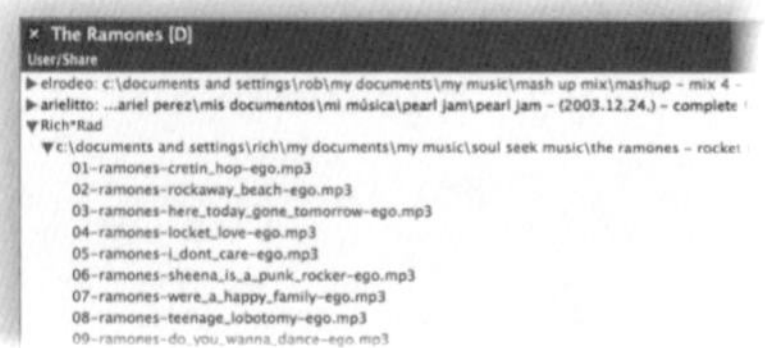

BitTorrents

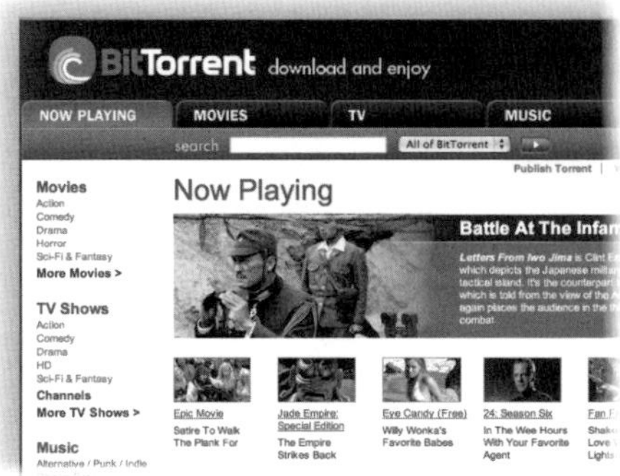

Although BitTorrent is now the most popular mode of sharing software, music videos, and digital books, by Internet standards its take-off was quite sluggish. The first torrent network was created in 2001 by a Python-language programmer named Bram Cohen. His intention was to share it freely. However, it wasn't until 2005 that the rest of the world caught on.

So how is BitTorrent different from previous P2P networks like Gnutella and Kazaa? As we've already said, the latter networks depend on the uploader repeatedly transferring files as requested. BitTorrent, on the other hand, is a true P2P network in that it is the user base as a whole that does the file serving.

How Does It Work?

Two key phrases to understand with torrent sharing are "swarming" and "tracking." Swarming refers to splitting large files into hundreds of smaller segments, and then sharing them across a "swarm" of linked users. Downloading a large number of small segments from many different sources at the same time prevents the bottlenecking that occurs with single-source sharing, and thus is much faster.

Tracking refers to specific servers that help members of the "swarm" find one another. Special torrent software (*see page 120*) is used to upload, download, and reconstruct the segments into complete files; torrent text files act as pointers during this process.

The way torrents work actively encourages users to share (or "seed") their files while punishing users who "leech"—take files without sharing. Download speeds are controlled by BitTorrent tracking servers, who monitor the swarm. If you are identified as a seed, servers will reward you by increasing your bandwidth; if you are a leech, the tracking servers can choke your download speeds almost to a standstill. Leeches are unwelcome in a BitTorrent!

It does take a while and a little technical know-how to set up a computer for dealing with torrents, but the results can be very worthwhile, especially if you intend to share large files.

How to Use Torrent Sharing

There are four different elements that you need (or need access to) to set yourself up for torrent sharing:

- BitTorrent client software for uploading, downloading, and constructing files
- Tracker server
- Torrent text file that points to the files you want to download
- Torrent search engine that helps you find torrent text files
- A high-speed Internet connection with an ISP that will allow torrent file trading

Now let's take a step-by-step walk through the complete torrent process. You may need some patience here—this is one area covered in this book that can be taxing from a technical point of view.

Client Software

Begin by downloading and installing your BitTorrent client software. (*A list is shown at the foot of the page.*) Initially, you don't need to launch the program, but it should be in place, ready for action.

Torrent Search Engine

Use a special torrent search engine to find torrent text files on the Internet. (*A list is shown on page 119.*) Although P2P sharing is a completely legal activity, the authorities are mindful of the fact that much of what takes place in the P2P online world infringes copyright law. Periodically you will find even some of the best-known

Torrent Software

ABC	http://pingpong-abc.sourceforge.net		
Anatomic P2P	http://www.anatomic.berlios.de	G3 Torrent	http://www.g3torrent.com
Azureus	http://www.azureus.com	iSwipe	http://www.hillmanminx.net
BitComet	http://www.bitcomet.com	TorrentSpy	http://www.torrentspy.com
BitLord	http://www.bitlord.com	Tribler	http://www.tribler.com
BitSpirit	http://www.167bt.com/intl	uTorrent	http://www.utorrent.com
BitTornado	http://www.bittornado.com	ZipTorrent	http://www.ziptorrent.com
BitTorrent	http://www.bittorrent.com		
Burst	http://krypt.dyndns.org:81/torrent		

Torrent Search Engines

BiteNova	http://www.bitenova.org	Torrentbox	http://www.torrentbox.com
Demoniod	http://www.demonoid.com	Torrentmatrix	http://www.torrentmatrix.com
Fenopy	http://www.fenopy.com	Torrentportal	http://www.torrentportal.com
IsoHunt	http://www.isohunt.com	TorrentReactor	http://www.torrentreactor.to
LegalTorrents	http://www.legaltorrents.com	Torrents	http://www.torrents.to
MegaNova	http://www.meganova.org	TorrentScan	http://www.torrentscan.com
Mininova	http://www.mininova.org	TorrentSpy	http://www.torrentspy.com
The Pirate Bay	http://www.piratebay.com	TorrentTyphoon	http://www.torrenttyphoon.com
Thinktorrent	http://www.thinktorrent.com	Torrentz	http://www.torrentz.com
Torrent	http://www.torrent-damage.net	Yotoshi	http://www.yotoshi.com

torrent search engines have been closed down pending legal action: they usually pop back up again within a matter of days. However, it's a good idea to keep abreast of these activities. If you type "Torrent Search Engines" into Google from time to time you should find up-to-date lists of currently active servers.

Now let's try a torrent search. In this example we'll use the popular IsoHunt, and we'll continue searching for items related to the Ramones.

• Enter the URL: **http://www .isohunt.com**. Type your search criteria into the box at the top of the screen, and then click on the button marked **Loading**.

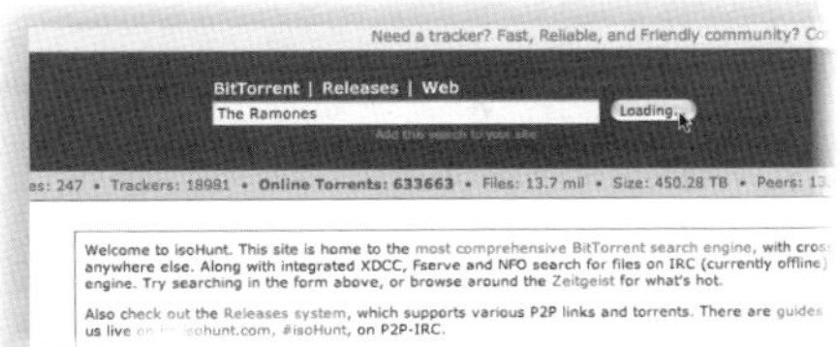

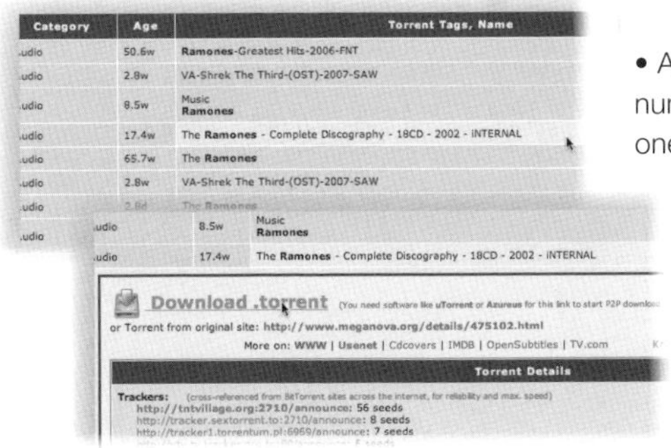

• As you can see, there are a number of matches. Click on one that interests you. The row will open out details of the trackers. Click on the button marked **Download .torrent**. The torrent text file will now download onto your hard drive.

Downloading

Now is the time to run your client program. In this example, we've downloaded and installed the current version of BitTorrent—the program designed by Bram Cohen.

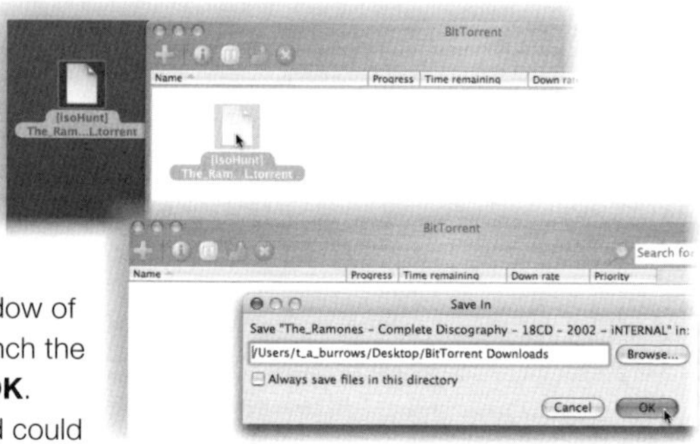

• Locate the downloaded torrent file on your desktop. Launch the BitTorrent software. Drag the downloaded file and drop it in the main window of BitTorrent. This will launch the **Save** panel. Click on **OK**. In theory, the download could now begin. However, before that happens there will be a good deal of background interaction between your program and the tracker server while it scours the Internet for people with whom to swarm. This can take several minutes. Both the client and tracker server will specifically be looking for other users who have the same torrent text file as you. As the server discovers users to swarm with, each one will be labeled as a leech or a seed: the more seeds the tracker finds for you, the faster your download will be.

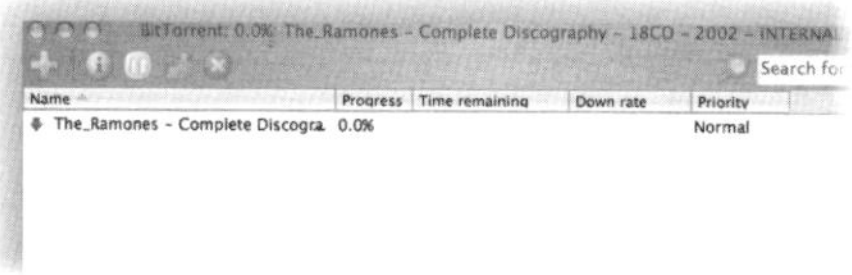

It's also good form in the file-sharing comminity to leave your torrent software running for a few hours after a download has completed, enabling you to share your reconstructed files with other users.

Uploading

Now we'll look briefly at the reverse of this process—uploading files to share. We'll use the BitTorrent client software once again.

• From the File menu, choose the option **Make New Torrent**.

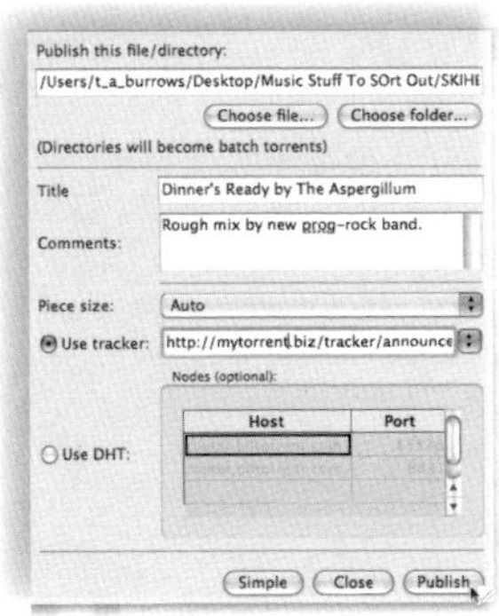

• The **Publishing** window will open. Enter the name of the file on your hard drive that you wish upload—you can type it in manually, or you can click on the **Browse File** button and navigate your hard drive until you find it.

• Add a title and comments for your file.

• You must now decide where to publish your tracker file. If you know the URL of a tracker site you intend to use, click on the **Use Tracker** button and enter it in the box alongside; if you don't have access to a public tracker you can use DHT—this essentially tells the BitTorrent software to act as its own tracker. This will be less effective than using a *real* tracker, though. (There are websites that contain lists of public tracker sites, such as **http://thebeehive.info**.)

• Click on the **Publish** button.

• BitTorrent will prepare your file. Click on the button marked **Start Seeding**.

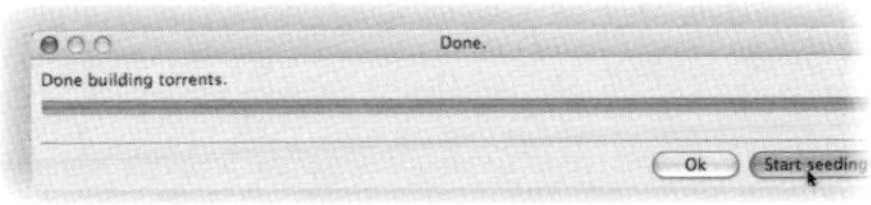

Your file is now being made available to other P2P users on the network.

Important Note

All peer-to-peer networking is completely legal. However, *everyone* knows that the majority of activity that takes place on these networks is not. In the future, this may well herald a completely new approach to the idea of intellectual property rights, or the way in which we receive our media content; or it may equally keep the legal profession in its accustomed style for decades to come. Whatever happens, we should stress firmly that this book (and this section in particular) is in no way intended to encourage copyright infringement. And that no illegal content has been downloaded intentionally in the making of this book. Our advice is simple: understand the law of your land, make your own moral judgements, and act accordingly.

Personal Management Tools

In this section we will be taking a look at web-based applications that are aimed at promoting greater personal efficiency. You'll see that some of these are perhaps more work-oriented, although they'll also come in useful for anyone leading a busy social life.

Diary Systems

In the not-so-distant past, the standard method of keeping your work and leisure time under control was to use a personal organizer system, such as those famously produced by Filofax or Time Manager International. These days, many of us are more likely to use computers for scheduling meetings and general project management. A new generation of web-based software takes this approach a stage further in that it enables groups of people to share such information. If, for example, you were to keep an up-to-date online diary then others would automatically be able to see when you were available. If someone was trying to organize a meeting with a large group of people, the software itself could even come up with convenient dates and times because it would have access to the availability of everyone involved. Let's begin with a brief look at some of the free online calendar systems available.

30 Boxes

http://www.30boxes.com

Launched in 2006, 30 Boxes was created by a small San Francisco–based company called 83°. Using AJAX technology, 30 Boxes combines a calendar with assorted social networking functions. However, its most innovative feature is its ability to integrate with many other applications, such

as Flickr, Webshots, Upcoming, LiveJournal, WordPress, Vox, and MySpace. This is such an in-depth application that we can only scratch the surface in a few pages, but it really is worth investigating in more detail.

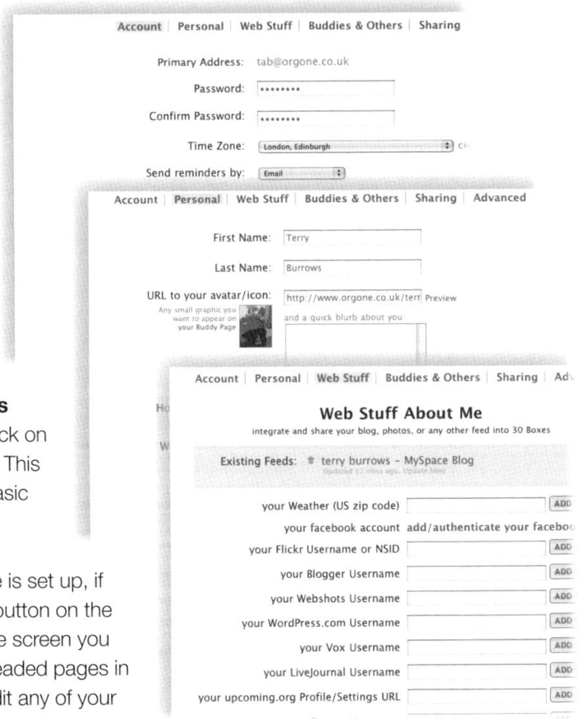

• Let's start off by entering the website's URL: **http://www.30boxes.com**. In the main page, click on the text **Just Get Started**. This will take you through the basic registration procedures.

• Once your calendar page is set up, if you click on the **Settings** button on the top right-hand corner of the screen you will find a number of tab-headed pages in which you can set up or edit any of your personal information.

• The **Account** tab requests details regarding your e-mail address and password—30 Boxes uses your e-mail address as your principal form of identity.

• The **Personal** tab contains name and location details. You can also link to any external image or avatar that you want to use within 30 Boxes.

• The **Web Stuff** tab is where you can enter user IDs for other applications, such as MySpace and Flickr.

On the next page, we'll take a look at how you can set up contacts in the **Buddies & Others** tab.

Creating Buddies

One of the neatest aspects of 30 Boxes is how well the social networking features are integrated. Here we'll look at how to create contacts.

• Still working under **Settings**, click on the tab labeled **Buddies & Others**. In the section headed **Your Buddies**, click on **Add Buddies**.

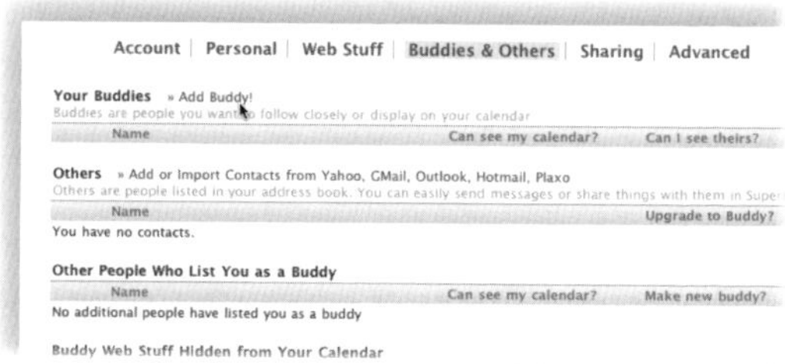

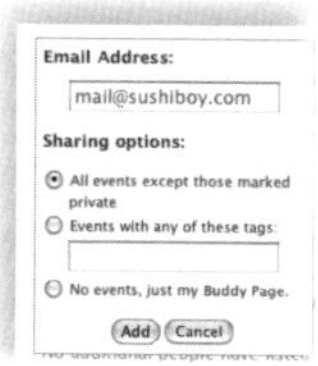

• In the pop-up window, add the e-mail address you want to add. Here you can also set up how much of your private data you wish to share with this contact. Click on the **Add** button to create your new "buddy."

• Your new contact will now appear in the section headed **Your Buddies**.

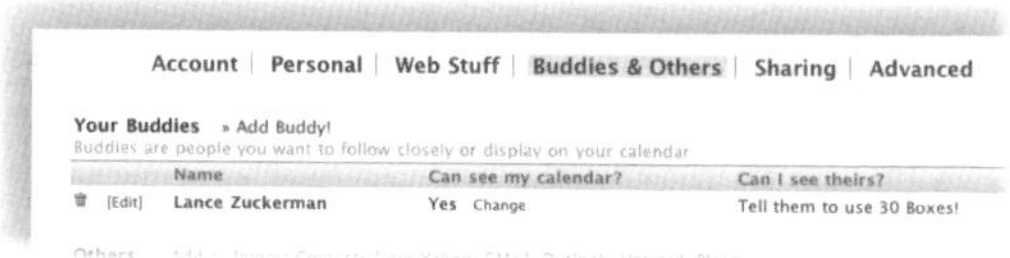

Add an Event to Your Calendar

Now let's take a look at your main calendar page. To do this, click on the calendar icon—the box displaying the number "30"—on the top left-hand corner of the window. The calendar will now appear.

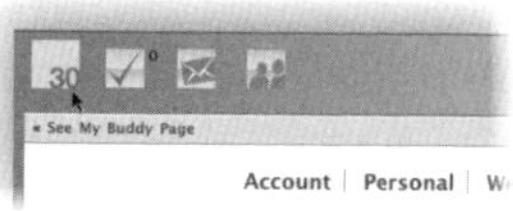

• To add an event to your calendar, highlight the day in question and then click on the **Add** button near the top of the window.

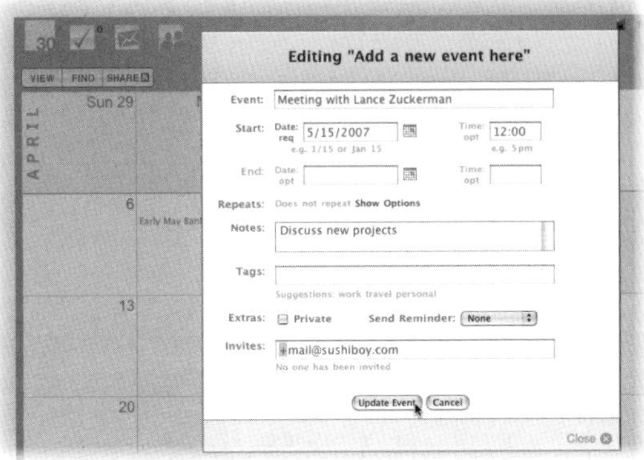

• The **Add a New Event** window will appear. Enter a name for the event, a time, and any descriptive notes you wish to include. If it is a meeting involving one of your 30 Boxes buddies, click on the box marked **Invites**, and a drop-down list showing all the e-mail addresses of all your buddies will appear. Select one of them from the list. Finally, click on the **Update Event** button to complete the operation. A confirmation window will appear—this indicates that the software has sent an e-mail to your buddy, but he or she has not yet responded.

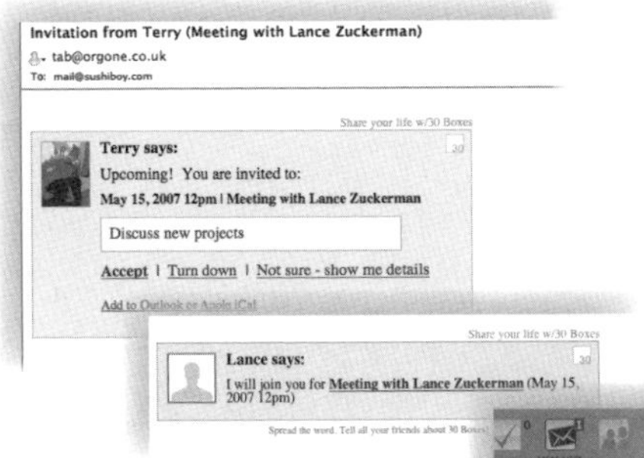

• Your buddy will receive an e-mail (*shown left*) with the option of accepting or declining the meeting, or requesting further information.

• You will then receive a standard e-mail with his or her response, as well as a "supermail" message from within 30 Boxes. (This is the software's internal mail system.) You will now see that your calendar page has also been updated.

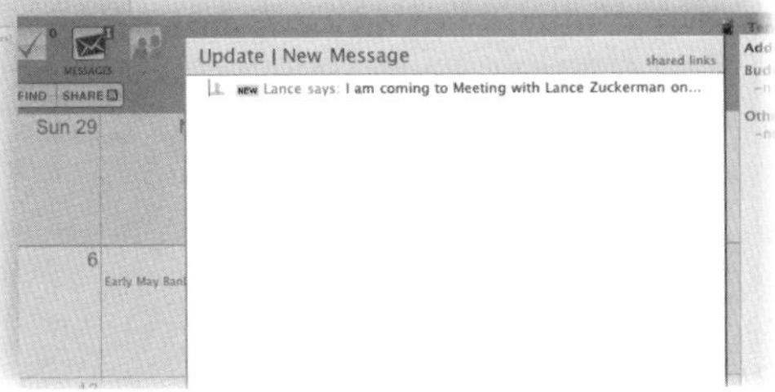

Other Time and Task Management Systems

Now let's take a brief look at some other calendar, project management, and to-do list applications.

HipCal

http://www.hipcal.com

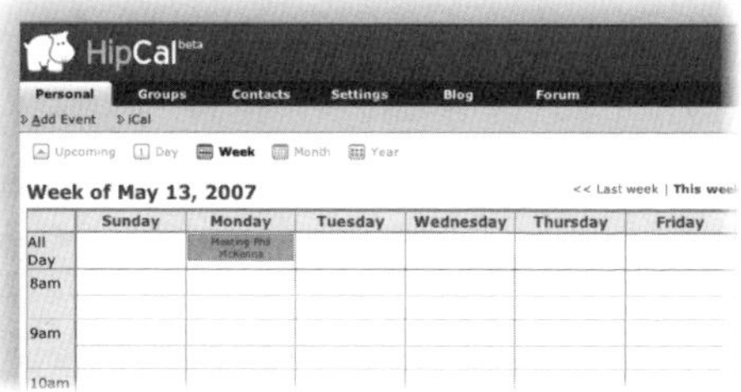

HipCal is online calendar system developed in 2005 by a bunch of painfully young entrepreneurs—in this case, five undergraduate fraternity brothers at Rensselaer Polytechnic Institute (RPI) in Troy, New York. It combines standard calendar features with a to-do list, and will send out event alerts to e-mail addresses or cell phones. It's especially strong for creating a group calendar for team or class projects.

MeetWithApproval

http://www.meetwithapproval.com

The product of UK-based design company This Side Up, MeetWithApproval is a simple web-based application that enables users to arrange meetings or events, work out which day is convenient for those invited, and keep track of who will be attending. It's extremely easy to use: the person creating the event completes a standard online form that creates a meeting page. Friends or colleagues are notified of the event via e-mail. They visit the meeting page and agree on a date. When everyone is happy, Meet With Approval confirms the arrangement.

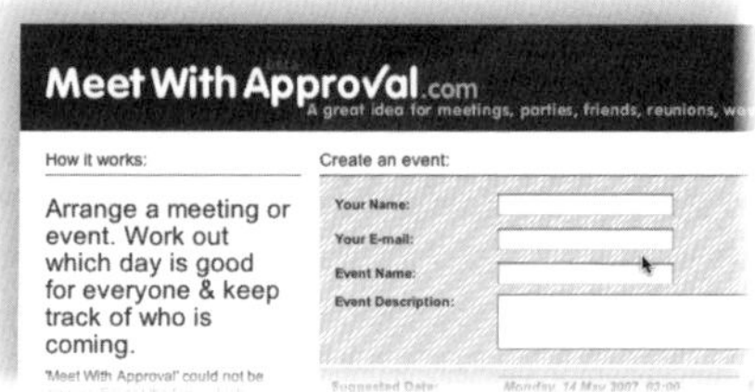

Planzo

http://www.planzo.com

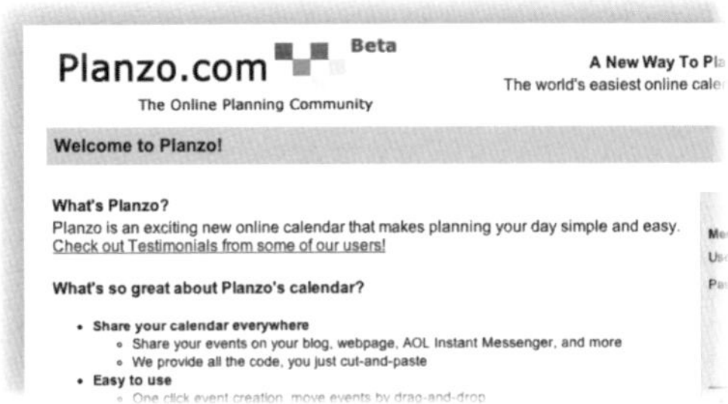

In addition to standard calendar and task features, Planzo also enables its users to share photographs, bookmarks, files, and text snippets. An AJAX-based application, Planzo allows users a greater degree of freedom than most applications to customize the look and feel of their calendars.

Remember the Milk

http://www.rememberthemilk.com

Remember the Milk is one of the more popular task-management web-based applications. It features an extremely user-friendly interface, and—thanks to an extensive set of keyboard shortcuts—can also be quite swift to use.

It's possible to have event reminders sent out using a variety of different means: e-mail, SMS texts, instant messenger (AIM, Gadu-Gadu, Google Talk, ICQ, Jabber, MSN, Skype, and Yahoo!). It's also possible to tag lists and look at outstanding tasks as an overview "cloud." A weekly planner can be printed out, showing tasks for completion during the week ahead. The calendar can also be viewed with Apple iCal or the Google Calendar. Any changes can be notified via RSS/ATOM feeds.

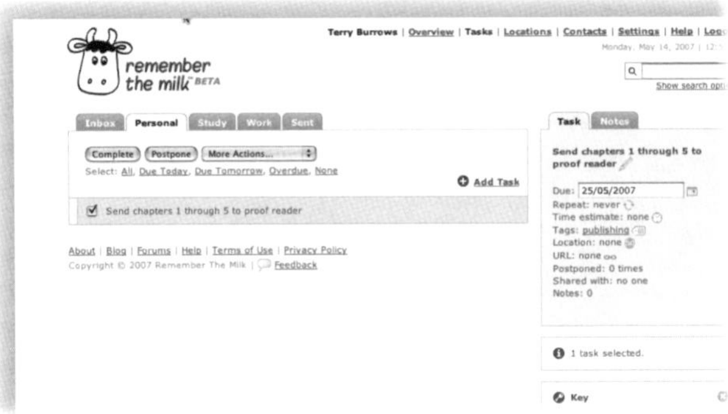

Skobee

http://www.skobee.com

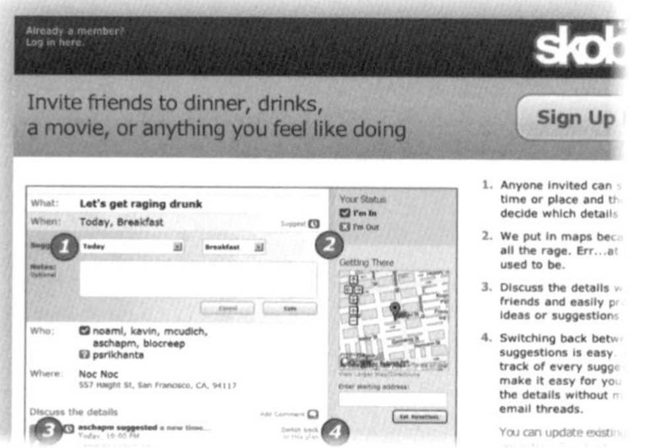

Another scheduling application, Skobee is aimed at social planning. Its basic thrust is "start general, get specific as needed." So it allows users to begin with what it terms "fuzzy" scheduling, which could in fact be little more than "Hey, shall we get together again some time in the future?" Skobee then produces invitation cards that are e-mailed to everyone listed. Details can then be fine-tuned communally. The Skobee invitation also generates a map, and can even use social networking techniques to tell you what is popular among other Skobee users in the same area.

Spongecell

http://www.spongecell.com

Spongecell is a social networking calendar. Users can create events online and distribute them via e-mail, web pages, blogs, iPods, and cell phones. Since the calendar is public, friends can leave comments or even upload files, such as videos.

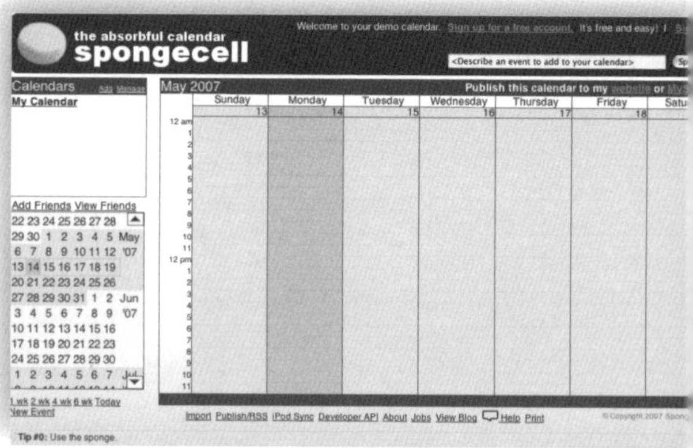

Ta-Da List

http://www.tadalist.com

A small Chicago-based company with the intriguing name of 37 Signals (which was so named after the 37 radio-telescope signals identified by astronomer Paul Horowitz as possible messages from extraterrestrial life forms) is responsible for a number of interesting Web 2.0 applications using Ruby On Rails technology. The company's flagship product is the sophisticated project management tool Basecamp (**http://www.basecamphq.com**), for which users pay monthly fees for varying levels of service. However, they are also responsible for the free task management application Ta-Da List. The user sets up a list with any number of tasks within. As tasks are completed, check boxes are ticked. Lists can also be shared with other users who can edit the contents.

• Enter the URL: **http://www.tadalist.com**. To get started, click on the text labeled **Create a New List**.

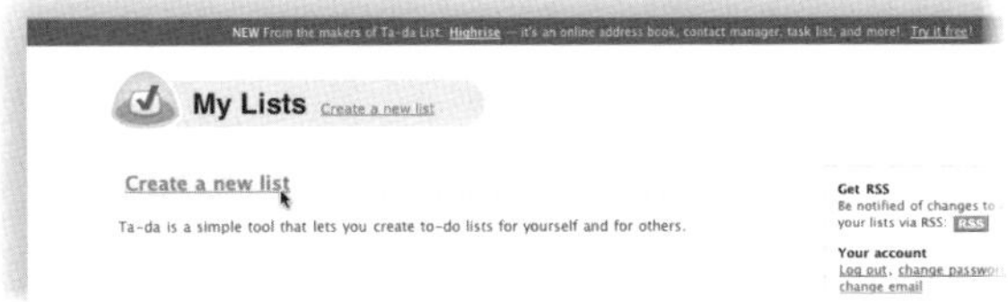

• Name your list—type your text in the box and then click on the **Create This List** button.

• In the page that follows, enter the name of a task and then click on **Add This Item**. Continue until you have set up all of your tasks within the list.

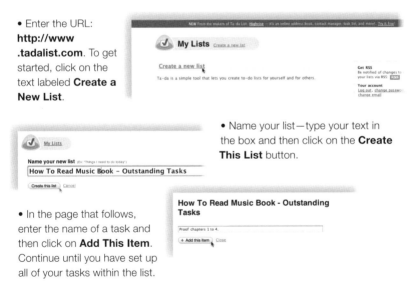

• You can now view your complete list. As you complete tasks you can tick them off by clicking on the check boxes to the left of each one. You can also e-mail a copy of the list to yourself, or be notified of changes made to your list via an RSS feed. The contents of the list can be modified or added to at any time by clicking on the **Edit** button above the list.

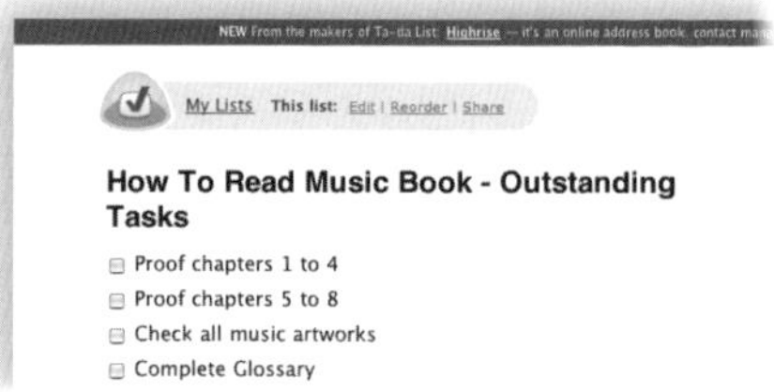

Sharing Your Ta-Da List

To share a list, click on the button marked **Share**. You have two different sharing options. The first is to enter one or more e-mails and then click on the button labeled **Share with These People**. You can also add a note that will appear in the body text of the e-mail. Take care to note that you are not only giving these individuals permission to look at your list, but also to *change* anything on your list. This is ideal for project lists where actions are to be taken by different individuals.

A second share option open to you is to tick the **Yes, Share Publicly** checkbox. This enables anyone to view your list, although they will not be able to make any changes themselves.

Tiktrac

http://www.tiktrak.com

Tiktrac is an AJAX-based professional project management tool aimed squarely at business users. Project tasks are broken down into component tasks and allocated to individuals

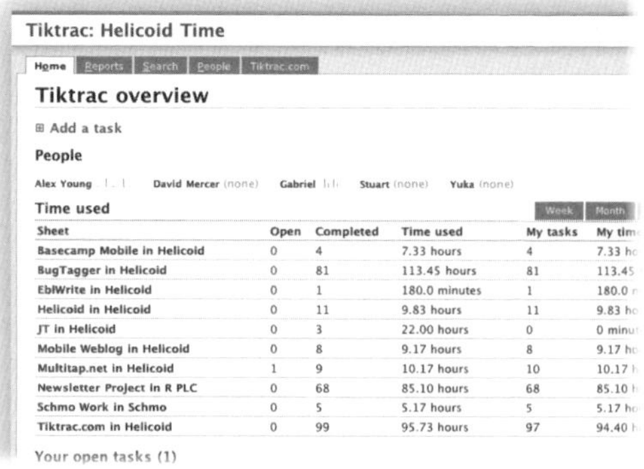

to create a set of timesheets; time is logged against tasks and project progress is monitored. Activity on any project can be tracked using RSS feeds, and reports can be generated with costings assigned. All in all, it's a pretty sophisticated project management system.

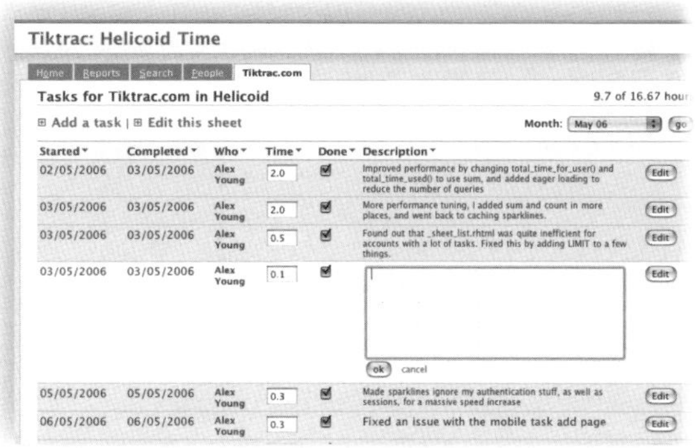

Tiktrac is currently free to use. However, it seems very likely that such a solidly business-oriented product will be accompanied by some kind of pricing structure at some time in the future.

Other Personal Management Sites

1Time	http://1timetracking.com	SunDial	http://www.clearwired.com/sundial
88 Miles	http://www.88miles.net	Taskfreak	http://www.taskfreak.com
Basecamp	http://www.basecamphq.com	Taskspro	http://www.taskspro.com
Calendarhub	http://www.calendarhub.com	Tilika	http://www.tilika.com
Citadel	http://www.citadel.org	Time 59	https://www.time59.com
ClockingIt	http://www.clockingit.com	Time IQ	http://www.timeiq.com
DekkoTime	http://dekkotime.com	ToadTime	http://www.toadtime.com
Dotproject	http://www.dotproject.ne	Toggl	http://www.toggl.com
Eventful	http://eventful.com	Trackslife	http://www.trackslife.com
Harvest	http://www.getharvest.com	Trumba	http://www.trumba.com
Inventiondb	http://www.inventiondb.com	Upcoming	http://upcoming.org
Ioutliner	http://www.ioutliner.com	Veetro	http://www.veetro.com
Mosuki	http://mosuki.com		
Myticklerfile	http://www.myticklerfile.com		
Near-time	http://www.near-time.net		
Projectplace	http://www.projectplace.com		
Projectspaces	http://www.forumone.com		
SlimTimer	http://www.slimtimer.com		
Sproutliner	http://sproutliner.com		

Photographs and Videos

As consumer broadband speeds continue to increase, home computers inevitably will be better equipped to rival television as a medium of entertainment. Nowhere has this been better demonstrated than with the massive success of the video-sharing site YouTube. Although nominally a place where people can share their homemade videos, it owes much of its growth and success to users illegally uploading commercial content—sometimes complete feature films—and thus creating a massive online video database. In turn, record labels, TV and film companies, and other content owners have viewed YouTube as a fertile ground for free advertising. However, like most other applications that find themselves placed under the Web 2.0 umbrella, YouTube and its photographic equivalents, such as Flickr, are also socially oriented, with users able to leave comments on each other's offerings, and perform searches based on category tags that they've created themselves.

Flickr

http://www.flickr.com

By any measure the world's most popular photo-sharing website, Flickr was launched in 2004 by Ludicorp, a company based in Vancouver, Canada. The application evolved out of a proposed multi-user game that was never released. Flickr first appeared as part of a chat room called FlickrLive, a place where users were able to exchange photographs. At this stage it was primarily a forum for sharing images collected from the Web. However, it quickly evolved as a means for users to show their own photography, and, in fact, the chat room itself was eventually dropped. Flickr's

enormous popularity was soon followed by the the inevitable corporate buy-out—in March 2005 Ludicorp was acquired by the Yahoo! company.

The premise behind Flickr is extremely simple: users may upload their own photographs for others to view. To aid searches, multiple tags can be applied to any photograph. Images can also be grouped in collections known as "sets." Although it's possible for anyone to view Flickr images, registered users can also leave comments on specific photographs, or even give them "favorite" ratings. It's also very easy to use.

Searching Flickr

Let's now look at Flickr in a little more detail. We'll begin by performing a simple search operation.

• Enter the URL: **http://www.flickr.com**. In this example, we'll look for pictures that have the words **Aldeburgh Cinema** either as tags or in titles and descriptive text. In the box marked **Find a Photo of**, type in the search text and click on the **Go** button.

• You'll now see a list of images that meet your search criteria. On the left of the screen is a thumbnail view of the image. Alongside, you can see the title of the photograph, the date it was uploaded, the name of the photographer, and the tag (or tags) that have been applied to the photograph. You can use the scroll bar to view other matching images.

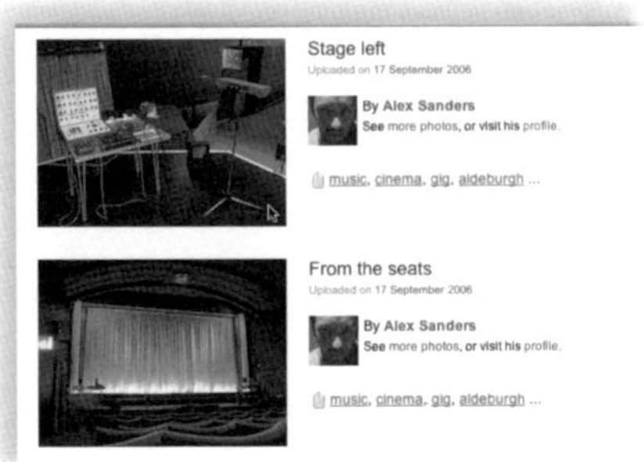

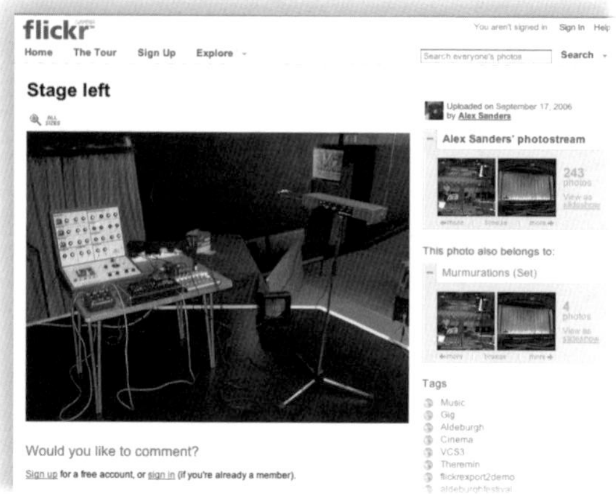

• If you now want to look at a full-size version of the photograph, click on the thumbnail view. As you can see, this image has been given eight different category tags. (In fact, it's possible to allocate up to 75 tags to any one photograph.)

• The information alongside the image tells you that it is a part of a set entitled **Murmurations**. If you click on the set name you can see the complete collection displayed. You can view a slideshow of the set by clicking on the text labeled **View as Slideshow**.

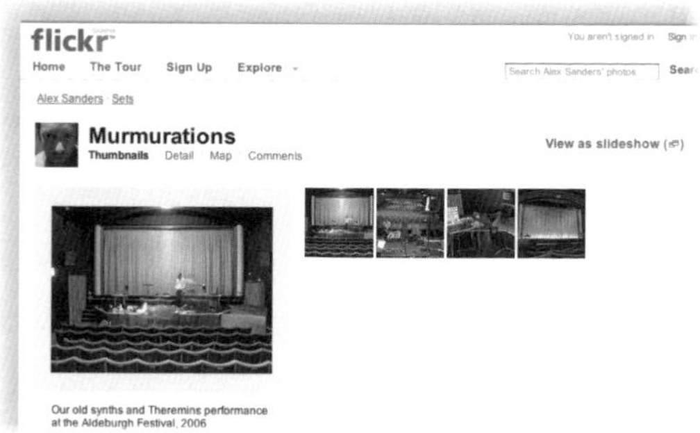

Uploading Photographs

To put a picture on Flickr, first ensure that the images are ready on your hard drive. Any of the standard file formats (JPEG, PNG, non-animated GIF, BMP, and TIFF) are allowable. Before you can upload photographs to the Flickr website you need to create a Yahoo! account for yourself. On the Flickr homepage, click on the **Sign Up!** button and follow the instructions.

• When you've set up your ID and password, sign in to Flickr. Click on **Upload Your First Photo**.

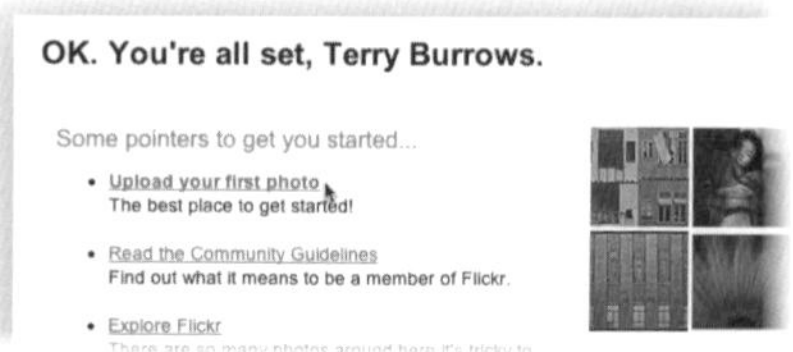

• You will now see the Flickr upload page. You can transfer up to six photographs at one time. Begin by locating the first image on your hard drive. Click on the first button marked **Choose File**. This enables you to browse your computer's hard drive until you have found the required file. Repeat for any other images you wish to upload. You can allocate a single tag for all of these images if you wish, or you can leave tagging until later. You can also decide on the privacy level for your pictures: by default they are "public," meaning that anyone can view them. However, they can also be set so they are only viewable by friends or family. When you're ready to begin the transfer click on the **Upload** button.

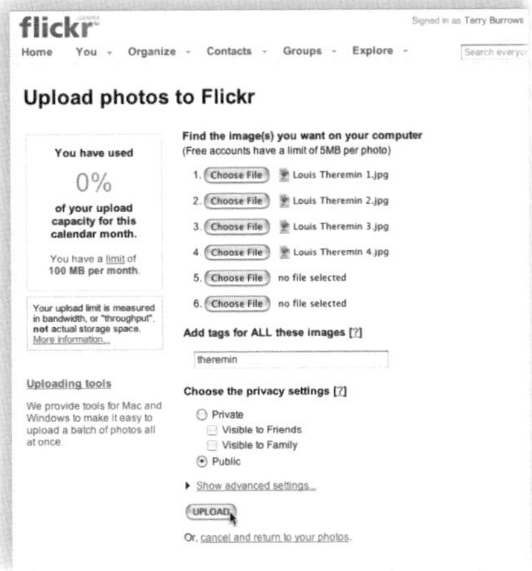

• Once the files have been uploaded, your pictures will be visible in a new window. Here you can give your photographs titles (by default their file names will be used), descriptions, and add (or edit) tags. Finally, click on the **Save** button.

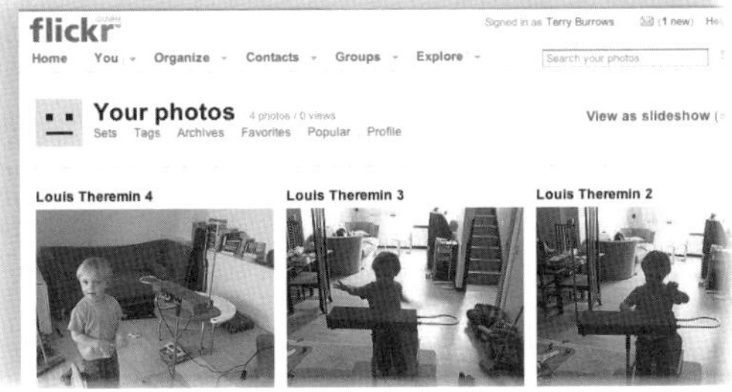

• Your photographs are now in place on Flickr.

Enhancing Flickr

When a web application becomes massively successful it's not unusual to find third parties prepared to provide services that aim to enhance their use. For example, there are numerous websites that will enable you to "pimp" your MySpace site. Similarly, there are those aimed at making the Flickr experience a little smoother.

Flappr (http:www.bcdef.org/flappr)

Flappr offers an alternative way to search for and view images on the Flickr database. If you enter some search text, Flappr will provide a screen of thumbnail views along with a cloud of tags. For a more detailed search, if you click on any tag it will be added to your original search criteria, and the list of thumbnails will be reduced. You can continue to add tags in this way. If you click on the image it will appear full size on the right of the screen, accompanied by the profile of the photographer.

FlickrFling (http://www.nastypixel.com)

FlickrFling provides a novel way of viewing Flickr photographs linked to popular news feeds. First select a news source from a drop-down list—in this example we have chosen **CNN.com**) FlickrFling will take the current RSS feed and use each word as a key for a Flickr search. In this example, the feed reads "**Sarkozy takes over in France. Sarkozy has been sworn in as France's new president, taking . . . .**" Some of the selections are extremely literal—the word "taking" has suggested an image of somebody taking a photograph! However, it does present an entertaining visual take on the news as it's coming in.

Slide

http://www.slide.com

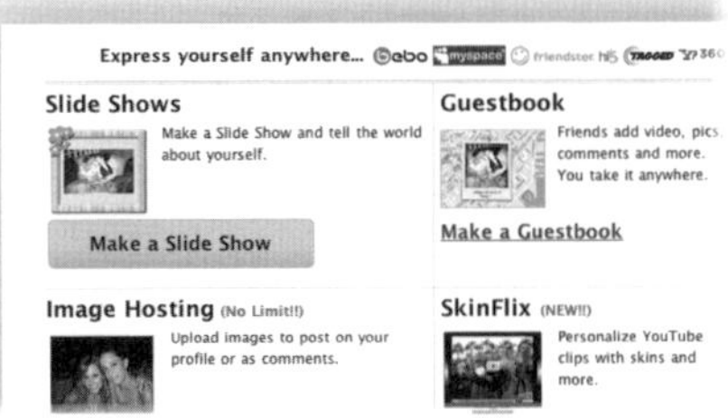

Launched in 2005 by Max Levchin, one of the founders of PayPal, Slide claims to be the biggest independent "widget" company on the Internet.

Slide is an application that enables the creation of customized slide shows of photographs that can be embedded in a blog or a MySpace page, sent out as an RSS feed, or streamed to a desktop as a screensaver. As of May 2007, the company was claiming that more than 200,000 new slide shows were being created each day.

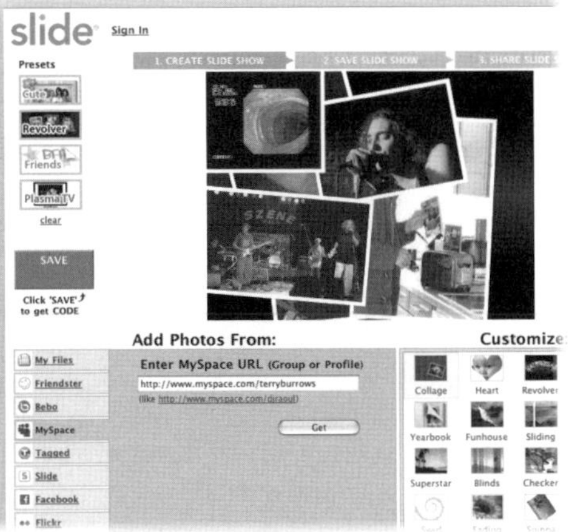

Let's look at how easily a MySpace photo gallery can be customized using Slide.

- Begin by entering the URL: **http://www.slide.com**. Click on the button marked **Make a Slide Show**.

- In the list of options on the left-hand side of the screen, choose **MySpace**. Enter the MySpace URL that contains the photo gallery you wish to customize. Click on the **Get** button.

- You will see the images appearing in the window at the top of the screen. You can alter the "theme" of your slide show using the **Customize** options in the bottom right-hand corner of the screen. When you click on the **Save** button, Slide will save your slide show and also generate the HTML code that can then be copied and pasted into your MySpace page. Slide also links up in the same way with Friendster, Bebo, Tagged, FaceBook, and Flickr.

Smilebox

http://www.smilebox.com

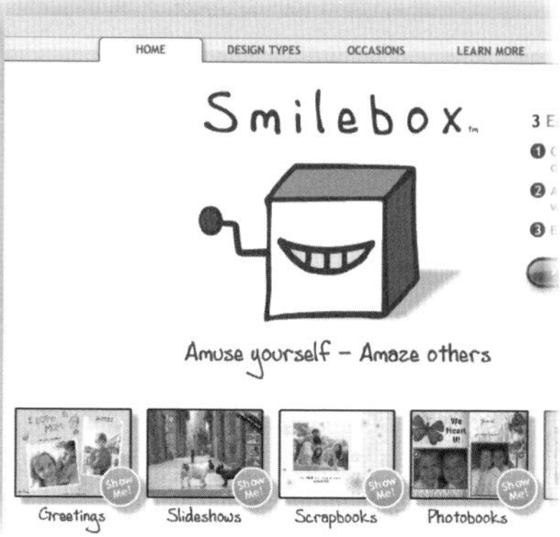

Smilebox takes a slightly different approach to other photo-sharing websites. It enables users to upload their photographs and videos in order to create animated scrapbooks, photo albums, slideshows, postcards, and greetings cards. Smilebox features a large database of ready-made templates into which personal content can be dragged, dropped, edited, and customized. Once saved, Smilebox sends out e-mails to any contacts you've entered. They can then view your work. The basic Smilebox service is free. However, a monthly subscription buys you a greater choice of templates and other benefits.

SmugMug

http://www.smugmug.com

SmugMug is arguably the most professional photo-sharing website currently on the Internet. Both simple and attractive in design, its popularity among its users stems from the fact that it is free from advertising banners. The downside is that there is a subscription charge for even the basic service. However, for that cost, SmugMug does offer unlimited safe storage for your digital images—as the company itself proclaims, "It's like Fort Knox for your photos!"

SmugMug also offers a variety of other commercial services, such as professional-quality printing, as well as the option of buying T-shirts, playing cards, ceramics, mouse pads, mugs, aprons, and jigsaw puzzles all using your own images. Holders of a SmugMug "professional" account are also able to sell their photographs as digital downloads.

Webshots

http://www.webshots.com

Webshots was one of the first sucessful photo-sharing websites. It started life in 1996 as a screensaver/wallpaper site, but later expanded into photo sharing. It is now one of the largest such communites on the Internet—by the start of 2007 there were more than 458 million photographs on the site.

Copyright Issues

The term "copyright" refers to a set of laws that prevents the work of artists, authors, composers, or others from being used without permission. With regard to posting images, videos, or music on the Internet, although specific copyright laws vary from nation to nation, there is one basic rule that holds true pretty well everywhere: if you didn't create it yourself then you probably don't have the legal right to upload it. So if you copy a video clip from the TV onto YouTube, you'll be in breach of copyright; similarly if you upload photographs to Flickr that you didn't take yourself. Of course, this hasn't prevented a great many people from doing just that. (And it's fair to say that in some cases, copyright holders haven't objected strongly—especially where video clips have acted as advertising tasters for more expensive end products.) The bottom line is, whatever your reasons or excuses, you *are* breaking the law when you do this, and—however unlikely it may seem—you could be leaving yourself open to legal action. So always consider the possible risks before you upload illegal content!

YouTube

http://www.youtube.com

YouTube is a video sharing website where users may upload and view video clips. Videos may be given star ratings (to a maximum of five stars) and commented on by other viewers—an average rating and the number of times a video has been watched are both displayed as part of the video's details.

YouTube was created in 2005 by former employees of PayPal. Within its first year of operation it had become the fastest growing site on the Internet, with over 100 million video clips being viewed daily. In October 2006, YouTube was acquired by Google for $1.65 billion worth of Google stock.

Much of the controversy relating to YouTube comes from users uploading copyrighted content. And the company has been the subject of numerous lawsuits from the major names in the television and film industries. However, as *Variety* magazine reported in March 2007, Hollywood has a complicated attitude toward the website: "The marketing guys love YouTube and the legal guys hate it." Legal threats have led the site to take a more proactive role in monitoring illegal activity. Yet it's fair to say that if you were to do a search for any well-known TV show you would still find plenty of content in place.

The success of YouTube has heralded a new trend in viewing, especially among the young, where many are reputed to have turned away from traditional television in favor of watching TV content on their computers. As a result, TV companies are increasingly offering their programs in a downloadable format.

YouTube Search

There are a number of different ways you can find video content on YouTube. A simple text search is usually the best bet for finding specific content. However, since all videos may be given multiple tags, you can sometimes discover material of interest by performing category searches.

- Start by entering the URL: **http://www.youtube.com**. In this example, we'll look for video clips by the lo-fi artist **R. Stevie Moore**. Enter the text and click on the **Search** button.

• Next, you will find a list of all videos that fit your search criteria. Each video clip shows a thumbnail image from the start of the film, the title, any details the uploader has chosen to include, the category tags allocated to the clip, the name of the uploader, the number of times the clip has been viewed, the average star rating it has been given, and the number of viewers that have given a rating to the clip.

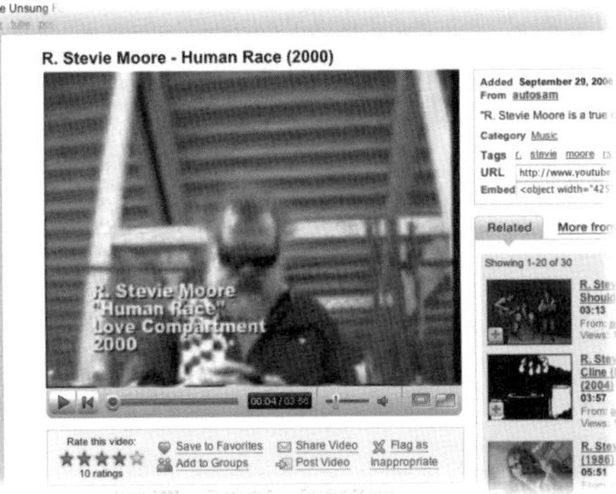

• You can watch the video by clicking on the title or the thumbnail image. It will appear in a new window at the top left-hand corner of the screen. You can control the video using the bar underneath the video clip. Let's look at what each of the controls does.

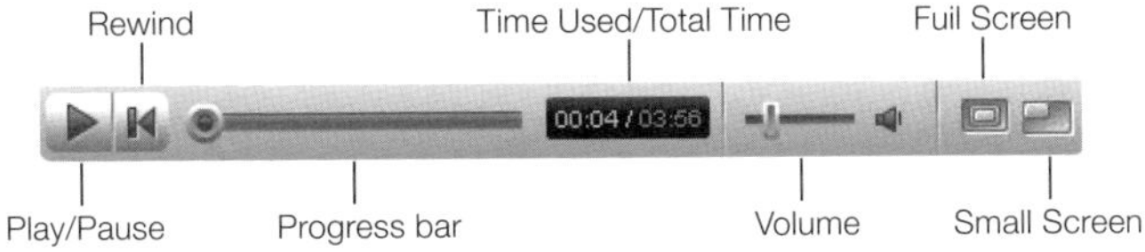

The **Play** button is a toggle switch—when you click on it, the video will begin and the button will change its appearance, becoming a **Pause** button—if you click on the button again, the clip will be paused, and the button will revert to its original appearance. If you click on the **Full Screen** button the video will increase in size to fit your screen. However, depending on the settings used when the video was made, that could well render the clip a jerky, bit-mapped mess, which may be imposible to watch.

Search by Category

In the YouTube home page, if you click on the **Categories** tab near the top of the screen you will see a vertical list of the most popular top-level catagories. In this example, we'll click on the label marked **Comedy**. The screen that follows contains a scrolling list of videos that fall under that category that have been selected by YouTube editors.

Uploading a Video Clip

Before you upload a video clip, first you need to ensure that it has been converted to a format that YouTube can handle, namely Windows Media Video (.wmv), Audio Video Interleave (.avi), Quicktime (.mov), or MPEG. To begin uploading, you must be a registered user and be logged in. If you are not a member, click on the **Sign Up** button at the top of the page and follow the registration instructions.

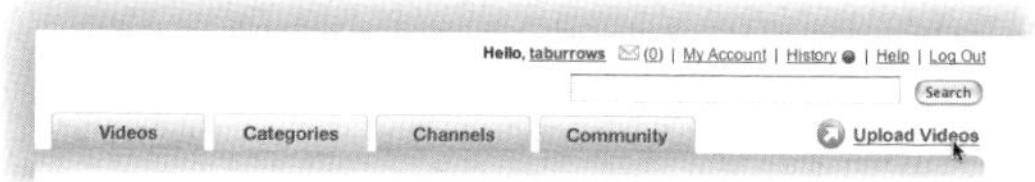

• On the YouTube home page, click the label marked **Upload Videos**. (If this is your first upload you may be asked to enter your e-mail address and then follow up a confirmation e-mail link.)

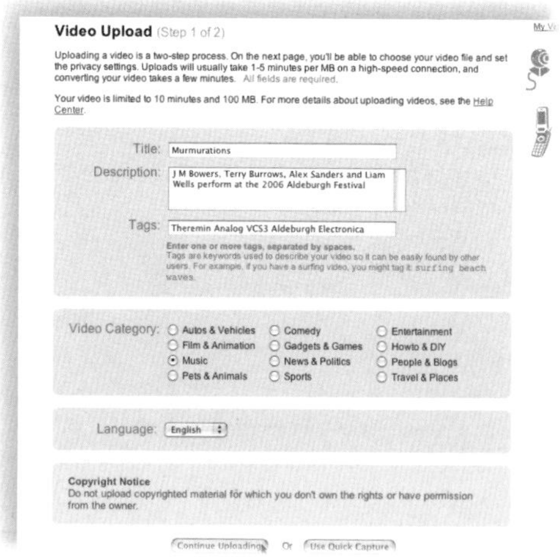

• You should now find yourself looking at the first **Video Upload** window. Here you can enter a title, description, and tags for your clip, as well as selecting from one of YouTube's top-level categories. Click on the button marked **Continue Uploading**.

• A second upload page follows. Click on the **Choose File** button and navigate through your hard drive until you find your chosen video file. On this page you can also select a privacy level: **Public** means that anyone can view it; **Private** means that it can only be accessed by people on your contacts list. Click on the **Upload Video** button.

• When the file has been uploaded you will see a confirmation window. On this page you will find the URL of your clip to send to anyone you wish to view it. You will also find a scrolling box that contains

the HTML coding that will create the links to your video. This can be embedded into a personal website, blog, or other applications, such as a MySpace page.

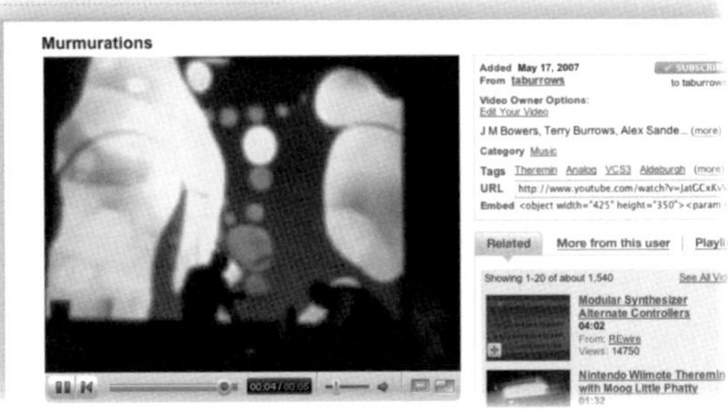

• If you now click on the button marked **My Videos** you will see that your new clip has been listed. You can now click on the title to watch the video.

Vimeo

http://www.vimeo.com

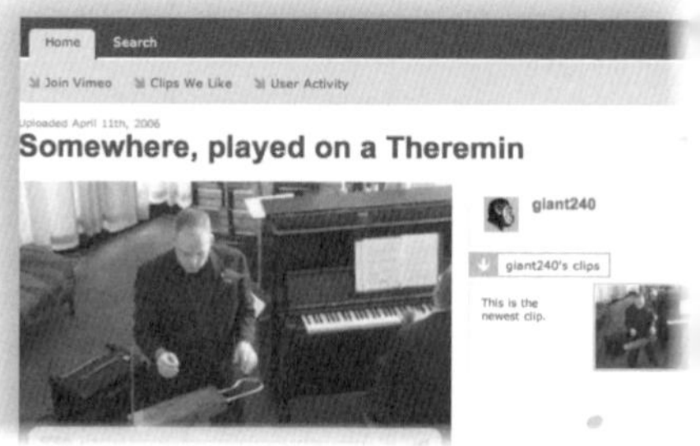

Vimeo is primarily a social networking site that also happens to have an built-in video sharing feature—a sort of hybrid of MySpace and YouTube. It promotes the idea of socializing with other members through the sharing of video clips.

VMIX

http://www.vmix.com

The VMIX application aims itself at the creative community—those who are making their own music, video, and films. It also makes claims for itself as a networking space for bringing together those with complementary skills—for example, filmmakers with composers of soundtrack music.

VSocial

http://www.vsocial.com

VSocial is another site that combines video sharing with social networking. On your **My VSocial** page you can create a personal profile, set up your contacts, and read and leave comments for others. There is also a "searchbox" where you can look for videos using assorted criteria, such as user, channel, or popular tags. VSocial has a reputation for being strong on animation, with a large amount of legitimate content provided by TV and film companies.

VSocial also scores well through the use of a number of production features, with a number of tools to help build and manage your own content. For example, it allows you to build a "video roll" that can then be exported to your blog.

More Photograph and Video Sites

23hq	http://www.23hq.com
Adultswim	http://www.adultswim.com
Ajaxilicious	http://movies.ajaxilicious.be
Blinkx	http://searchus.blinkx.com
Blip.TV	http://www.blip.tv
Bolt	http://www.bolt.com
Broadbandsports	http://www.broadbandsports.com
Clipshack	http://www.clipshack.com
DailyMotion	http://www.dailymotion.com
Dropshots	http://www.dropshots.com
Flickrlicious	http://www.flickrlicio.us
Flyinside	http://www.flyinside.com
Fotoflix	http://www.fotoflix.com
Fotolia	http://www.fotolia.com
Google Video	http://video.google.com
Grouper	http://www.grouper.com
Groupr	http://groupr.200ok.net
JumpCut	http://www.jumpcut.com
Mefeedia	http://www.mefeedia.com
Metacafe	http://www.metacafe.com
Mightyv	http://www.mightyv.com
Openvlog	http://www.openvlog.com
Phlog	http://phlog.net
Photobucket	http://www.photobucket.com
Photomap	http://photomap.mozdev.org
Revver	http://one.revver.com/revver
Slidestory	http://www.slidestory.com
Stickam	http://www.stickam.com
StupidVideos	http://www.stupidvideos.com
Tagworld	http://www.tagworld.com
Truveo	http://www.truveo.com
VidiLife	http://www.vidilife.com
Veoh	http://www.veoh.com
Videobomb	http://videobomb.com
Videoegg	http://www.videoegg.com
ZippyVideos	http://www.zippyvideos.com
Zooomr	http://beta.zooomr.com/home

Podcasts

A podcast is an audio or video file that is distributed automatically to a subscribed user. That person can then play it back on a computer or mobile device, such as an mp3 player or cell phone. You could think of it as an Internet radio or TV show for which each episode is automatically delivered to the subscriber.

The Evolution of Podcasting

The word *podcast* was originally coined by the British technology writer Ben Hammersley in an article for the *Guardian* newspaper in 2004, and is a portmanteau of the words "iPod" and "broadcasting." The term could be seen as misleading in that it suggests that you need an iPod to listen to a podcast; in fact any mp3 player could be used. Apple, the manufacturer of the iPod, initially took legal steps to prevent the term being used commercially. However, when the editors of the *New Oxford American Dictionary* declared "podcasting" to be the word of the year in 2005, and thus gave it a definition—"a digital recording of a radio broadcast or similar program, made available on the Internet for downloading to a personal audio player"—there was clearly no going back.

Although the main technical developments took place in the United States, it was across the Atlantic in the UK that the idea first achieved mainstream popularity at the end of 2005 when comedian Ricky Gervais began his own podcast show. It remains the most widely received podcast worldwide, with an average of around 300,000 downloads per episode. Gervais broke further new ground a year later with his second series, which became the first major podcast to charge consumers for each download.

This "content-on-demand" idea is certain to evolve over the coming years, and may provide a glimpse of how we receive our TV shows in the future. Recently, although podcasters have largely taken the traditional radio broadcast as a primary model, other approaches are slowly appearing.

Over the next few pages, we'll take a look at everything you need to subscribe and listen to a podcast, and also how you can go about creating and distributing your very own transmissions. Note: there is also some crossover here with the section on blogging (*see page 20*)—that's because a podcast is in essence an audio or video blog.

How It Works

On the surface, a podcast may seem similar to other existing digital delivery technologies, such as downloading and streaming. The key difference, however, is that files are downloaded *automatically*. This is achieved using software that can read a *syndication feed*—a specific kind of data format used for providing the end user with content that changes frequently.

The mechanics of the process are easy to understand. The content provider creates a podcast "episode," which is usually an mp3 file, and references a syndication feed file, usually in RSS format. This is a list of the web URLs used to find specific podcast episodes. It is posted to the server at its permanent URL address. The podcaster then makes the feed known to his or her target audience.

The receiver uses a type of software known as an aggregator (or podcatcher) to subscribe to and manage their feeds. This is typically a program that launches when the computer is switched on and runs permanently in the background, periodically checking if feed data has changed. If it has, a new episode is automatically downloaded. This can then be heard using suitable playback software, or downloaded to an mp3 player or suitably equipped cell phone.

Podcasting: Other Uses

Music Replacement for live performance audio streams.

Adding content Enables news organizations to distribute audio or video to supplement or complement existing news.

Promotional tool Disney/Pixar famously trailed their film *Cars* with a series of video podcasts.

Avoiding regulatory bodies Enables broadcasts that may not be allowed in traditional media.

Education Podcasts are increasingly used in universities and high schools as a way of disseminating lectures.

Commentary Alternative audio commentaries can accompany DVDs or TV shows. Podcasts have been made by the creators of popular shows to accompany specific episodes. There are also examples of fans providing their own commentaries to accompany releases.

Politics and religion Political parties have adopted the podcast as a way of reaching younger audiences. Some churches issue their own "Godcasts" of sermons and lectures.

Receiving a Podcast

There are three simple steps you need to take to receive a podcast. First you need some podcast software, then you need to subscribe to the podcast, and finally, select your medium for listening or viewing the podcast.

Podcast Software

To begin, you will need to install a piece of software on your computer that is able to search the Web for podcasts, and then automatically deliver the latest episode to your computer. Most of this software can be downloaded free of charge. The three most popular applications are iTunes, Juice, and Doppler. You can find a more extensive list of other podcasting software on the next page.

iTunes

http://www.apple.com

There are a variety of ways you can subscribe to a podcast, some of which will depend on the software you use. Apple's iTunes (which also works on PCs) is a popular choice for dealing with podcasts, primarily because so many people use it to organize and play their mp3 collections. You can download iTunes from the Apple website: **http://www.apple.com**. The software also doubles as a storefront for the company's highly successful commercial music and video download store.

Let's begin with a simple and common example of a podcast link found within a website. Here we'll

Podcasting Software

Almost all of the software needed to capture and listen to podcasts is free to download. This is a small list of some of the better-known products. If you enter the name of the software into any search engine you will find links to where they can be downloaded. (Note: The letters in parentheses indicates the platforms on which the software operates: **L**—Linux; **M**—Mac; **W**—Windows.)

@Podder (W)	**Client for the visually impaired.**
BlogMatrix Sparks! (W)	**Record, mix, share, publish, store, and listen to podcasts.**
Doppler (W)	**Podcast aggregator—a tool to subscribe to RSS feeds.**
HappyFish (W)	**Syncs podcasts to most mp3 players.**
iPodderX (W/M)	**Handles podcasts, vlogs, and other distributed files.**
iTunes (W/M)	**All-in-one downloading and listening solution.**
Juice (W/M)	**Enables users to select and automatically download pocasts.**
NetNewsWire (M)	**RSS and Atom newsreader for Mac OS X.**
NewsFire (M)	**Newsreader and podcast client.**
NewsMacPro (M)	**Supports podcasting and syncs with Palm and iPod.**
Peapod (L)	**Podcast client for Linux.**
Poddumfeeder (M)	**Applescript-based podcast client.**
Podspider (L)	**Podcast client with integrated podcast directory.**
PulpFiction (M)	**Powerful RSS/Atom feed reader.**
Replay Radio (W)	**Captures podcasts, broadcast radio shows, and XM Radio.**
RSSRadio (W)	**Podcasting software for Windows.**
Synclosure (W)	**RSS aggregator.**
TVTonic (W)	**A video podcast reader optimized for Windows Media Center.**
WinAmp (W/M)	**Commercial audio application with free "iite" option.**
Yamipod (W/M/L)	**iPod management.**

look at the online version of the British newspaper, the *Guardian*, which creates a large number of weekly podcasts as a means of providing additional related news content. In fact, the *Guardian* has an entire menu of podcasts as well as a hefty archive, many of which can be obtained free of charge through iTunes.

• To begin, select a podcast from the list and then click on the text marked **Subscribe Free Via iTunes**. This kicks off the download process, and will automatically launch your own copy of iTunes, linking you to the iTunes store.

• You will then see the podcast's header page, with a description of its content, episode details, and viewer/listener reviews. Click on the **Subscribe** button.

• If you look in the Podcast section of your iTunes library, the most recent episode of the podcast you subscribed to will have been downloaded. You will also see that, in this example, you have been notified of a number of earlier episodes. If you want to download any or all of these, click on the **Get** button. From this point, each time you launch iTunes when connected to the Internet, your computer will search for new episodes of that podcast.

Juice

http://juicereceiver.sourceforger.net/index.php

We'll now look at subscribing to a podcast using a piece of aggregator software. In this example we'll use a popular free program called Juice.

Begin by downloading the software from the URL above. Install it on your computer. When you launch the program for the first time, Juice opens up with a pair of default subscriptions. Juice also has a useful podcast directory, which lists numerous broadcasts from various global sources.

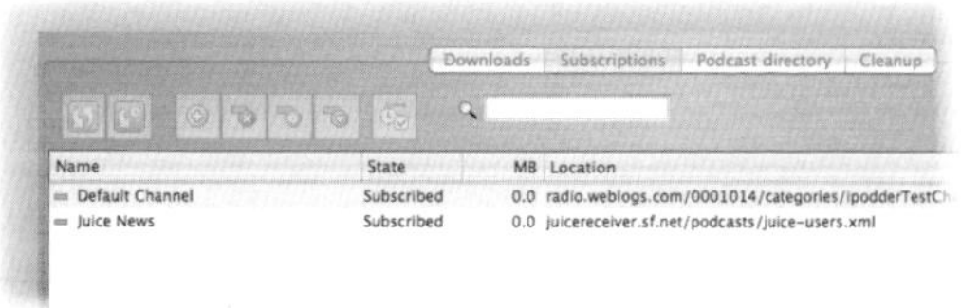

• Click on the button marked **Podcast Directory**. The podcasts are grouped within folders; double-click on any folder to see what is available inside. In this example, we've chosen **Adam Curry's Pod Squad**—a list of favorites selected by the noted online celebrity.

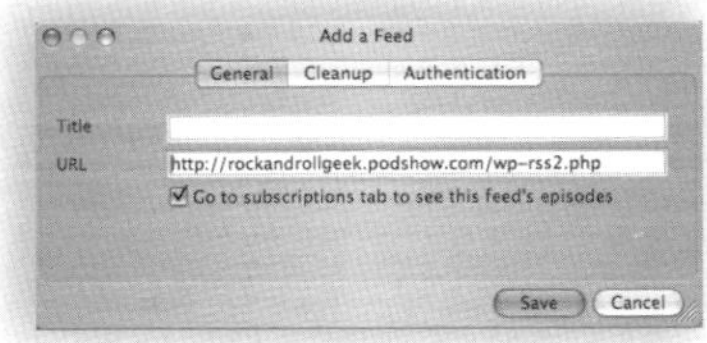

• If you highlight one of the podcasts you will see the URL of the feed appearing in the box near the top of the window. To subscribe to that podcast, click on the **Save** button.

• If you click on the **Downloads** tab and look in the column headed **State**, you will see that your selected podcast is indeed being transferred to your computer. The column headed **Progress** indicates how much of the file has so far been downloaded, and the current speed of the transfer. When the file has arrived on your hard drive you can play it using your chosen mp3 software, or transfer it to an external mp3 player or a suitably equipped cell phone.

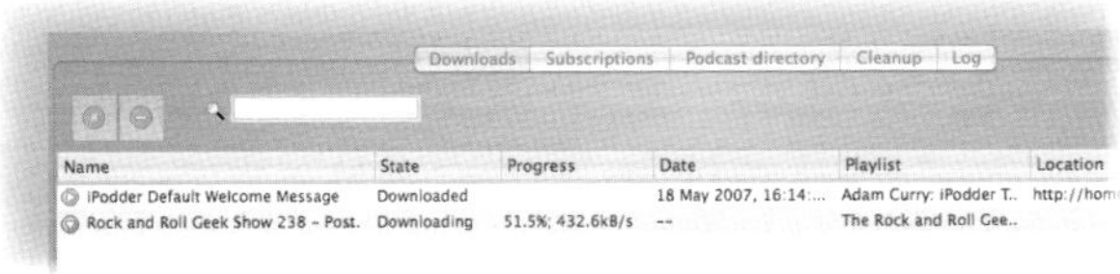

Adding Your Own Podcasts

Directories like those found in Juice and other similar types of software are all well and good for introducing you to selections of the most popular podcasts, but in most cases you are going to want to subscribe to the ones that you find for yourself, or that are recommended to you. To include these, you need to add the "feed" of the podcast manually. (The feed is the URL address the software will go to each time it wants to look for a new episode.)

There are many places you can look for podcast feeds—most news and entertainment websites will have plenty. There are also numerous web-based podcast directories. When you find your chosen podcast, it will usually be accompanied by a button labeled something like **Subscribe**. (The orange-colored XML button is also commonly used for podcast feeds.)

• In this example, we'll use a web directory called Podcast Alley. When you've located the podcast that interests you—in this case, the comedy show **Nobody Likes Onions**—click on the **Subscribe** button.

• In the page that follows, highlight and copy the URL in the box. (**Command + C** for Macs; **Ctrl + C** for PCs.)

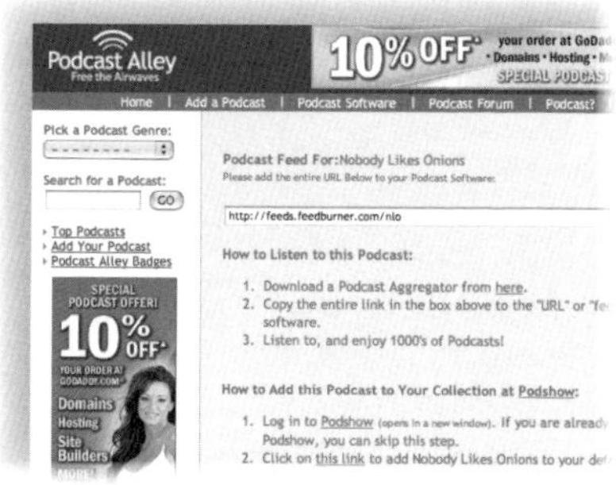

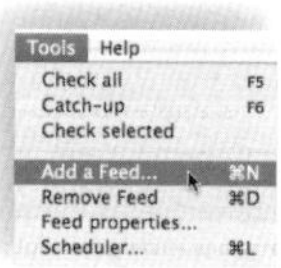

• Launch the Juice application. From the **Tools** menu, select **Add a Feed**.

• In the **Add a Feed** pop-up window, click on the empty box labeled **URL**. Paste the URL into the box. (**Command + C** for Macs; **Ctrl + C** for PCs.) At the same time, you also have the option of entering a title for the podcast.

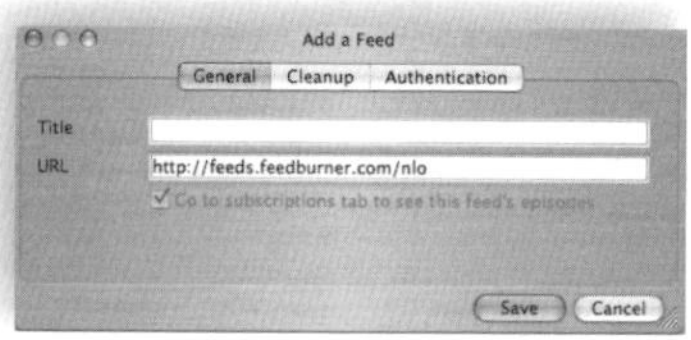

• To complete the subscription, click on the **Save** button.

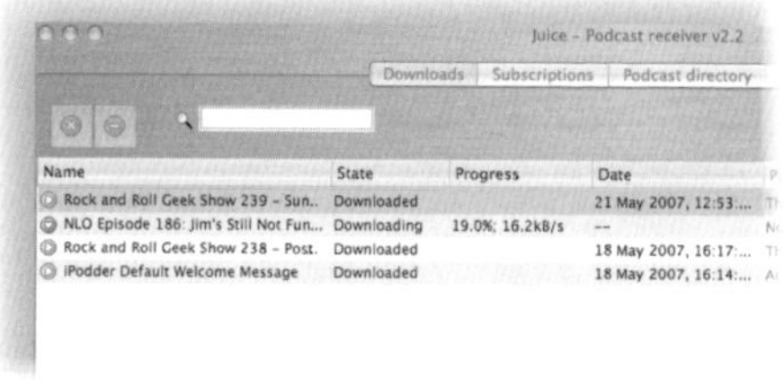

• The selected podcast now appears in Juice's download list. Once it has been transferred you can play the file on your computer or copy it to an mp3 player.

Podcasting Directory

The list below represents a small sample of the podcast (and video podcast) directories available on the Internet. Although most cover a wide array of categories, some are more specialized in their content.

All Podcasts	http://www.allpodcasts.com	General
AmigoFish	http://www.amigofish.com	General
AudioFeeds.org	http://www.audiofeeds.org	Independent music
Blubrry	http://www.blubbry.com	Social networking
ClickCaster	http://www.clickcaster.com	General
EveryPodcast.com	http://www.everypodcast.com	General
Feedzie	http://www.feedzie.com	Podcast search and tagging
fluctu8.com	http://www.fluctu8.com	General
GoFish	http://www.gofish.com	Directory of RSS content
HardPodCafe	http://hardpodcafe.com	General
IdiotVox	http://idiotvox.com	General
iPodderX	http://ipodderx.com/director	General
Learn Out Loud	http://www.learnoutloud.com	Education
Loomia	http://www.loomia.com	General
LoudPocket	http://www.loudpocket.com	Business
Melodeo	http://melodeo.com	Cell phone content
MusicOnlyPodcasts	http://www.musiconlypodcasts.com	Music
New Time Radio	http://newtimeradio.com	Comedy
Nimiq	http://www.nimiq.nl	General
Odeo.com	http://www.odeo.com	General
Pluggd	http://www.pluggd.com	General
Podcast Alley	http://www.podcastalley.com	General
Podcast Blaster	http://www.podcastblaster.com	General
Podcast Central	http://www.podcastcentral.com	Podcast Charts
Podcast Directory	http://www.podcastdirectory.com	General
Podcast Empire	http://www.podcastempire.com	Directory, forum, and blog
PodcastPickle	http://www.podcastpickle.com	Rated content
Podcast Pup	http://podcastpup.com	General
Sportpodcasts.com	http://www.sportspodcasts.com	Sports
StreetIQ	http://streetiq.com	Business/finance
VlogList	http://vloglist.com	Video blogs
Vodstock	http://www.vodstock.com	Video podcasting

Making Your Own Podcast

There are two distinct phases in making your own podcast. The first step is to create the audio or video file that you want to broadcast; the second is to upload your podcast file to a specific location and then let the world know how to get hold of it.

Writing and recording a podcast is well outside the scope of a book such as this—the best we can come up with is a list of basic commonsense tips (*see page 159*). However, if you are interested, there is a huge amount of information on this topic to be found on the Internet. The remainder of this segment assumes you have already recorded your podcast and are happy with its content.

Uploading Your Own Podcast

For anyone to watch or listen to your podcast it must first be uploaded to a location on the Internet that can be accessed by the public. In other words, it needs its own exclusive address. If you have your own website or access to an FTP server this is very straightforward: all you need to do is create a folder in your "public" area and upload the file to that folder. When you've done that, make a note of the full URL of the file you've copied across. (It's likely to be something like **http://www.yourdomain.com/podcasts/myveryimportantpodcastepisode1.mp3**.)

If you don't have an FTP server, you'll need to find a site that will host your podcast on your behalf. There are a number of free or cheap options here that we'll look at shortly. However, there are two critical issues that we should first address: server space and bandwidth.

Server Space

The amount of server space you need for your podcasts will depend on four factors:

- The length of each episode
- The audio quality of your mp3 files
- How often you produce episodes
- How many episodes you want to make available at any time

If you were to use standard CD-quality digital audio for your podcast, the files would be much too large for most subscribers to download quickly. This is why podcast audio files are "compressed" in the mp3 format. (And, indeed, this is the reason that mp3, for all its sonic limitations, is so hugely popular.) Compression enables files to be reduced to a tenth of their size or more without too drastic a drop in sound quality. This also means that upload and download times are reduced by a similar factor. The key component here is the "bit rate" of the audio file, which you are able to set when you create your final mp3 file. The rule here is simple: the higher the bit rate, the better the sound, but the larger the file. So it's all a matter of balancing trade-offs. As far as podcasters are concerned, 128 kilobytes per second would be adequate for most music; for spoken word, 64 or 96 kilobytes per second should be ample. This means that:

- A 128 kbps stereo file will take up around 1 megabyte/minute
- A 96 kbps stereo file will take up around 0.7 megabytes/minute

So if, for example, you were to create a 30-minute stereo podcast using a bit rate of 96 kbps, each episode would take around 21 megabytes of storage space. If you were to record one episode each week, and wanted make a year's worth of episodes available online at all times, you would need 1,092 megabytes—or just over a gigabyte—of server space. Many hosting services will offer a limited basic package of up to a gigabyte, and then charge incrementally for larger amounts of space.

Bandwidth

The second major factor to consider when choosing a server for your podcasts is the "bandwidth." This is the amount of data that your host server allows to be transferred back and forth each month. Each time you upload a podcast, some of your bandwidth allowance is used; more significantly, each time anyone downloads your podcast, that *also* will eat into your allowance. If your podcasts suddenly start becoming popular then you must ensure that your host allows you enough bandwidth to accommodate your audience, otherwise, depending on the deal you have with your host, you may have to pay excessive fees, or even find that your account is frozen or removed. If this thought seriously worries you, and you have ambitions of reaching a large audience, you should look for a host server that offers you unlimited bandwidth.

So how do you assess your likely monthly bandwidth requirement? The calculation itself is a very simple piece of arithmetic but is made very difficult by one simple fact: you have to estimate how many people are going to attempt to download your podcast. Once you're up and running you'll quickly get a feel for the size of your audience, but to begin with you really just have to guess! So, for example, if our 21-megabyte podcast is downloaded by 200 people in a month, and one episode is issued every week, then a monthly bandwidth of 16.8 gigabytes would be needed. As with space, if you want a lot of bandwidth you'll have to pay for it.

Simple Hosting

Selecting the best place to host a podcast will depend on how seriously you intend to take your podcasting. If you just want to give it a try, and don't envision doing it very frequently, you should be able to find a free solution. Let's take a look at one of these services—PodBean.

PodBean

http://www.podbean.com

PodBean is a typical podcast host and directory. It offers a basic package, which is free, with allowances of 100 megabytes of storage and 5 gigabytes bandwidth. (As you can see, the weekly podcast example we showed above would already be struggling here.) There are a number of other packages offering unlimited storage and bandwidth for a small monthly charge.

- Enter the URL: **http://www.podbean.com**. First you must register as a user: to do this, click on the **Sign-Up** label and follow the instructions. Once you've registered you can log in.

- To begin uploading, click on the **Publish a Podcast** tab.

• PodBean recommends that you begin by filling out details of the podcast that will appear in your menu. Click on the button marked **Add Your Audio/Video**. A new box will open out: click on the text labeled **Upload New Files**.

• The **Media Manager** page will open. Click on **Upload** and then the button marked **Choose File**.

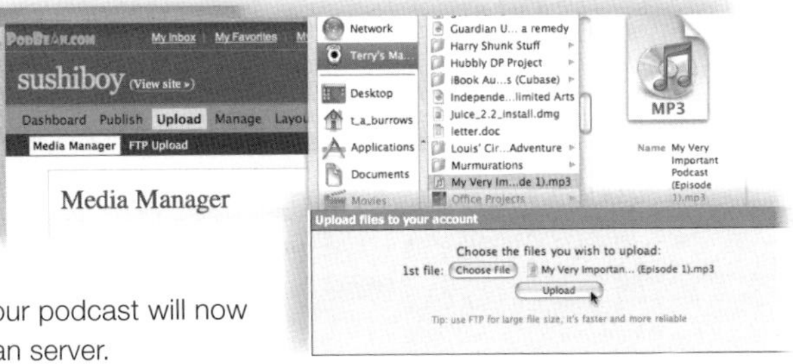

• Navigate through your hard drive until you find your podcast file. Finally, click on the **Upload** button. Your podcast will now transfer to the PodBean server.

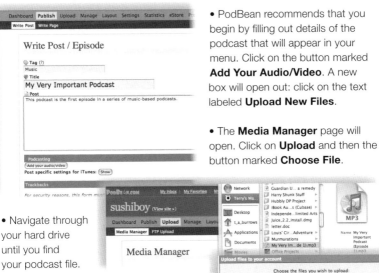

• If you click on the **Layout** tab, you will be able to select a "theme." This is the layout and text style that others will see when they discover your podcast. This page contains a number of different designs—scroll down the list to view all the options. To make your choice, click on the title above the thumbnail image. You can see how your page will look by clicking on **View Site**—a small piece of text that appears next to your username near the top of the screen.

• Your podcast is now uploaded.

Accessing Your Podcast

This is how your podcast page will look to another user. They will also be able to comment on and rate what you have done. And they can contact you using PodBean's internal mail system.

• The podcast will become available when a user clicks on the **Subscribe** button. This will open their **My Subscriptions** page, which gives an overview of all subscribed podcasts, along with their average ratings.

• If you click on the orange **RSS** button (it appears alongside the podcaster's ID) this will open a new page, which gives the option of adding that podcast to a number of popular "podcatcher" programs. The box beneath shows the URL of your podcast feed. This can be copied and pasted into other podcast software, in the same way as we did with Juice (*see page 152*).

Creating an RSS Feed

As we have seen in the example above, hosts such as PodBean can offer an appealing all-in-one solution to the different processes required to launch a podcast. However, there will be other occasions when you may need to do things manually—for example, if you are creating a feed for your own website. So let's now look at some other ways of creating a "feed."

Good Podcasting Tips

What's your point? If your podcast is themed, follow the three classic rules of public speaking: say what you're going say; say it; and then say what you just said.

Keep it short We've all got short attention spans these days—15–30 minutes should be ample for most podcasts.

Structure There may be a few gifted individuals who can switch on a microphone and talk engagingly for 30 minutes without much preparation, but if you or I try it, the results are sure to be mind-numbingly bad. Structure your program so that it can be broken into smaller chunks. If you are interviewing someone, prepare the questions in advance.

Create an identity Every TV and radio show has a theme tune that heralds it arrival and departure. Your podcast should be no different.

Technical quality Recording audio is a skill in its own right. But while lo-fi sound has its place in popular culture, having to endure a tinny, hissy, crackly, low quality podcast can be a painful experience. While most computers can record high quality digital audio, almost any built-in microphone will sound poor. Invest in, or borrow, a reasonable microphone and a pop screen to prevent those "P" syllables from leaping out.

Quiet Unless you are specifically doing an on-location podcast, always do your microphone recording in quiet surroundings. Routinely, you don't want to hear traffic noise, dogs barking, or your family talking in the background.

Edit before broadcast Most computers now come equipped with some kind of basic digital sound editing software. If yours does not, try Audacity, which is cross-platform, open-source, and free (**http://audacity.sourceforge.net**). Use it to construct and edit your podcast. Study other radio shows or podcasts that you like, listening for production techniques such as using background music for transitions.

Identify your podcast If you plan to podcast regularly, it may be a good idea to begin your program with some "meta" information, such as date, epsidode number, and subject. This will give an overall sequence to your shows.

Easy listening Make it as easy as possible for users to subscribe.

First, what exactly *is* an RSS feed? RSS is an acronym for **Really Simple Syndication** and is one of a number of web feed formats used to publish frequently updated digital content. This includes not only podcasts, but blogs and news feeds as well. In simple terms, you could think of an RSS feed as a table of contents. The feed does not itself contain the podcast, but links to it using its URL. While RSS is by far the most widely used type of feed, it is by no means the only one. ATOM, another XML-based feed, is rated more highly by the technical community. However, there are certain compatibility issues between the two, so, as far as podcasters are concerned, they need only worry about RSS for the time being.

An RSS feed is a text file created using a language called XML (Extensible Markup Language). Anyone familiar with XML can easily create their own feed files—it's not terribly difficult, and not that different from the HTML used in website design. However, the strong recommendation here is that if you *have* to create your own feed files, then make life a little easier by using one of the many online RSS generator websites. Two good examples are Podcast Generator (**http://www.tdscripts.com**) and Listgarden (**http://www.softwaregarden.com/products/listgarden**). Both work in a similar way: you input the required information into the table and then click on a button to generate the coding to paste into a simple text file. Ensure that you save the file with a suffix of ".rss" and then upload the file to your website (*see page 150*). This is the file that then needs to be linked to an RSS button on your website, passed on to podcast directories, or just given out to anyone interested in receiving your podcast.

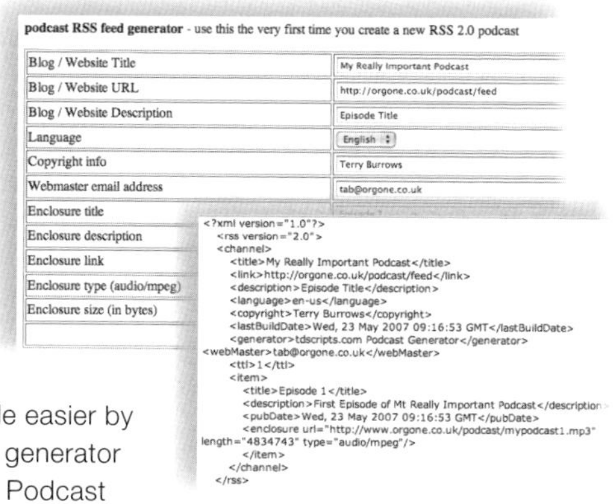

Before promoting your podcast, there's one more thing you need to do: check that your feed is working. Once again, there are free web applications to help you with this. For example, go to **http://rss.scripting.com**, enter the URL address of your RSS file, and click on the **Validate** button. If you get an error message, then there will be something wrong with your XML coding.

Promoting Your Podcast

With millions of other podcasters busy doing their thing all over the Internet, you can't simply expect to upload your program and suddenly find yourself with a massive audience. That means taking every opportunity possible to publicize what you are doing. So here are some ideas to help you reach a greater number of listeners and viewers.

Podcast directories We've already seen the importance of podcasting directories as a source of available content (*see page 153*). As a podcaster, it's *critically* important that you register your work with the main podcast directories. Inclusion in podcast search engines and directories will open up a potentially enormous audience. You can find a massive selection of directories to contact at **http://www.podcasting-tools.com/submit-podcasts.htm**. This may be daunting and tedious work, but it's the single most important thing you can do to get your podcast known.

Let people know Send something resembling a press release about your podcast to absolutely anyone who you think may be interested in what you have to say. If you have a social networking site send out a bulletin or message to all your "friends."

Look the part Add suitable images to your website that will let visitors know that a podcast is available. Popular icons include the orange rectangles used to indicate RSS feeds, but many others are now used. A nice selection of free downloadable podcast icons is available from **http://www.feedforall.com /podcasting-graphics.htm**.

Be descriptive People browsing websites rarely read every word in front of them, so make sure that your RSS feed contains the kind of keyword information that will grab the interest of potential listeners.

Educate your listeners Remember that podcasting is a relatively new idea: there may be a large potential audience out there made up of people who have little or no understanding of what podcasting is all about, let alone how to subscribe to one. Therefore it may be worth your while to explain on your website a little about the nature of podcasting, or at least create a link to a podcasting FAQ site, such as **http://www.podcastingnews.com.**

Portals

A portal is a website that acts as a centralized point of information and contains links to other significant or related web pages. Business organizations have long understood their significance—they represent a first point of online contact, and so are an important part of the modern branding process. A portal has a slightly different meaning for most individual users. Here it generally refers to a user-defined home page that appears each time a browser is launched. Whilst it would be possible to program a custom-made web page according to your own needs, there are now many simpler solutions available.

Your Own Front Page

So what do you want to see on your screen when you first launch your browser? In the past, among the most common approaches were to set the browser preferences to a preferred search engine or news page. In recent times, however, the "dashboard" approach has become increasingly popular. This is a type of portal that is made up of what are called "widgets"—each of which can be an individual application in its own right. Examples of widgets include calendars, diaries, news items, search engines, weather reports, and games. The key factor here is that the *specific* content and appearance is defined by the user.

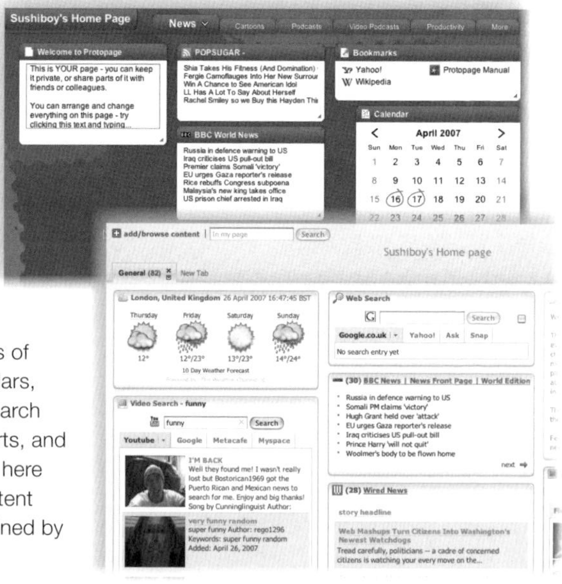

iGoogle Homepage

http://www.google.com/ig

Let's look at one of the most popular user-definable portals—Google's personal home page. This brings an assortment of function from across the Web into a single page, while keeping the popular search engine feature in place.

• Begin by typing in the URL **http://www.google.com/ig**. The screen that appears is the default homepage.

• The screen comprises a number of individual windows—these are the widgets. Each of these windows can be repositioned around the screen by clicking and dragging on the menu bar. On the top right-hand corner of each menu bar you'll see that there are three buttons. Clicking on the **downward arrow** generates a drop-down menu with a variety of edit options or recommendations; the **dash** button collapses the widget leaving only the menu bar visible; the **cross** button causes the widget to close completely.

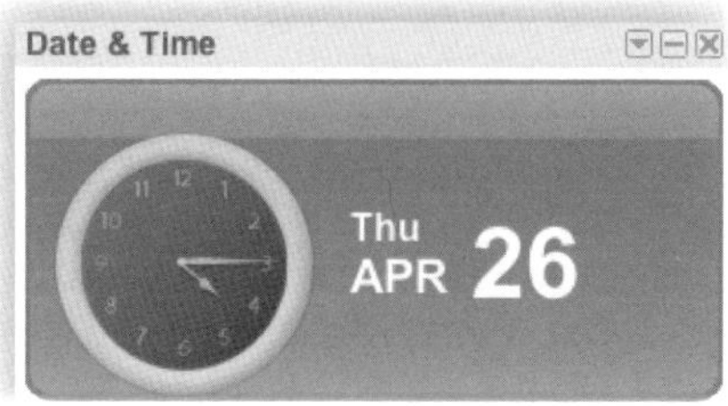

Adding Widgets to Your Home Page

Let's now take a look at how easy it is to customize your home page. Google itself offers a great number of options, from Google Maps and GMail to puzzles and games. Additionally, there is an ever-growing list of third-party widgets available.

• Click on the text marked **Welcome to Your Google Homepage. Make It Your Own**. (You can find it beneath the search box near the top of the page.)

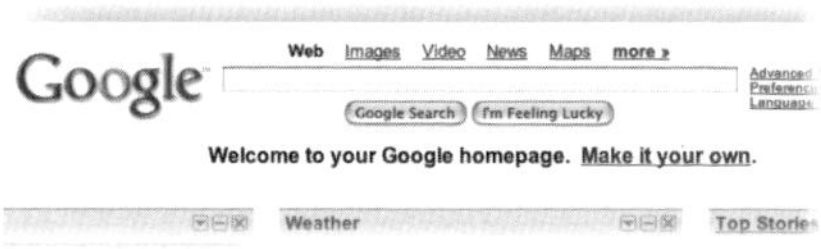

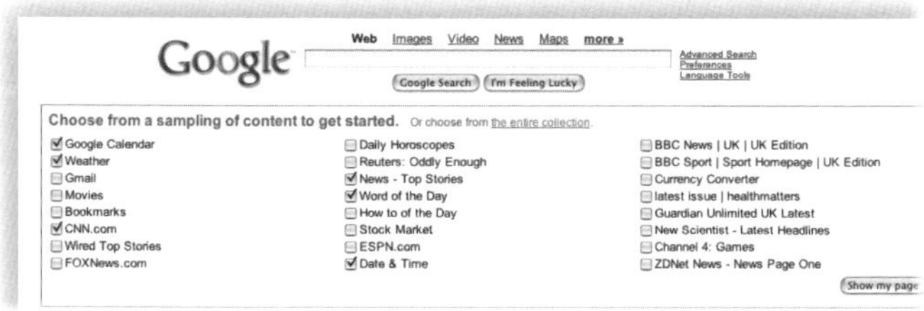

• The window that opens contains a list of Google's most popular widget options. To add any of them to your home page, click on the checkbox alongside your choice. (Similarly, you can remove widgets by clicking on the ticks in the checkboxes.) For a complete list of options, click on the text labeled **Or Choose from the Entire Collection**. When you've finished your selection, click on the **Show My Page** button. You will then be returned to your newly adorned homepage.

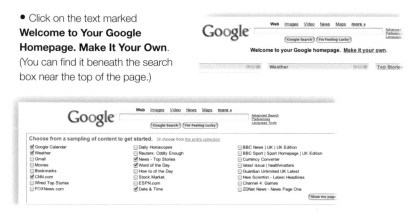

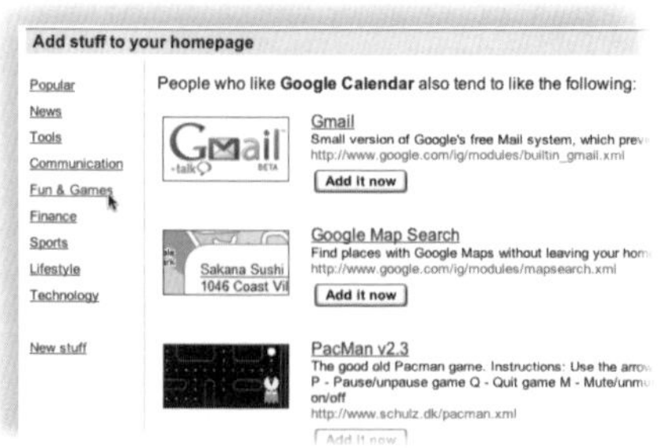

• For a wider selection, including many third-party widgets, click on the **Add Stuff** button on the top right of the window. The screen that follows contains a variety of options, all of which can be previewed. Alternatively, you can choose from the categories listed on the left of the screen. In this example we've selected **Fun & Games**.

• You will now be able to see a scrolling window of games widgets. To select one of them to add to your home page, click on the **Add It Now** button beneath the preview screen. When you return to your home page you will see the widget in place.

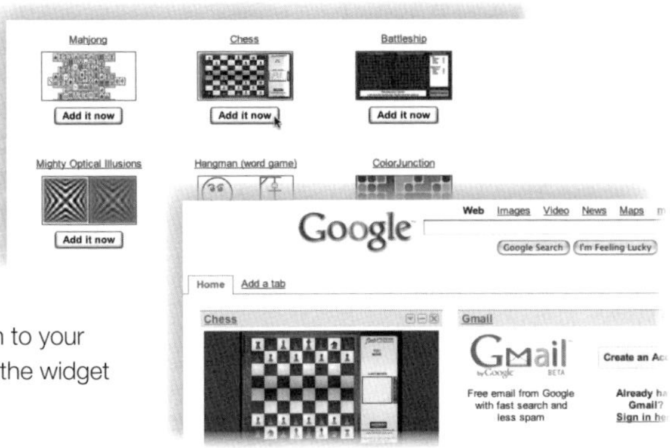

Adding a Theme

You can customize the look of your home page by adding what is called a "theme." This alters design aspects of the page—color, layout, images—without changing the content.

• To call up the list of options, click on the **Select Theme** button. The selection will appear in a window on the page. Click on one of the options—in this example we've chosen **Tea House**—and then **Save**.

• You'll now be able to see the effect this has had on the design of your homepage.

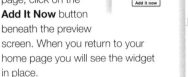

Netvibes

http://www.netvibes.com

Whereas Google's Personal Homepage is aimed squarely at the average Internet user, the AJAX-based Netvibes portal is perhaps of interest to those with more experience. It works in broadly the same way—a series of user-defined modules—but also incorporates RSS feeds, podcasts, and a limited social networking capability, in that you can send recommendations to other users or e-mail them to friends. Many of these modules can also be integrated into your own websites using html commands.

• Enter the URL **http://www.netvibe.com**. A default home page will load. To alter to the content of your page, click on the button marked **Add/Browse Content**.

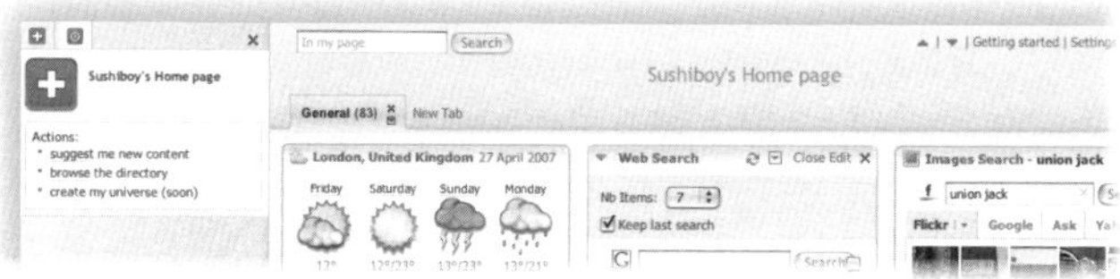

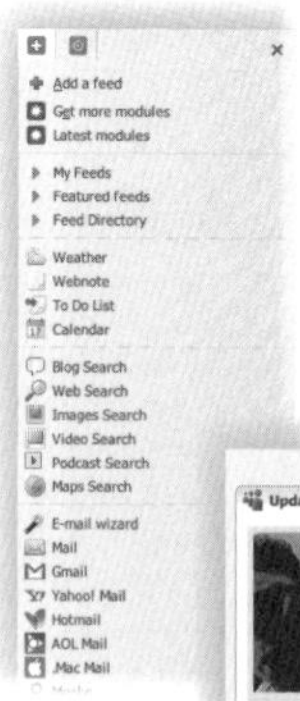

• A drop-down menu will appear on the left-hand side of the window. This contains the most popular Netvibe modules. For a more complete list of options, you can click on the **Get More Modules** button near the top of the list. To select a module, simply click the icon alongside its name and it will appear in the main window. In this example we've chosen MySpace.

• The MySpace module will appear floating in the main window. If you click on the **Edit** button you can enter the URL of your chosen MySpace page and display different components, such as pictures or comments. If you want to add this module to your Netvibe homepage, click on the button marked **Add to My Page**.

• When you click on the **Get More Modules** button, a new page of options appears. You can view different categories—**Modules**, **Feeds**, **Podcasts**, **Events**—by clicking on the different tabs.

• You can choose from the list of modules in each category. Clicking on the NetVibes button gives you a preview of the module. If you like what you see, click on the button labeled **Yes, Add It to My Page**.

Additional portal sites

24eyes	http://www.24eyes.com	Inbox	http://www.inbox.com
Browsr	http://www.bloxor.com	Itsastart	http://www.itsastart.com
Eskobo	http://www.eskobo.com	Klipfolio	http://www.serence.com
Favoor	http://www.favoor.com	Mobileglu	http://www.mobileglu.com
Feedication	http://www.feedication.com	Pageflakes	http://www.pageflakes.com
Feedpile	http://feedpile.com	Pobb	http://www.pobb.net
Feedtv	http://www.feedfeeds.com	Protopage	http://www.protopage.com
Fold	http://www.fold.com	Pushy	http://www.pushy.com
Fyuze	http://www.fyuze.com	Start	http://www.start.com
Googlemodules	http://www.googlemodules.com	Superglu	http://www.suprglu.com
Goowy	http://www.goowy.com	Windowslive	http://www.live.com
Gritwire	http://www.gritwire.com	Wrickr	http://www.wrickr.com

Search Engines

If there was a single type of web-based application that could be said to be at the heart of the Internet, it is the search engine. Whether your favored search site is Yahoo!, Google, or any of the many other available possibilities, the basic concept is similar: you type in a keyword, string of text, or a Boolean search, which results in a list of websites that most closely contain your search criteria. You can then click on any of the items from that list to open the website.

Search History

The first ever application for searching on the Internet was a program called Archie that was created in 1990 at McGill University in Montreal, Canada. Archie downloaded directory listings located on anonymous FTP sites to create a searchable database of filenames. However, it could not read the contents of the files, so depended on a logical naming structure being in place.

The first web search engine, Wandex, appeared in 1993. This compiled its information, like most subsequent engines, using a "web crawler"—an automated program that browses the Web collecting data. The following year saw the launch of many of the most popular search engines of the 1990s, such as Lycos, Excite, Infoseek, Inktomi, Northern Light, Ask Jeeves, Yahoo!, and AltaVista. Indeed, it was commercial interest in these so-called "first generation" search engines that fueled much of the first Internet stockmarket boom.

The second generation of search engines began to appear toward the end of decade, among them, in 1998, Google, the most popular search engine of them all. The success was based in part on the use of link analysis and the PageRank analysis algorithm—a numerical weighting system which helped to make searches more relevant and accurate. In fact, such search engines typically use more than 150 different criteria to determine relevancy.

The most recent developments in web searches—"Search 2.0" sites—have aimed to refine relevancy even further. We'll take a look at a selection of these on page 172.

Google

http://www.google.com

Google is perhaps the most astonishing success story in the history of the Internet. It began in 1996 as a research project by Larry Page and Sergey Brin, two doctoral students at Stanford University, California. Their basic idea was that a search engine that analyzed the relationships between websites would produce better results than existing techniques, which largely ranked results according to the number of times the search term appeared on a page. The name "Google" originated from a misspelling of the term "googol," which refers to the number 1 followed by 100 zeros. The business was initially run from a friend's garage, but by 2007 Google employed over 12,000 full-time staff and had an estimated stock market value of $23 billion. Such is its ubiquity that in 2006 the term "to google" was given its own entry in the Oxford English Dictionary.

Simple Search

• Begin by entring Google's URL: **http://www.google.com**. (If you are outside the United States, you might find yourself automatically transferred to one of Google's local sites.) One of the reasons Google was instantly popular was because it was so simple to use. All you have to do is type in some text and click on the **Search** button. In this example we've entered the word **fish**.

• You will see a list of what Google considers to be the 10 most relevant websites that match your search criteria. If you want to see the next 10 ranked websites, then click on the button marked **2** at the foot of the page. You continue to view more search results by clicking on the subsequent numbers.

Alternative Searches

When you launch Google, it immediately assumes that you want to do a web search—and this is what the vast majority of users do want. However, above the search box you see further options: besides Web, you can search for **Images**, **News**, **Maps**, **Products**, and **Groups**. And if you click on **More**, then you will see a whole new page of options.

- Let's use our existing search text to look for images. With the word "**fish**" still in the search box, click on **Images**.

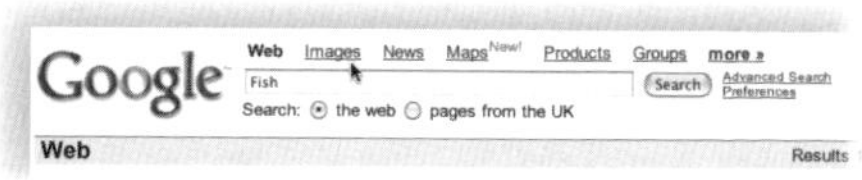

- Google now provides you with a page of thumbnail views of websites that it believes match your search requirements.

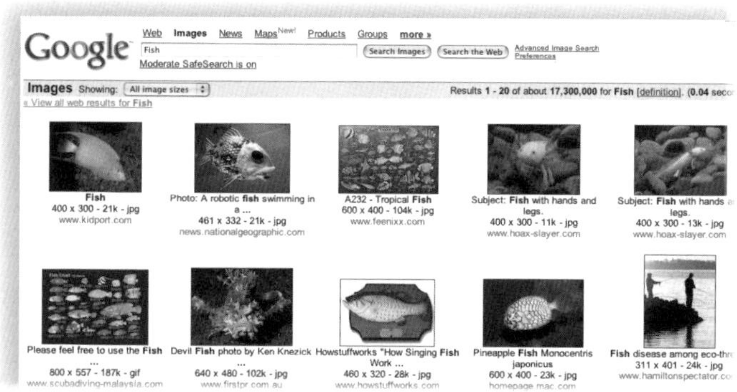

- To get a full-size view of any of the websites shown on the page, you simply click on the image.

The other search types Googles offers are:

News	Searches dedicated news sites.
Maps	Maps from around the world.
Products	Commercial products related to your search.
Groups	Searches related newsgroups and displays them in your web browser.

Search Criteria

Doing a search is very straightforward—you simply enter a word and click on the **Search** button. There is an art in choosing the correct terms, though. Here is a brief guide:

Choose your words with care Start with the obvious. If you want general information about, say, London, try typing in **London**! If you want to find a place in London to rent a car, try **London car hire**. Google, like most search engines, is not case sensitive, so if you enter **London**, **london**, **LONDON** or **lOnDoN,** it will generate the same results.

Exclude common words If you are searching on multiple criteria, there is no need to include "and" between terms. Also, many search engines ignore common terms, such as "how" and "where," as well as certain single digits and letters. Google will tell you if it has omitted a common word. If your search critically requires this word to be included you can place a "+" sign in front of it.

Exact phrases Sometimes you will want to search for a very specific phrase—for example, a line from poem, or a person's name. To do this, place quotation marks around your search term. So if you want to do a web search for Tony Blair, enter "Tony Blair"—otherwise you may find options that list the words "Tony" and "Blair."

Negatives Some words have multiple meanings. You can use the "minus" sign to filter unwanted items. For example, bass might refer to a fish or a musical instrument. If your intended search is the latter, you could enter bass -fish. This should avoid any fish-related sites being selected.

More Google

If you click on the **More** button you will find further search options and other Google tools. On the left of the screen you will see such possibilities as the **Google Book Search**, which gives you details of complete works that are available to read online. Or the **Google Notebook**, which enables you you to take "clippings"—text, images, or links—from other websites.

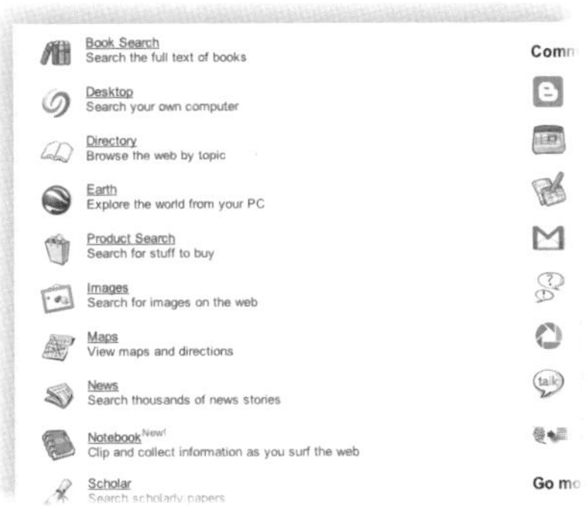

Search 2.0

Let's now take a look at some of the newest approaches to data retrieval. These are all third-generation search engines. They don't represent a radical overhaul of the commercial big guns, such as Google, MSN, and Ask, but rather an enhancement—most of what they offer will doubtless be subsumed by the industry leaders in the future.

Clusty

http://www.clusty.com

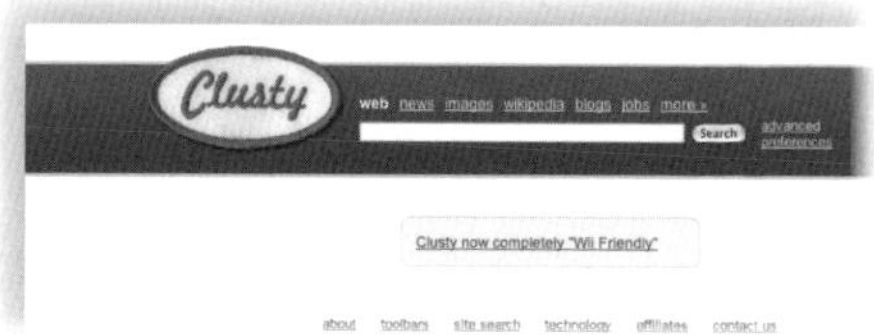

Clusty is a "clustering" engine that groups similar items together and organizes search results into folders. It's a "meta-search" system, so it searches other search engines. The categorization makes for a neater and more refined search experience. So if you're looking for a specific subject you are likely to get the best results by navigating the categories and their subdivisions.

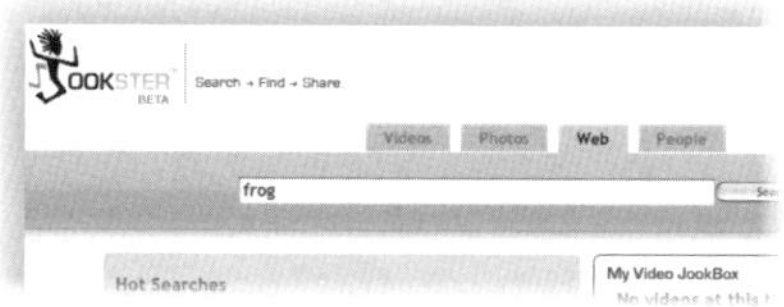

Jookster

http://www.jookster.com

Jookster is part social networking tool and part search engine. It works as a browser toolbar and searches through the browser's bookmarks and also websites of interest that have been derived from the user's social network.

Rollyo

http://www.rollyo.com

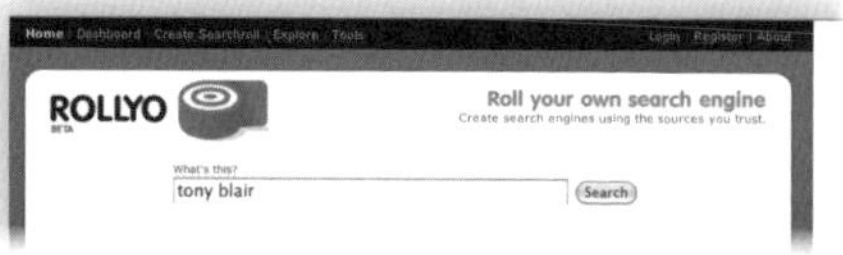

This is a community-powered, theme-based search. Rollyo allows users to create and publish their own personal search engines. This is achieved by creating custom "SearchRolls" made up of URLs that the user knows to be useful in a specific category. This means that while it's nothing as exhaustive as a traditional search engine, you get results based on the recommendations of real people, rather than a mathematical algorithm.

SearchMash

http://www.searchmash.com

SearchMash is a part of the ever-growing Google family. Although it uses the same search criteria as Google, its use of AJAX technology provides a vastly improved user interface. This is an excellent site for those who want an enhanced version of a traditional search engine.

Snap

http://www.snap.com

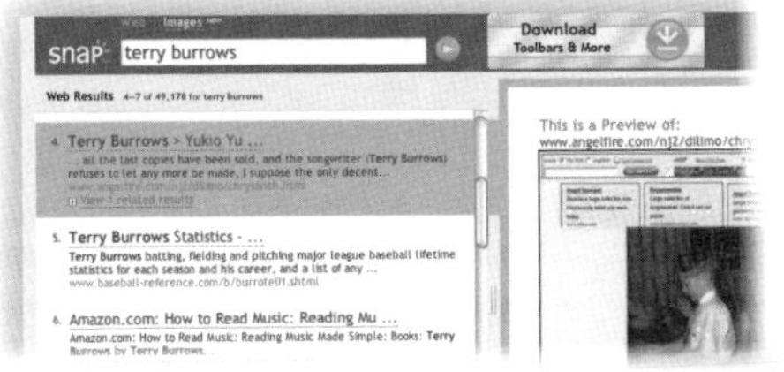

Snap is a preview-powered search engine. When you perform a search, your results page contains a conventional scrolling list on the left of the window. If, however, you highlight any of those entries you will see a screenshot of the web page on the right-hand side of the window. This can save huge amounts of time since you don't necessarily need to visit the site to assess its usefulness.

Swicki

http://www.swicki.eurekster.com

Like Rollyo, Swicki is a social networking search engine that allows users to create focused searches based on the input of other Swicki users.

Curiosities

Most search engines stand or fall on how well they do their job—namely to find and retrieve relevant information. There are a few, however, that have some mysterious agenda of their own. They may not be of great practical value, but they *are* fun to play with.

Retrievr

http://labs.systemone.at.retrievr

This a very strange approach to searching. It's one that has a pretty limited application, and yet it's extremely attractive. Retrievr is a search engine that uses the vast image base of Flickr (*see page 132*) as its population. You have two options. You can draw an image in the Flash panel and Retrievr will list photographs from Flickr that look a bit like it! Or you can upload your own photograph and, again, you will get a list of "similar" photographs.

• Enter the URL: **http://labs.systemone.at.retrievr**. To draw an image, select the size of your pen and a color, and start drawing in the box—position the arrow where you wish to start drawing, press the mouse button to release the ink, move the cursor around to draw, and release the mouse button when you want to stop the ink. Here you can see we've drawn a very crude cartoon figure.

• While you are drawing, Reteivr gets to work, coming up with photographs from Flickr that have some kind of visual link—be it shape or color—to your sketch. These are the suggestions that Retrievr produced (*see left*). As you can see, there is *some* kind of connection between them!

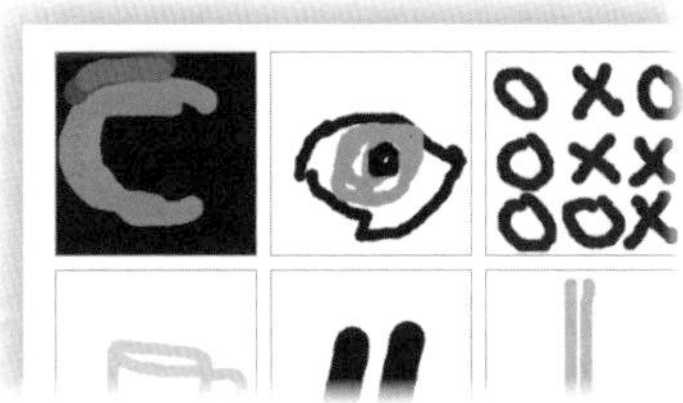

• Finally, Retrievr enables you to look through a library of sketches that have been produced and give them a rating.

More Search Engines

1000tags	http://1000tags.com	Qwerky	http://qwerky.stellify.net
Blogpulse	http://www.blogpulse.com	Releton	http://www.releton.com
Blue	https://www.blue.us	Riya	http://riya.com
Browster	http://www.browster.com	Rollyo	http://rollyo.com
Collaborativerank	http://collabrank.org	Surfwax	http://www.surfwax.com
Ditto	http://ditto.com	Talkdigger	http://www.talkdigger.com
Doubletrust	http://sushil01.securesites.net/~ashish/doubletrust		
Exalead	http://www.exalead.com	Technorati	http://www.technorati.com
Factbites	http://www.factbites.com	Whonu	http://www.whonu.com
Feedster	http://www.feedster.com	Wikimatrix	http://www.wikimatrix.org
Filangy	http://www.filangy.com		
Gadabe	http://www.gada.be		
Gahooyoogle	http://www.gahooyoogle.com		
Gravee	http://www.gravee.com		
Hakia	http://www.hakia.com		
Healthline	http://www.healthline.com		
Icerocket	http://www.icerocket.com		
Jookster	http://www.jookster.com		
Kinja	http://www.kinja.com		
Lexxe	http://www.lexxe.com		
Liveplasma	http://www.liveplasma.com		
Lumrix	http://wiki.lumrix.net		
Makidi	http://www.makidi.com	Wink	http://www.wink.com
Nextaris	http://www.nextaris.com	Yoono	http://www.yoono.com
Omgili	http://www.omgili.com	Yubnub	http://www.yubnub.org
Prase us	http://www.prase.us		
Prefound	http://www.prefound.com		
Quintura	http://qube.qelix.com		

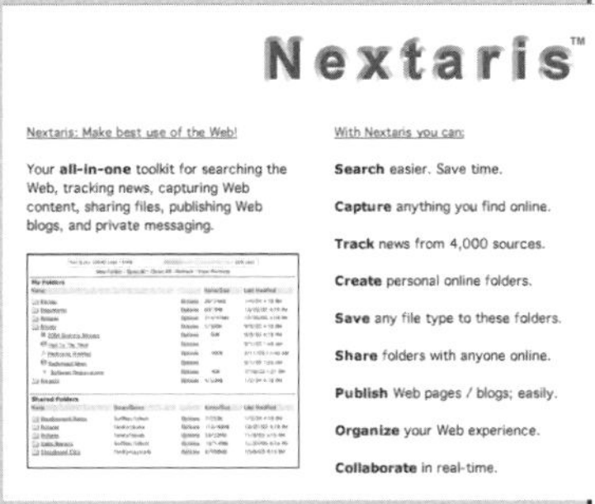

Nextaris™
Nextaris: Make best use of the Web!
Your all-in-one toolkit for searching the Web, tracking news, capturing Web content, sharing files, publishing Web blogs, and private messaging.
With Nextaris you can:
Search easier. Save time.
Capture anything you find online.
Track news from 4,000 sources.
Create personal online folders.
Save any file type to these folders.
Share folders with anyone online.
Publish Web pages / blogs; easily.
Organize your Web experience.
Collaborate in real-time.

Social Networking

In its brief life, the Internet has been responsible for introducing the world to a wide array of buzzwords. Most of these terms have emanated from the technical, scientific, and academic communities, disseminated through the media, before merging into the mainstream and eventually becoming unutterable clichés. One recent addition to this canon is the term "social networking"—the practice of expanding social contacts by making connections through others. It's rather like the concept of "six degrees of separation," the idea that it would be possible for any two people on the planet to make contact through a chain of no more than five intermediaries. In a similar way, social networking on the Internet enables people to make new and relevant contacts with those they would have been unlikely to have otherwise met.

Background to Social Networking Sites

It's fair to say that social networking of some sort has been taking place almost as long as societies themselves have existed. However, the number of people who now have access to the Internet means that what once would had to have taken place face-to-face in a fixed location can now occur between two computer screens anywhere in the world.

Unsurprisingly, social networking was one of the earliest types of website to achieve popularity. One of the first to be launched was Classmates.com, which began in 1995. Like many others that followed, it existed primarily as a way of keeping old school and college friends in touch with one another. Inspired by its popularity, Friend's Reunited enjoyed similar success in Europe when it launched four years later. Others sites emerged, usually with a target audience in mind. MySpace, for example, was initially only really attractive to teenagers; Facebook was aimed at university students. However, all have had to evolve as their users have grown up, and most are now globally inclusive.

Estimates of the numbers of people actively engaged in social networking make for some fascinating reading. There are thought to be over 300 web-based social networks on the Internet, and in the U.S. it's thought that two in every three people visit one of them regularly. MySpace estimate that more than 40 million people—that's around a third of their total number of resgistered users—log on for more than one hour a week.

MySpace

http://www.myspace.com

MySpace is the most stunning phenomenon of the "new" Internet era. Founded in 2003 by Tom Anderson, Chris DeWolfe, and a small group of programmers, MySpace is an interactive social website where individuals create their own personal profiles and build networks of "friends." Content of profiles may include anything from photographs to audio and video clips to lists of personal preferences. MySpace also has its own internal e-mail, instant messaging, and chat systems. Users invite friends—other MySpace profiles—to sign up to their own pages, and in this way large personal networks can evolve quickly. MySpace was an immediate success, and just two years after its creation it was sold to Rupert Murdoch's News Corporation for a reported $580 million.

Initially, the MySpace community largely comprised teenagers and students, however an increasingly mature market has accounted for its recent growth—by the end of 2006 there were in excess of 120 million registered accounts, with MySpace among the five most heavily trafficked websites in the world.

Easy to Use

Many people choose to create a MySpace presence rather than building their own web pages. Part of the appeal is that MySpace is a self-contained system. Furthermore, while not as intuitive as other web-based applications, MySpace requires no technical ability to make it work—although those with HTML and CSS programming skills can significantly alter their pages.

My Friend Tom

All new MySpace registrants receive an invitation to be a friend of "Tom." This is, in fact, Tom Anderson, the founder of MySpace. At first this became something of a joke in the MySpace community, and has been referred to in a number of songs and comedy routines. In fact, a few years ago, T-shirts bearing the logo "Tom is my only friend" even became quite fashionable in certain circles.

Setting Up a MySpace Page

The process of creating a basic MySpace presence is very simple. Before you start, think about the MySpace name you want to use, and also have a photograph in a digital format ready to upload.

• Start by going to the MySpace website. To do this, enter the URL: **http://www.myspace.com**. In the **Member Login** box, click on the **Sign Up** button. (You can also click on the **SIgn Up** button on the top right-hand corner of the window.)

JOIN MYSPACE HERE!

Please enter a valid e-mail address. You will need to confirm your e-mail address to activate your account.

Email Address:	mail@mrsushiboy.com
First Name:	mr
Last Name:	sushiboy
Password:	••••••••
Confirm Password:	••••••••
Country:	United Kingdom
Region/County:	London and South East
Post Code:	EC1 1AV
Date Of Birth:	July 22 1963
Gender:	○ Female ● Male
	☑ Allow others to see when it's my birthday
Preferred Site & Language:	U.K.

☑ By checking the box, you confirm that you know MySpace.com is a website operated by MySpace U.S., and you consent to the transfer of your personal data to the U.S. , where your personal data will be subject to U.S. law and where the level of data protection is different compared to your country. You also agree to the MySpace Terms of Service and Privacy Policy which describe how your personal data will be used.

Sign Up

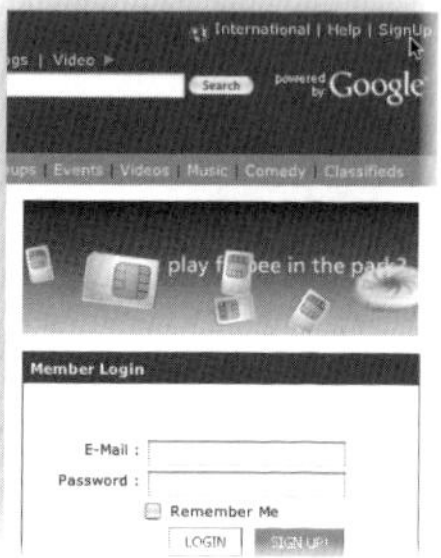

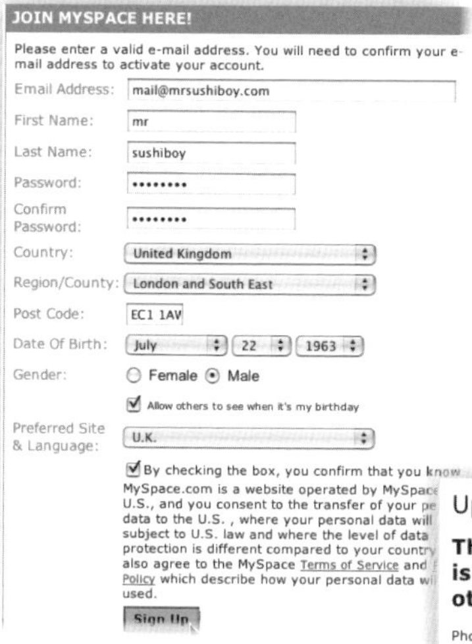

• A window labeled **JOIN MYSPACE HERE!** will appear. Complete the registration details and click on the **Sign Up** button. You'll then be asked to verify your account by entering a series of letters that will appear in the window. When you've done that, click on the button marked **Continue to My Account**. So far, so easy.

Upload Some Photos!

The second step in creating your profile is sharing your photos to let friends and other members see who you are.

Photos may be a max of 600K in these formats: GIF or JPG [Help]

Photos may not contain nudity, violent or offensive material, or copyrighted images. If you violate these terms, your account will be deleted. [photo policy]

If you don't see the Upload Photo form below, click Here

Upload Photo
(Choose File) tb.face.jpg (Upload)

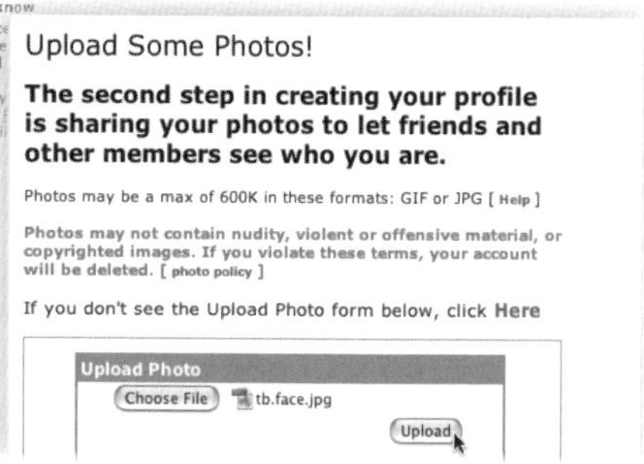

• A new window will now appear, asking if you would like to upload a photograph for your profile. Click on the **Browse** button and navigate your computer's folder hierarchy until you find your chosen image. Click on the **Upload** button. If you don't wish to add a photograph at this point, click on the **Skip for Now** button. A further screen will appear that enables you to invite others with MySpace profiles to be your friends. You can enter their e-mail addresses, separated by a comma, and click on the **Invite** button. You can also skip this section as well—as we will, since we'll look at creating "friends" over the coming pages. Your first MySpace page is now set up.

Components of a MySpace Page

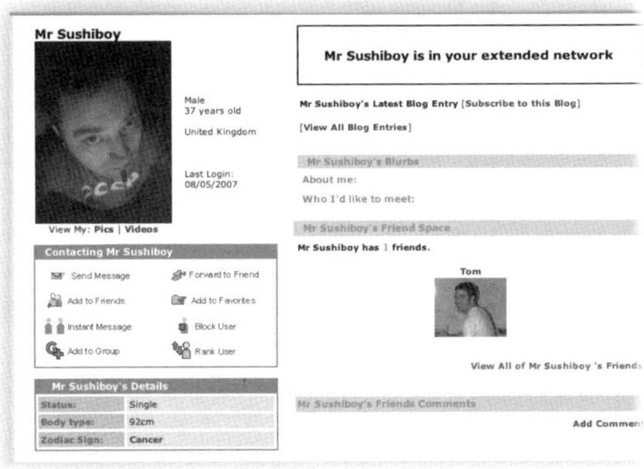

Let's now take a look at what information makes a simple MySpace page.

In the top left-hand corner you can see the basic profile data. This can be edited and added to at will. Further personal details can be found on the bottom left of the page.

On the top right of the screen, you can create your blog entries. Beneath that you'll find the list of MySpace "friends"—when you first create your account you will always find you have one friend, Tom Anderson! Finally, beneath that you'll find a space for other users to leave their comments.

As far as other people viewing your MySpace page are concerned, the **Contact** box is the means by which you can be contacted. The eight buttons within provide for the following options:

- **Send Message** enables users to send you a private e-mail;
- **Add Friends** is where users can make requests to be your friend;
- **Instant Message** enables chat between two friends using the MySpace instant messenger—MySpaceIM;
- **Add to Group** enables you to join or create a user group;
- **Forward to a Friend** enables you to forward a profile to any of your friends;
- **Add to Favorites** allows you to include a MySpace profile among your favorites list;
- **Block User** enables you to prevent a MySpace user contacting you;
- **Rank User** allows other users to "vote" for which photograph should be used on your profile—for this you must have multiple photographs uploaded.

Making Friends

The whole purpose of MySpace is to allow its users to create their own social networks. This is achieved by making "friends." There are numerous ways in which you can do this, but we'll concentrate on a very basic one—using the search facilty. Like many features of MySpace, you must be signed in to make the best use of its features.

• From within your MySpace page, look at the search box at the top of the screen. Enter the name of the person you wish to find, and then click on the **Search** button.

• MySpace will list any pages that match your search text.

• Click on the profile image or the URL to visit your chosen profile.

• To make a "friend" request click on the **Add Friend** button. A pop-up window will appear asking you to confirm that you wish to add this person as a friend. An e-mail will then be sent to the other party. They can then accept or decline your request. If they accept, they will thereafter appear on your list of friends.

Sense and Safety

At its purest and least commercial, social networking is all about self-expression as well as connecting with and making friends. However, you should remember that you are, in effect, speaking to the world and what you post publicly could later come back to haunt you, or—at worst—expose you to danger. Here are some commonsense guidelines that you should follow when using any social networking site.

Public space Your profile is a public space, so don't post anything you wouldn't want the world to know, such as your address or telephone number. Above all, avoid posting information that could make it easy for a stranger to find you.

Embarrassment Think twice before posting a photo or making public comments. Can you think of *anyone* who you might not want to view your online behavior? Your family? Your friends? Your boss?

Appropriate content Harassment, bullying, hate mail, and other inappropriate content should always be reported to the site authorities.

Beware of strangers Take care when adding strangers as friends—people aren't always who they claim to be. Think VERY carefully before agreeing to meet someone in person whom you have met in this way. If you *must* meet someone, do it in a public place and take a friend along with you.

Scams Be on the lookout for fraudulent activities like "phishing"—a method used by criminals to try to get personal information by pretending to be a familiar site. Remember the golden rule of online common sense: if someone makes you an offer that looks too good to be true, then it probably *is* to good to be true.

The sites listed below all provide detailed advice regarding online safety. They are especially useful if your concerns are for the online activities of children or teenagers.

OnGuard Online:	**http://onguardonline.gov/socialnetworking_youth.html**
Internet Crime Complaint Center	**http://www.ic3.gov**
NetSmartz	**http://www.netsmartz.org**
SafeTeens	**http://www.safeteens.com**
WebWiseKids	**http://www.webwisekids.org**
SafeFamilies	**http://www.safefamilies.org**

Communicating with Friends

The two most common methods of "talking" on MySpace are either to make comments, which, with your friend's approval, will appear in public on the profile; or to send them a private message.

Making a Comment

To send a comment you must be signed in, and also be a MySpace friend of the intended recipient.

• Look at the profile we set up earlier: you'll see that a new friend has been added. Click on a chosen profile in your friends list. This will take you to that friend's MySpace page.

• The **Friends Comments** list at the bottom of the page contains all the comments that other MySpace users have posted. Click on the text marked **Add Comment**.

• Write your comment in the pop-up window. When you've finished, click on the **Post a Comment** button.

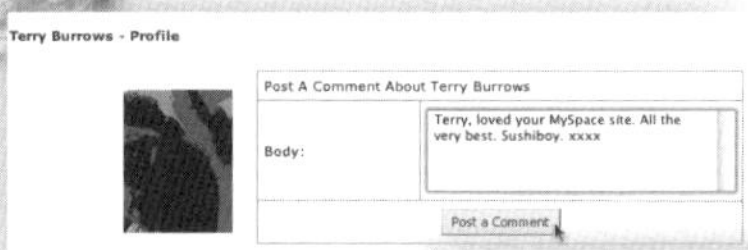

• A new pop-up window will appear asking you to confirm your comment. If you want to make any changes, click on the **Edit** button. When you are happy with what you've written, click on the button marked **Post a Comment**.

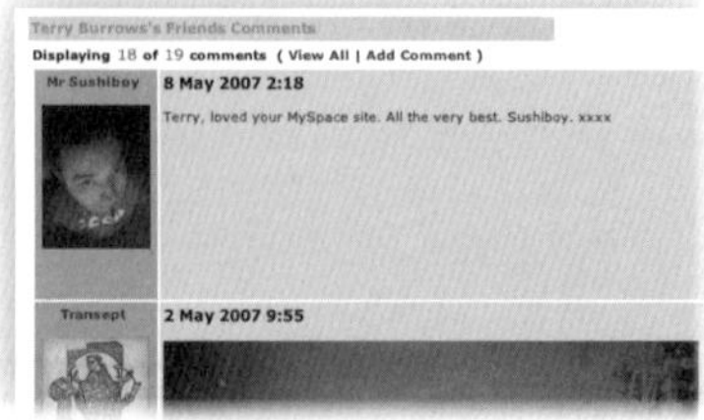

• Your new comment should now appear on your friend's home page.

Sending a Private Message

As with MySpace comments, to send a message you must first be signed in and you must also be a friend of the proposed recipient.

- Begin by opening your friend's MySpace page. Then click on the **Send Message** button.

- The message window appears. Enter a subject for your message, and then the message itself. When you've finished, click on the **Send** button to transmit your message.

- You will receive a confirmation note telling you that the message has been sent.

Sending a Bulletin

MySpace also has a feature that enables users to send a message to *everyone* on their friends list. Bulletins are especially popular on the MySpace music pages, where bands can keep their followers up-to-date on their activities. It's also useful for setting up social events.

Unlike posting comments and messages, which can be done by visiting the intended recipient's MySpace page, to send a bulletin you have to be logged into your MySpace home page. (Note: this is not the same as your own MySpace content page.)

- Enter the URL: **http://www.myspace.com**. Enter your ID and password.

- In your home page, look down the screen to the **My Mail** box, and click on the button marked **Post Bulletin**.

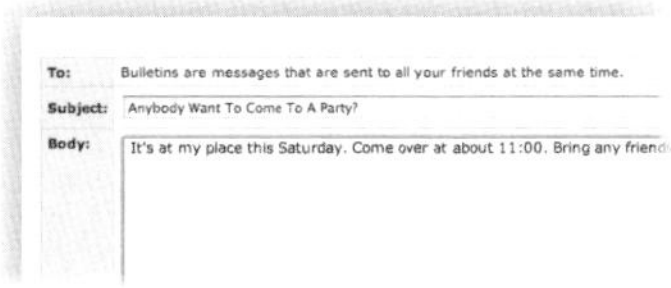

- Enter the details you wish to send and click on the Post button. Your bulletin will now be sent to all of your friends.

Pimping Your MySpace Page

By default, all MySpace pages look largely the same—pretty unpleasant! However, the application was designed in such a way that with a bit of knowledge of HTML or CSS programming you can heavily personalize your space. However, if that idea fills you with dread, have no fear: there are plenty of templates produced by third parties that are available free of charge. One versatile possibility comes from a site called Pimp-My-Profile, which has created a code generator. The user works through a series of tabbed menus, selecting different colors, fonts, and other design factors. At the end of the process a piece of HTML code is generated automatically—this is copied and pasted into a chosen MySpace page.

Pimp-My-Profile

http://www.pimp-my-profile.com

Editors
Myspace Layout Editor
Create a custom profile for your myspace page or choose
MYSPACE
hi5.com Editor
Customize the look of your hi5.com profile here

• Enter the URL: http://www.pimp-my-profile.com. Scroll down the page looking for the **Editors** list. Click on the button marked **MySpace Layout Editor**.

• The MySpace Layout Generator opens. This page features nine options that can all be accessed from the tabs running horizontally along the top of the window. You can navigate by using these tabs, or you can work through each page in sequence by clicking on the **Start** button. (This becomes the **Next** button on subsequent pages.)

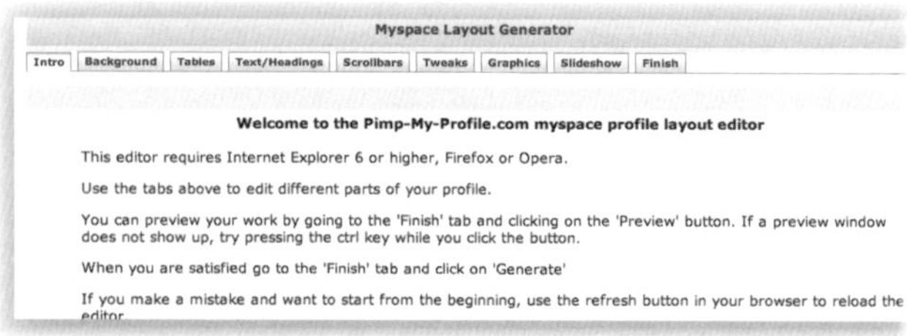
Myspace Layout Generator
Intro
Background
Tables
Text/Headings
Scrollbars
Tweaks
Graphics
Slideshow
Finish
Welcome to the Pimp-My-Profile.com myspace profile layout editor
This editor requires Internet Explorer 6 or higher, Firefox or Opera.
Use the tabs above to edit different parts of your profile.
You can preview your work by going to the 'Finish' tab and clicking on the 'Preview' button. If a preview window does not show up, try pressing the ctrl key while you click the button.
When you are satisfied go to the 'Finish' tab and click on 'Generate'
If you make a mistake and want to start from the beginning, use the refresh button in your browser to reload the

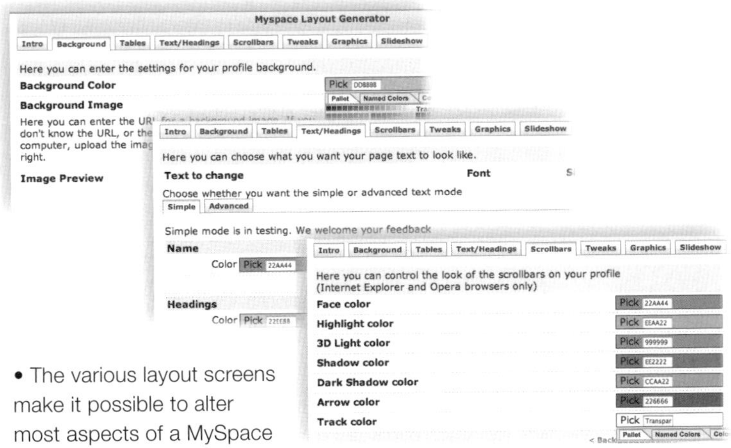

• The various layout screens make it possible to alter most aspects of a MySpace page in some way. Work through the options making any changes that you require. If at any time you want to see what your design looks like, click on the **Preview My Layout** button. A dummy MySpace page will now appear in a pop-up window showing all of your design changes. If you are happy with what you see, click on the button marked **Generate My Code**.

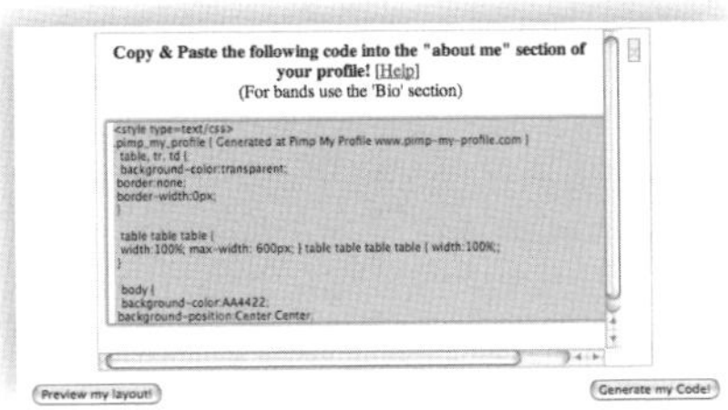

• A new scrolling window opens, showing the HTML code that contains your layout. Highlight and copy the code. (**Ctrl + C** for PCs; **Command + C** for Macs.)

• Now go to your MySpace home page. Enter the URL: **http://www.myspace.com**. Once you've logged in, click on the **Edit Profile** button. At the very top of the **About Me** section of your profile, paste the HTML. (**Ctrl + V** for PCs; **Command + V** for Macs.) Your MySpace page has now been updated. If you have a music page, then the HTML code should be pasted in to the **Bio** section of your profile.

Other Networks

MySpace may be the most popular social networking website around—indeed, if you take a look at the Alexa web rankings (**http://www.alexa.com**), you will find it regularly among the top five websites worldwide in terms of traffic. This is not to say that MySpace is necessarily the "best" such website. Indeed, many would argue that MySpace is a little old-fashioned, clunky in design, and not as user-friendly as it might be—for example, a basic knowledge of HTML, at the very least, is needed to make the simplest of design changes to a page. And even then, the scope of possibility is still limited. When you take into account all the advertising and banners most would have to conceded that it's pretty difficult to make an attractive looking MySpace page.

However, there are a great number of other social networks from which you can choose. Some, such as Bebo, work in much the same way as MySpace; others are more specialized—ChainReading, for example, enables users to compare and recommend reading lists.

43 Things

http://www.43things.com

43 Things is a social networking site that uses "tagging" principles to link people together. Users create accounts and then make a list of their hopes, goals, or dreams. These are then connected with users who have created lists with similarly worded ideas. 43 Things was created using the Ruby On Rails programming language, and officially launched on January 1, 2005. At the end of April 27, 2007, it reached the landmark of having over one million registered users.

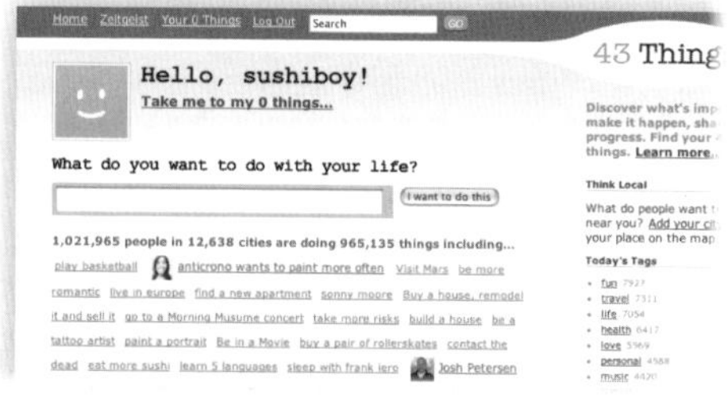

• Enter the URL: **http://www.43things.com**. Go through the registration process and sign in.

• The main 43 Things page contains a "cloud" of tags based on information entered by other users. Like most clouds, tags that have a greater number of entries attached to them are shown more prominently. You can browse the cloud and click on any individual entry, or you can make your own entry. Let's do the latter, and create a goal to swim the English Channel.

• Look for the box beneath the question: "What do you want to do with your life?" Enter **Swim the English Channel**. Click on the button marked **I Want to Do This**.

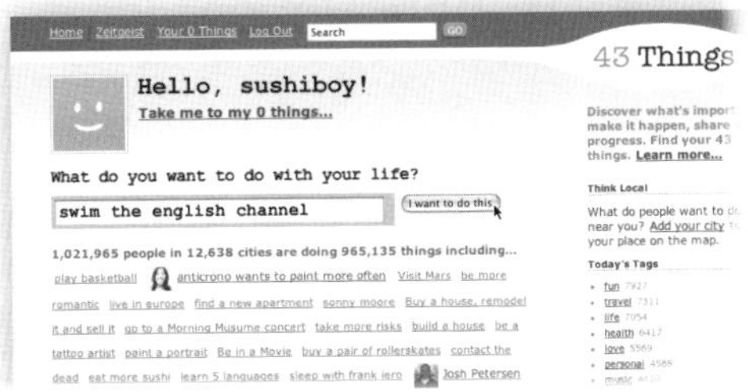

• The results screen will appear. As you can see, in this example there are 58 users who have swimming the Channel as one of their goals. The top half of the screen lists the 10 most recent people to list the same goal. If you scroll to the bottom of the list you can see if any of the users sharing this goal have posted comments.

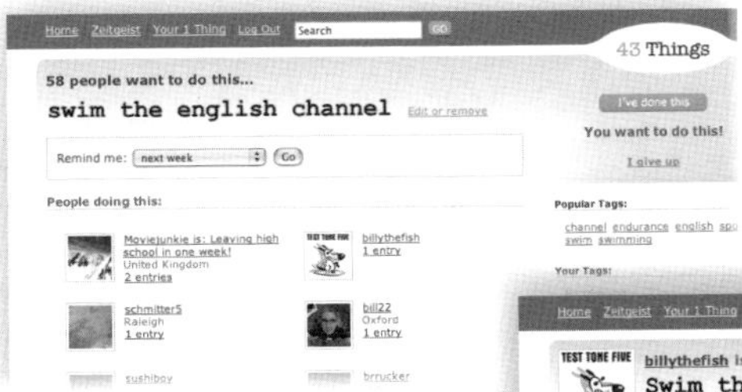

• The user profiles also indicate if any individual has made a comment relating to this goal. If we look at the user **billythefish** we can see that he has made one comment. To see it, click on the text that reads **1 entry**.

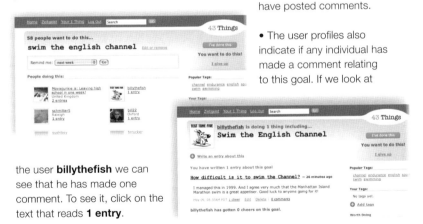

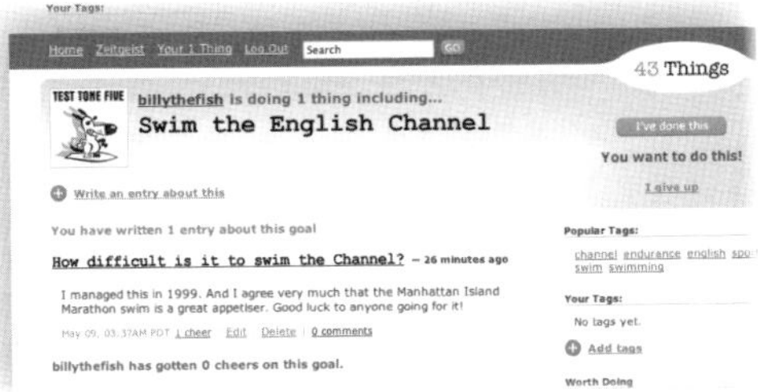

• We can see that this user claims to have already swum the English Channel. What's more, he also offers advice on how to do it. And this is the essence of 43 Things—if you have a goal in mind, getting help from someone who already been there can only be a good thing.

Bebo

http://www.bebo.com

Launched in 2005, Bebo is almost as widely used in some parts of Europe as MySpace and Facebook (the other major social networking site). Functionally, Bebo covers most of the same ground as MySpace. However, it does so with a little more elegance.

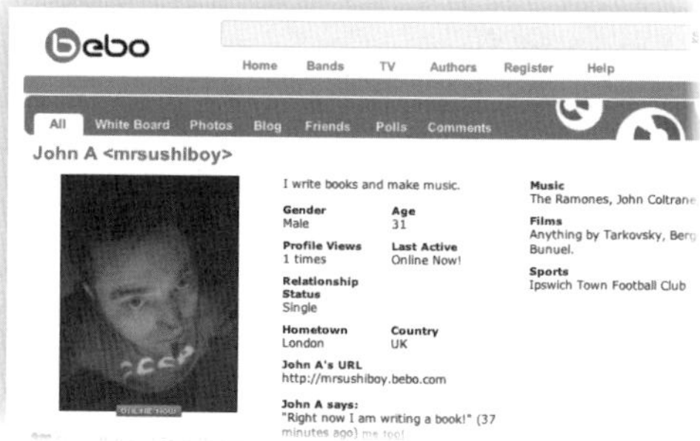

The user creates an account in much the same way as with MySpace. However, profile pages are presented in a much neater way. The front page contains a summary of the user's personal information. Further specific details can be accessed by clicking on the tab buttons near the top of the page. The **All** tab contains summary data; the other tabs are **White Board**, **Photos**, **Blog**, **Friends**, **Polls**, and **Comments**. The white board is an interesting feature in that it allows the user to create computer artworks using a system called **ffART**, which produces shapes using the mouse. Artworks can be saved in a portfolio.

The social networking aspect is little different than most of the other systems in that you make "friends" and use a variety of different means to send them messages.

Bolt

http://www.bolt.com

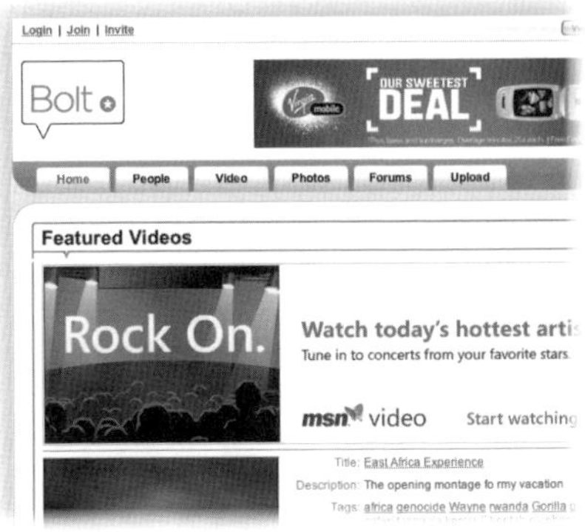

Bolt is another tab-driven social networking site. Unlike the other major sites, Bolt also integrates user videos, much in the same manner as YouTube. Bolt dates back to mid-1990s and was originally a teenage network. However, as its users became older it gradually evolved and has since been through numerous changes. It has a user base of around four million, the vast majority of which reside in the U.S. Bolt originally had a user-uploadable music feature that was dropped as a consequence of a media industry lawsuit.

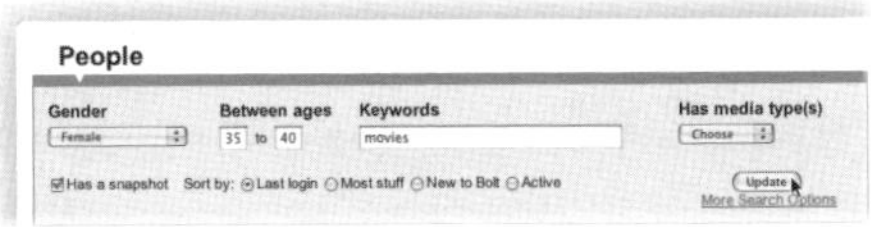

Bolt offers of simple tag-based search facilty to find people within specific age ranges or interests. If you click on the **People** tab you will see the search box. Select a gender, an age range, and enter keywords to hook you up with like-minded folks. In this example we've selected **females** within the ages of **35 to 40** who have declared and interest in **Movies**. You could also select from different media types, such as video, photo, or blog. Finally, to kick off the search, click on the **Update** button. The next screen you see will contain profiles that fit your search criteria.

Chain Reading

http://www.chainreading.com

There's a growing trend for the development of social networking sites that focus on specific interests, such as jobs, music, and travel. Chain Reading is website for book lovers. It can be used actively or passively: you can create a personal profile, make recommendations on the books you've read, tag them under multiple categories, and write your own reviews; or you can simply follow anonymously what others have been doing. The quality of the writing within is extremely variable—some reviews look to have been written by academics, others by barely literate school children. Indeed, the user reviews in shop sites such as Amazon are arguably as useful.

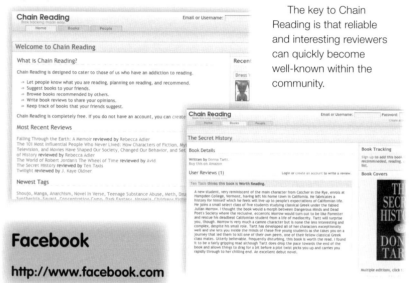

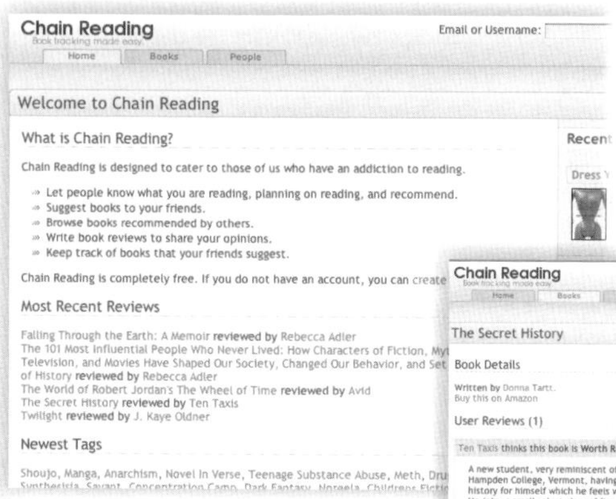

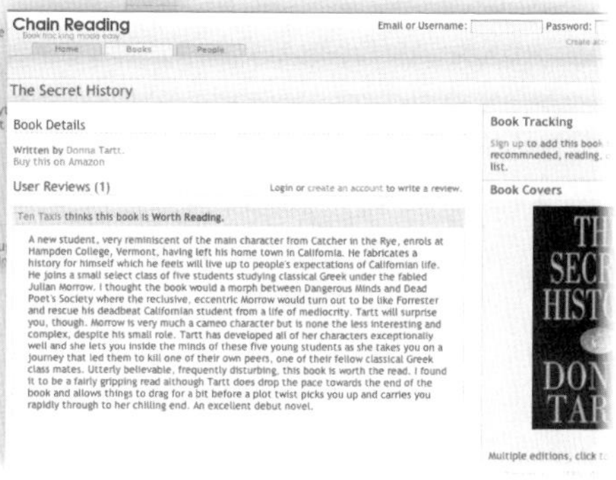

The key to Chain Reading is that reliable and interesting reviewers can quickly become well-known within the community.

Facebook

http://www.facebook.com

As modern-day Internet success stories go, Facebook represents one of the most remarkable examples. Launched in 2004, it was created by Harvard University student Mark Zuckerberg and two of his roommates. The project started as a computer game, but gradually evolved into an online social networking utility for the use of other Harvard students. Such was its success that within a few weeks over half of the undergraduates on campus are said to have registered. Facebook quickly expanded further, first inviting students from other Ivy League colleges, and then opening it up to all students. Facebook is now open to all users.

Following this immediate success, advertising revenue rose at such a dramatic rate that Zuckerberg left Harvard to run Facebook full time. He has since turned down a number of multi-million dollar takeover deals. Facebook is now a permanent fixture among the world's top 20 heavily traffic sites, and is second only to MySpace as the world's most popular social networking site.

In practice, Facebook works in much the same as MySpace or Bebo. You set up a personal profile and search for friends. However, there is a strong emphasis on creating specific social networks within schools, universities, and workplaces.

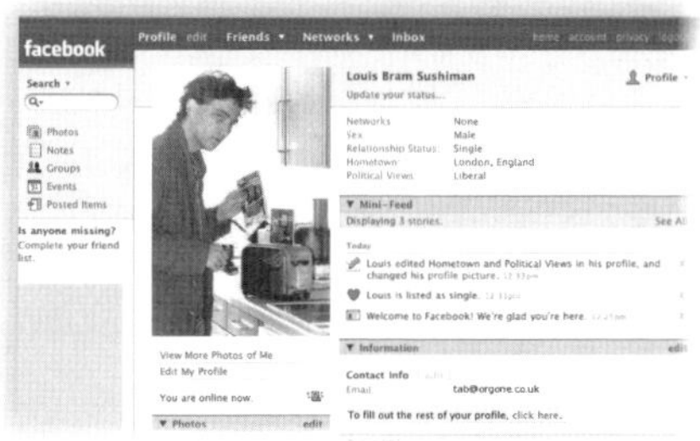

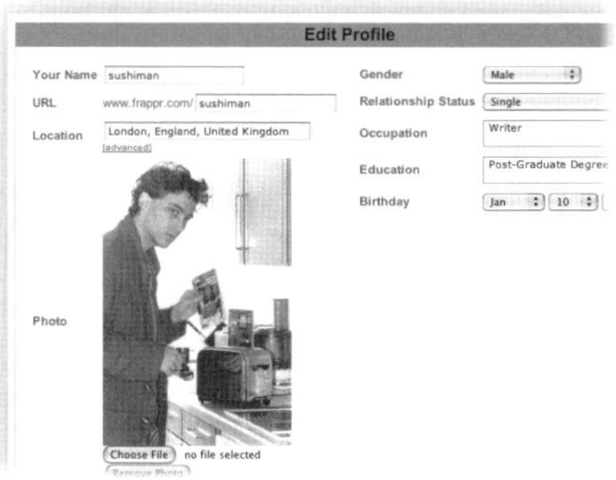

Frappr!

http://www.frappr.com

Launched in 2005, Frappr! is an online community mapper. Members position themselves on a map and create personal profile pages. They can then interact with friends via online chat and blogs. The Frappr! Map can be exported and embedded into other personal or social networking websites.

Creating A frappr! Map

Let's now produce a map using Frappr!

- Start by entering the URL:**http://www.frappr.com**.

- Click on the button marked **Get Your Own Map**.

- A new **Frappr! Map** opens up with a suggested location based on settings on your computer.

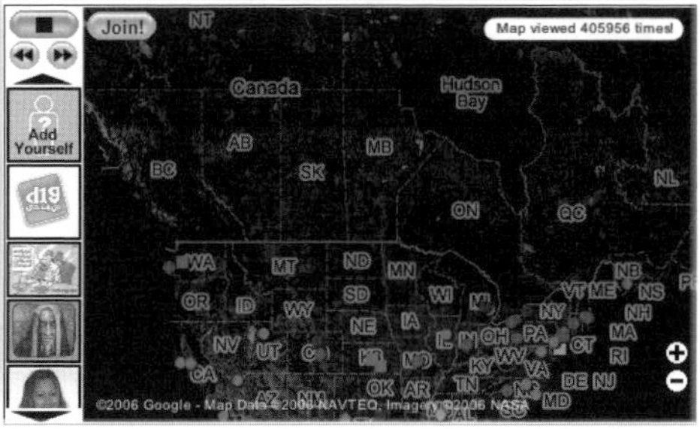

• If the settings are not correct, click on **Move This Pin** and enter new location information in the window. To continue, click on the text labeled **Hi! Please Add Yourself!**

• In the pop-up window enter your chosen name and e-mail address, upload a photograph, and, finally, enter a "shoutout"—this is the phrase that will greet anyone who finds you on the map. Click on the **Add Me!** button. Click on the **Continue** button to see your finished map.

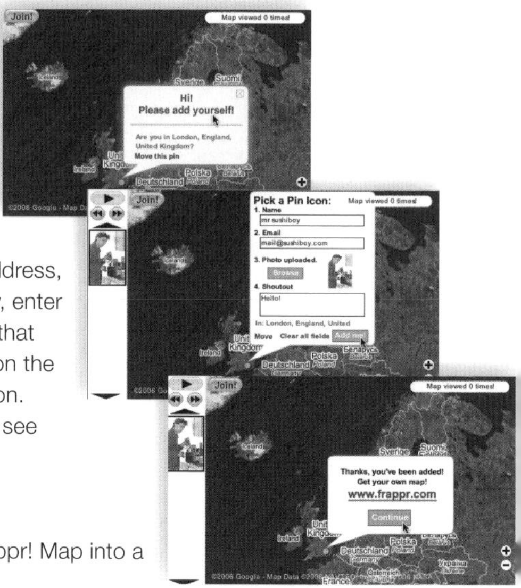

Exporting Your Frappr! Map

Now let's see how to copy a Frappr! Map into a MySpace page.

• To the right of your map, you should see a green button labeled **Put This Map on MySpace or Any Website**. In the pop-up window that follows, select the size of your map and then click on the **Save** button.

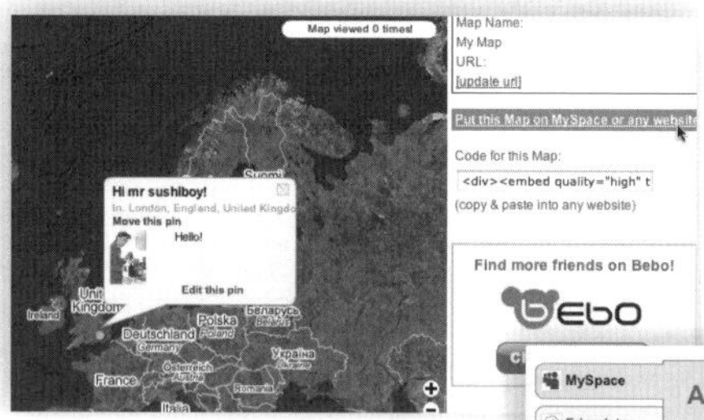

• The "export" window has default settings for MySpace. Enter your MySpace e-mail address and password and click on the **Add** button. There are also tab options for Xanga, Blogger, Friendster and Hi5. Alternatively, if you are HTML-savvy, then you can copy and paste the code directly.

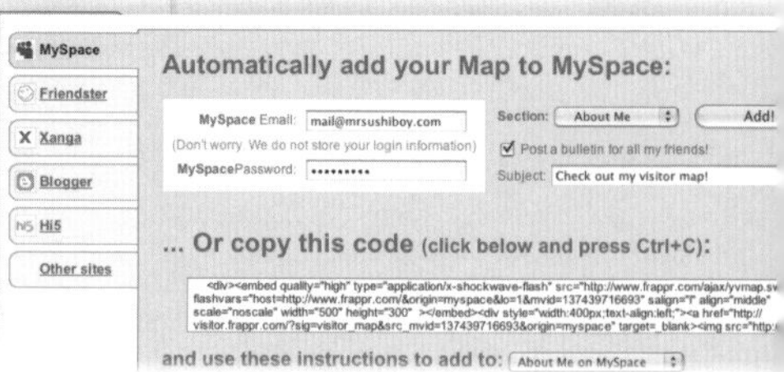

Social Networking Websites

43people	http://www.43people.com
43places	http://www.43places.com
Blogtronix	http://www.blogtronix.com
Communitywalk	http://www.communitywalk.com
Consumating	http://www.consumating.com
Dodgeball	http://www.dodgeball.com
Doostang	http://www.doostang.com
Friendster	http://www.friendster.com
Giftbox	http://www.giftboxhome.com
Greedyme	http://www.greedyme.com
Groups	http://grou.ps
Ikarma	http://ikarma.com
Linkedin	Http://www.linkedin.com
LiveJournal	http://www.livejournal.com
Lovento	http://www.lovento.com
Mapmix	http://www.mapmix.com
Meetro	http://www.meetro.com
Meetup	http://www.meetup.com
Metawishlist	http://www.metawishlist.com
Mologogo	http://www.mologogo.com
Mozes	http://mozes.com
Myprogs	http://myprogs.net
OpenBC	http://www.openbc.com
Opinity	http://www.opinity.com
Orkut	https://www.orkut.com
Partysync	http://group.partysync.com
Peerprofile	http://www.peerprofile.com
Peertrainer	http://www.peertrainer.com
Phusebox	http://phusebox.net
Piczo	http://piczo.com
Placesite	http://www.placesite.com
Plum	http://www.plum.com
Poddater	http://www.poddater.com
Pooln	http://www.pooln.com
Rabble	http://www.rabble.com
Tagalag	http://www.tagalag.com
Tinfinger	http://www.tinfinger.com
TheBlackStripe	http://www.theblackstripe.com
Towncrossing	http://towncrossing.com
Twocrowds	http://www.twocrowds.com
Vcarious	http://www.vcarious.com
Wallop	http://mywallop.com
Xanga	http://www.xanga.com
Zaadz	http://www.zaadz.com
Ziggs	http://www.ziggs.com

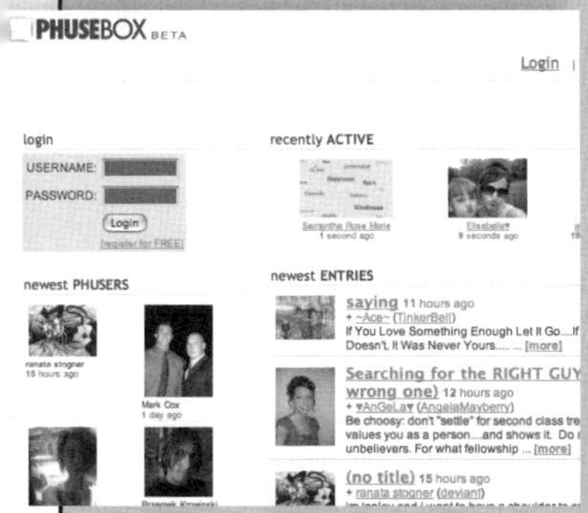

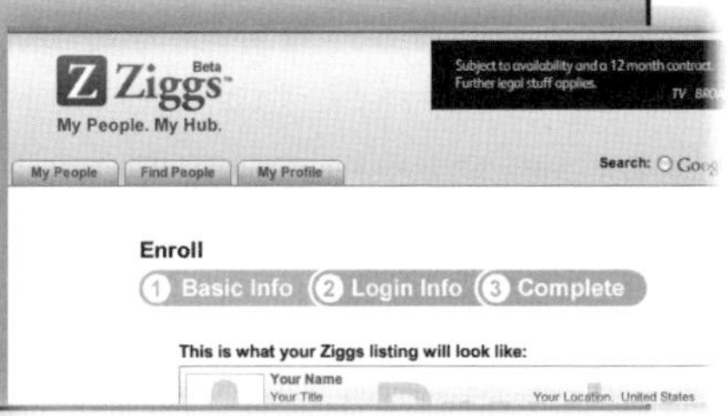

Web-Based Office Software

The world of technology frequently throws up unexpected quirks on an unsuspecting world. Who, for example, would have imagined that SMS messaging—developed primarily for business users—would have been seized by teenagers and used to create a new type of language? However, one future development that now seems highly predictable is the gradual and continued migration of software from the desktop to the Web. This transformation is very much in its early days, but products such as ThinkFree and Zoho give a clear indication of how things are likely to develop in the near future.

ThinkFree

http://www.thinkfree.com

Microsoft Office is the world's most popular so-called "productivity suite." It comprises a set of industry-standard programs, among them the word processor Word, the spreadsheet Excel, and the presentation software PowerPoint. Although rumors have circulated on Internet news sites for several years, Microsoft has yet to make a firm commitment to creating a web-based version of Office. In the meantime, there has been no shortage of new start-ups prepared to fill this hole in the marketplace. Let's look at one of the most prominent of them, ThinkFree.

Webtop Word Processing

ThinkFree is a suite of "webtop" office applications—word processor, spreadsheet, and presentation—each of which bears more than a passing resemblance to its Microsoft counterpart: each of these applications, in fact, is capable of reading and writing the relevant Microsoft file formats, so the clear aim here is universal compatibility. Let's now take a look at ThinkFree's word processing capabilities.

• Begin by enter the URL: **http://www.thinkfree.com**. Before you can use ThinkFree you must first go through the registration process. Click on the button labeled **Sign On** in the top right-hand corner and follow the instructions. When you have finished, use your ID and password to log in.

• Click on the button marked **ThinkFree Online** in the menu bar at the top of the screen (*see above*).

• Your **MyOffice** page will now open. To begin word processing, click on the blue **New Document** button. (You'll notice that ThinkFree has even helpfully used the same colors as its Microsoft counterpart!)

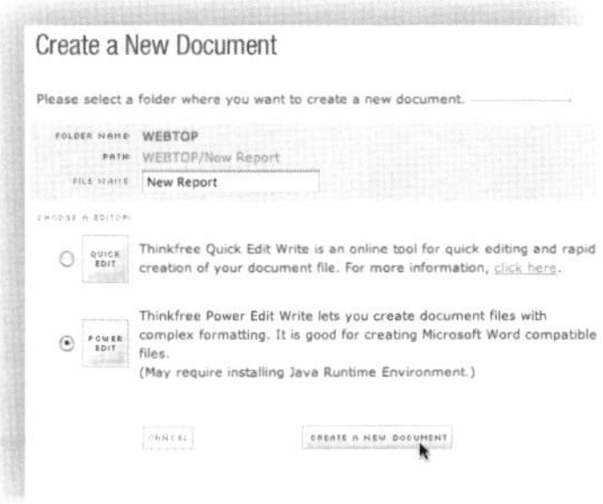

• The **Create a New Document** window opens up. In the **File Name** box you can give your document a title. You can now choose between **Quick Edit** or **Power Edit**: the former produces a simple text file; the latter is used for Microsoft Word format. Click on the **Power Edit** button, and then on **Create a New Document**.

• An empty word processing document will appear in the screen that follows. You will notice that it contains the same principal features as most other word processors.

• Type in your text and when you've finished choose **Save** from the **File** menu. You will be returned to your own **MyOffice** page where you'll see your document in place.

Lazybase

http://www.lazybase.com

Lazybase is an extremely neat online database system, created by California-based New Zealander Toby Segaran. Databases can be designed and built from scratch or using existing templates. They can also be given a unique URL and shared. There is no registration process as such; the user enters a database name and e-mail address, and as long as that combination is unique it can be saved.

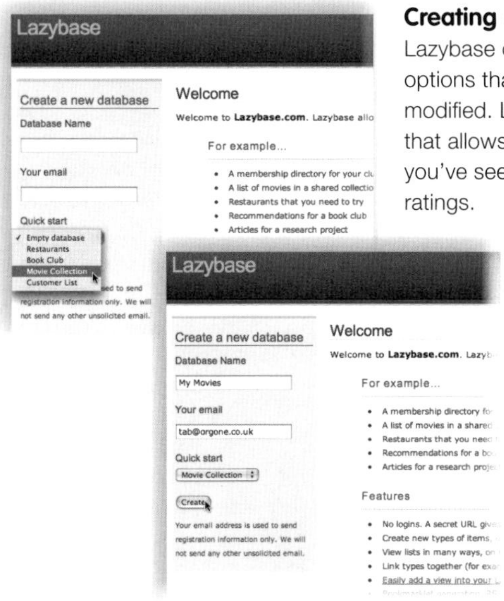

Creating a Quickstart Database

Lazybase offers a number of "quick start" options that can be used off the shelf or modified. Let's set up a simple database that allows you to keep a list of movies you've seen, along with some category ratings.

- Enter the URL **http://www.lazybase.com**. From the **Quick Start** drop-down menu, select **Movie Collection**.

- Enter a name for your database, your e-mail address, and then click on the **Create** button. A confirmation window will open with two web links: one is the URL that enables you to access and edit your database; the other gives read-only access to others you may want to inform. Click on the uppermost link.

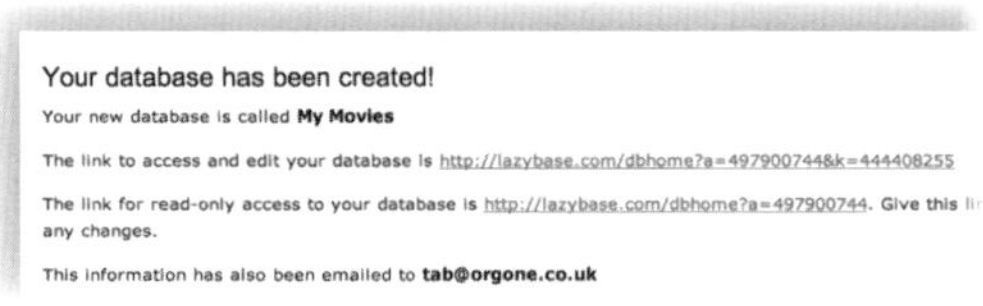

Welcome

Welcome to the **My Movies** shared database.

Movie

Recently changed: Office Space, view all »

Add a Movie | Search Movie List

Genre

Recently changed: Documentary, Thriller, Drama, Action, Comedy, v

Add a Genre | Search Genre List

Create a new type of item

My Movies

Item Types	New Movie
Movie (1 Items)	Enter the details for this Movie (or create a bookm
View all, Search, Add new	
Genre (5 Items)	Name Raging Bull
View all, Search, Add new	Keywords DiNiro Boxing
	Genre Drama
Quick Search	Comedy ★☆☆☆☆
	Drama ★★★★★
	SFX ★☆☆☆☆
Go	(Save this Movie) (Save and add more)

My Movies

Item Types

Movie (4 Items)
View all, Search, Add new

Genre (5 Items)
View all, Search, Add new

Quick Search

Go

Options

My Movies

Item Types	Movie
Movie (4 Items)	Here are the results of your search. Click on a column heading
View all, Search, Add new	
Genre (5 Items)	
View all, Search, Add new	

Name	Genre	Comedy	Drama	SFX
Office Space	Comedy	★★★★★	★★☆☆☆	★☆☆
Raging Bull	Drama	★☆☆☆☆	★★★★★	★☆☆
King Of Comedy	Drama	★☆☆☆☆	★★★★★	★☆☆
Young Frankenstein	Comedy	★★★★★	★★☆☆☆	★☆☆

Quick Search

Go

You can also view this list:

- As of chart of Comedy vs Drama , Comedy vs SFX , Dram
- As a CSV File, RSS feed or on your own page

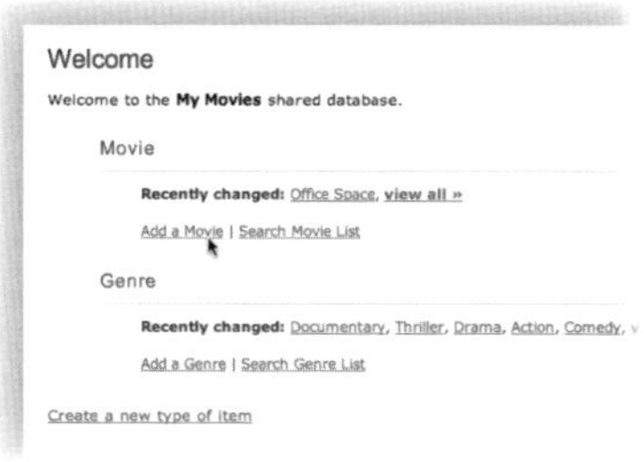

• You can now begin entering information into your database. You have the option of adding a new movie or adding a movie genre. For now, click on button marked **Add a Movie**.

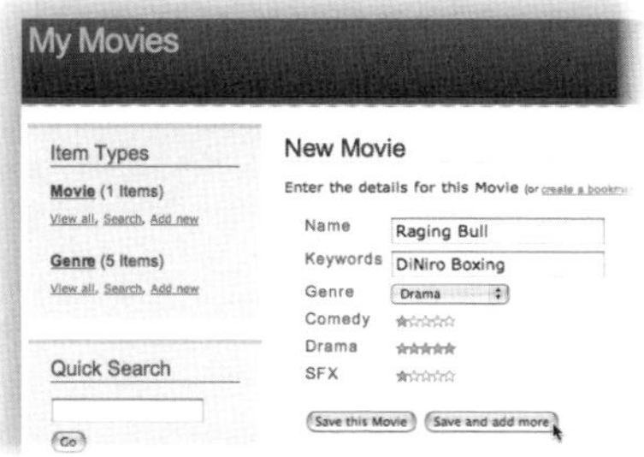

• The screen that appears can be thought of as an entry screen for a single record in your database. Enter the name of the film—in this case, **Raging Bull**. You can now add any suitable tags that you think will assist with searches: here we've added **Di Niro** and **Boxing**. From the drop-down menu choose a genre—**Drama**. You can now give the film a star rating in various categories. When you've finished, if you want to add another record, click on the button marked **Save and Add More**.

Viewing Your Database

Once you have more records in your database you can view your information in a number of different ways.

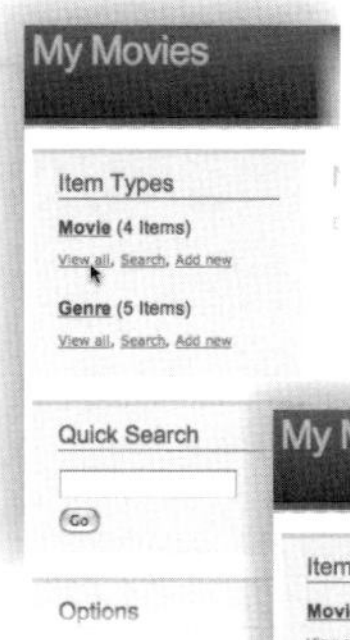

• Under **Item Types** on the left-hand side of the screen, click on **View All**. The page that follows shows all the records on your database. You can sort them in any order you choose by clicking on any of the headings. It's also possible to perform a variety of keyword searches on your data.

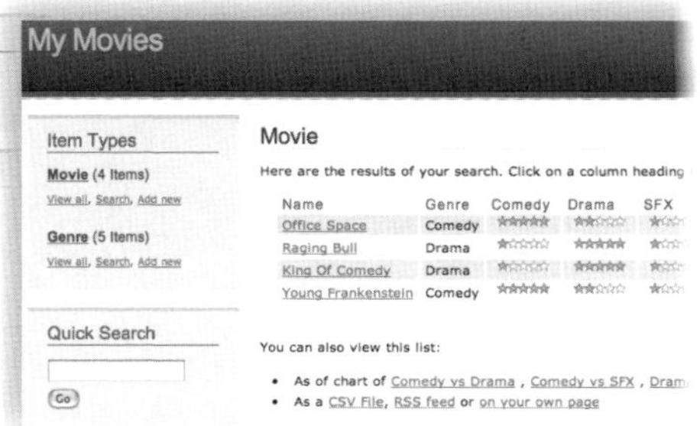

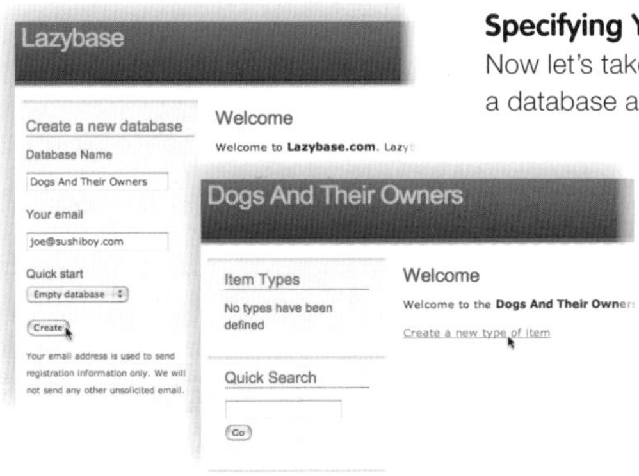

Specifying Your Database

Now let's take a brief look at how to set up a database and specify your own fields.

- Enter the URL: **http://www.lazybase.com**. Enter a name for your database, an e-mail address, and click on the **Create** button. (The **Quick Start** menu should be left on its default setting—**Empty Database**.)

- You're now ready to specify the fields you want for each of your records. In the **Welcome** screen, click on the text labeled **Create a New Type of Item**. In this example, we'll create a dog owners' database: the "key" will be the owner's name, the fields will be made up from information about their pets.

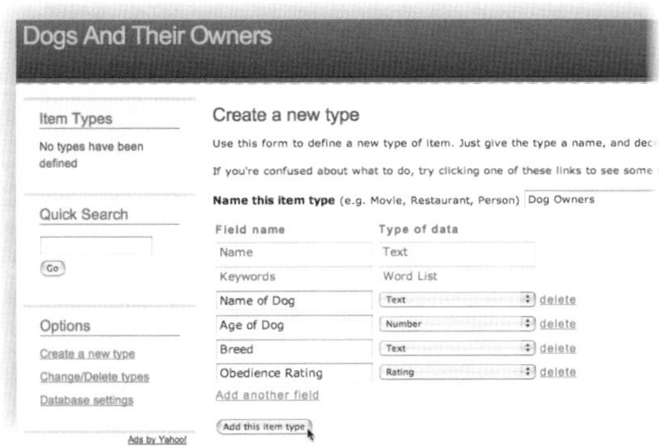

- Begin by naming the item type—the dog owner's name. Now add the individual fields—name and age of dog, breed, and an obedience rating. Alongside each field, choose a data type from the drop-down menu (for example, text or numeric). Fields are added one at a time—after each one, click on the text labeled **Add Another Field**. When you've specified your last field, click on the button marked **Add This Item Type**. The database is now complete.

Zoho

http://www.zoho.com

Zoho claims to be the world's first AJAX-based suite of web-based office programs. It's certainly wide-ranging in its scope, including takes on the most popular types of office software. For example: Zoho Writer is a word processor; Zoho Sheet is a spreadsheet system; Zoho Show is a presentation program; Zoho Projects and Zoho Planner are project management tools; and Zoho Chat is an instant messenger. Most of these tools are capable of importing and exporting the most widely used file formats.

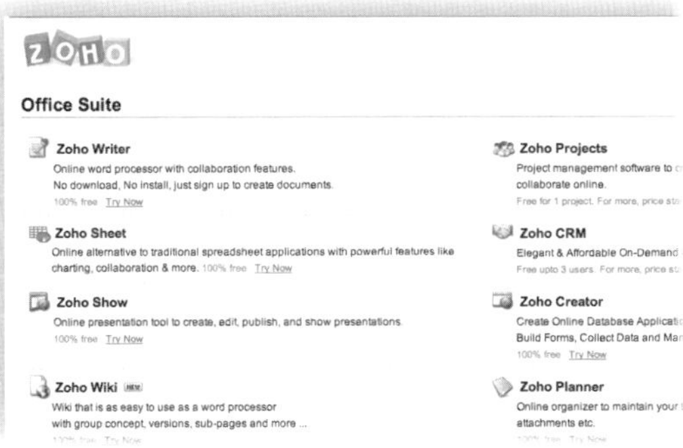
ZOHO
Office Suite
Zoho Writer
Online word processor with collaboration features.
No download, No install, just sign up to create documents.
Zoho Sheet
Online alternative to traditional spreadsheet applications with powerful features like charting, collaboration & more.
Zoho Show
Online presentation tool to create, edit, publish, and show presentations.
Zoho Wiki
Wiki that is as easy to use as a word processor
with group concept, versions, sub-pages and more ...
Zoho Projects
Zoho CRM
Zoho Creator
Zoho Planner

Let's begin with a look at Zoho's spreadsheet program, and how it reads a standard Microsoft Excel file.

Zoho Sheet

Enter the URL: **http://www.zoho.com**. To use any of the Zoho applications you must first register.

• As we want to use the spreadsheet software, begin by clicking on the button marked **Zoho Sheet**. Sign in and click on the **Submit** button.

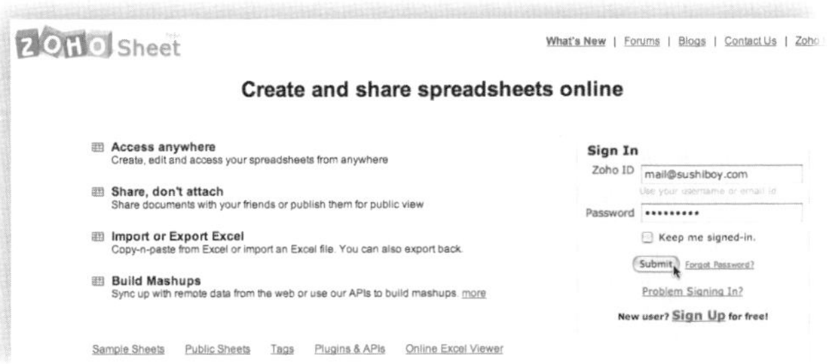
ZOHO Sheet
What's New | Forums | Blogs | Contact Us
Create and share spreadsheets online
Access anywhere
Create, edit and access your spreadsheets from anywhere
Share, don't attach
Share documents with your friends or publish them for public view
Import or Export Excel
Copy-n-paste from Excel or import an Excel file. You can also export back.
Build Mashups
Sync up with remote data from the web or use our APIs to build mashups. more
Sign In
Zoho ID
mail@sushiboy.com
Password
Keep me signed-in.
Submit
Problem Signing In?
New user? Sign Up for free!
Sample Sheets
Public Sheets
Tags
Plugins & APIs
Online Excel Viewer

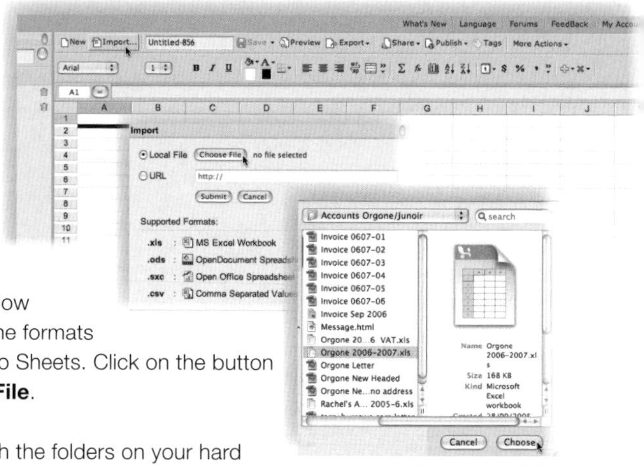

- An empty spreadsheet will open. To begin importing an existing document, click on the **Import** button.

- The import window opens. This lists the formats supported by Zoho Sheets. Click on the button marked **Choose File**.

- Navigate through the folders on your hard drive until you find the require Excel-format file. Click on the **Choose** button.

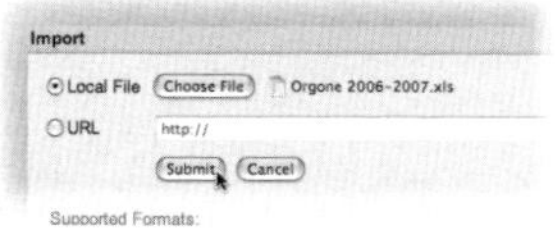

- When the import window opens you should see the name of the file you have selected. Click on the **Submit** button. The Excel document will open (*see below*).

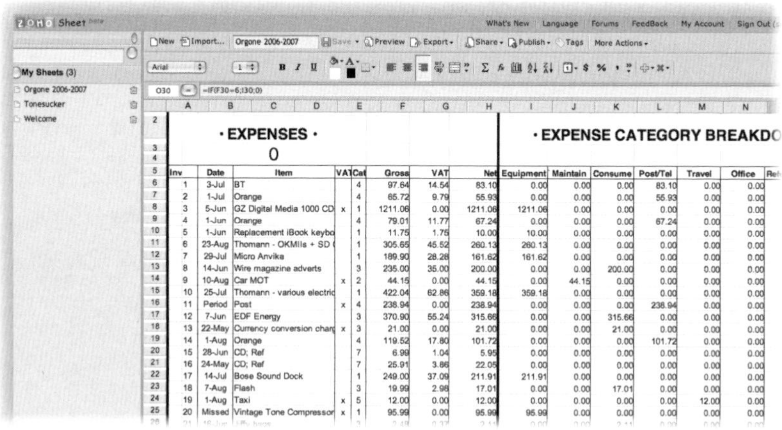

Zoho Show

Using the presentation application Zoho Show, you can create slide shows or import Microsoft PowerPoint documents (*see right*).

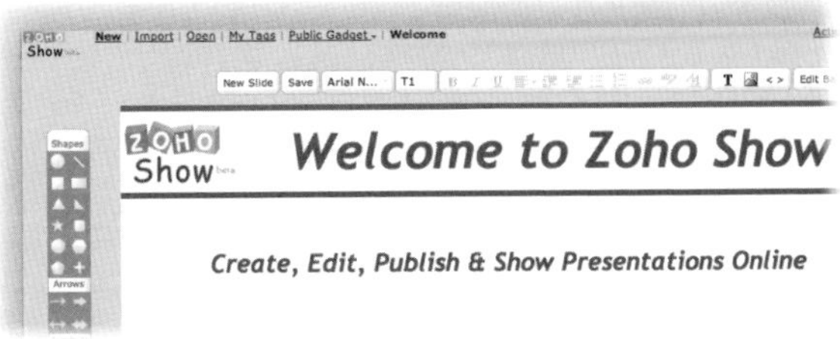

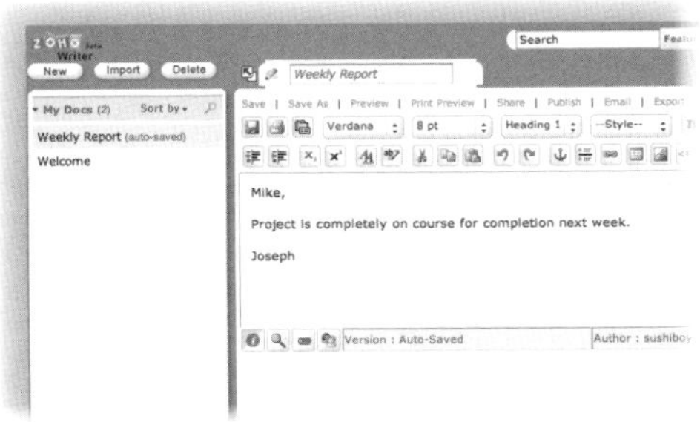

Zoho Writer

The Zoho suite also incorporates a well-specified word processing application called Writer. This operates in a very similar fashion to Microsoft Word, and can import and export files in that format.

More Data Hosting Sites

Ajax13	http://us.ajax13.com/en	Office suite
Ajax Office	http://ajaxoffice.sourceforge.net	Office suite
Edit Grid	http://www.editgrid.com	Spreadsheet
FCK Editor	http://www.fckeditor.com	Word processing
Glide	http://www.glidenext.com	Word processing
Gliffy	http://www.gliffy.com	Diagram
GOffice	http://www.goffice.com	Office suite
Google Docs	http://docs.google.com	Word processing
iRows	http://www.irows.com	Spreadsheet
Numbler	http://numbler.com	Spreadsheet
NumSum	http://numsum.com	Spreadsheet
Peepel	http://www.peepel.com	Office suite
S5	http://meyerweb.com/eric/tools/s5	Presentation
WebNote	http://www.aypwip.org/webnote	Notebook
Zimbra	http://www.zimbra.com	Office suite

Wikis and Collaboration

The notion of an application having its "worth" enhanced by the more people that use it is completely central to the Web 2.0 debate. We've already seen a few collaborative applications at work—for example, online project diaries or calendars that can be updated by different members of a group. A "wiki" works in a similar way. It is a website that allows its users to add, change, or delete content within its pages. The term is used to describe collaborative authoring applications, of which the most famous (or infamous, perhaps) is Wikipedia. The word wiki comes from the Hawaiian language, where it means "quick," so any such application will enable its content to be accessed swiftly and simply.

The Wiki Debate

The idea of collaborative writing is an interesting one. A person can place an article on a wiki website; another can edit or rewrite it; and a third person can, if they choose, delete it altogether. So what are wikis good for? Certainly it's possible to set up a wiki web page far more quickly than by using a dedicated web design program. And, once set up, wikis are very easy to maintain. Their collaborative potential is extremely good for brainstorming, compiling notes from a conference, meeting, or event, or preparing a document with others who are in different locations. However, there are potential pitfalls: if a wiki's content is open to all, then we can (and arguably should) have little or no control over those who may later edit the work. It is this very fact that has made Wikipedia—the world's largest online encyclopedia—such a controversial subject. Whereas most of us would expect contributors to anything claiming to be an encyclopedia to have some kind of expert credentials, absolutely *anyone* can write or edit a Wikipedia article. Thus, a fundamental criticism of Wikipedia is that its accuracy must *always* be in question, and it would certainly not be suitable as a primary source of reference. Other concerns include a lack neutrality normally expected from an encyclopedia, and that some contributors may be working with a background agenda.

In spite of such criticisms, in 2006 *Nature* magazine did a comparative study of science articles found on Wikipedia and their equivalents within *Encyclopaedia Britannica*. It found both to be similarly accurate. Some who have argued in favor of the wiki approach claim that any errors made on Wikipedia tend to be corrected quite quickly, and so articles gradually become refined over time.

Wikipedia

http://www.wikipedia.org

The most important collaborative text application on the Internet, Wikipedia was first launched in 2001, and is run by the Wikipedia Foundation—a nonprofit organization set up by cofounder Jimmy Wales. The encyclopedia holds well over seven million articles written in 252 languages. Massively popular, it has long enjoyed a permanent place in the top 10 trafficked websites across the globe.

Searching for an Article

Wikipedia is extremely straightforward to use, and usually provides very swift results.

- Enter the URL: **http://www .wikipedia.org**. Enter a keyword for your search in the box on the main page. Wikipedia is available in many different local language versions, so select English from the drop-down list. Click on the arrow button (**>**).

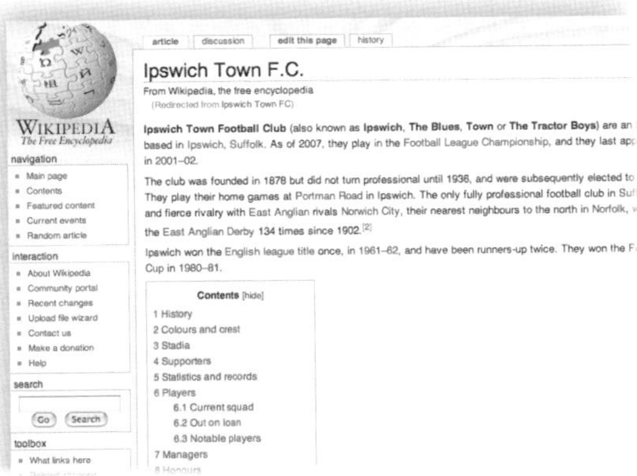

- You will either see the article you have requested or, if there is more than one that matches your search text, what Wikipedia refers to as a "disambiguation list." This is a list containing a number of possible results. Click on any item in the list to open the article.

Editing an Article

Now let's look at how to make changes to an article on Wikipedia. Before going any further, decide whether or not you wish to register. It *is* possible to edit anonymously, but you should be aware that your IP address (the unique address of your computer connection to the Internet) will be logged, so your identity could, if necessary, be established without too much difficulty.

Let's make a change to the page we already have open.

article
discussion
edit this page
history
Ipswich Town F.C.
From Wikipedia, the free encyclopedia
(Redirected from Ipswich Town FC)
WIKIPEDIA
The Free Encyclopedia
navigation
Main page
Contents
Ipswich Town Football Club (also known as Ipswich, The Blues, Town or The Tractor Boys)
based in Ipswich, Suffolk. As of 2007, they play in the Football League Championship, and they
in 2001–02.
The club was founded in 1878 but did not turn professional until 1936, and were subsequently ele

- At the top of the window, click on the tab marked **Edit This Page**.

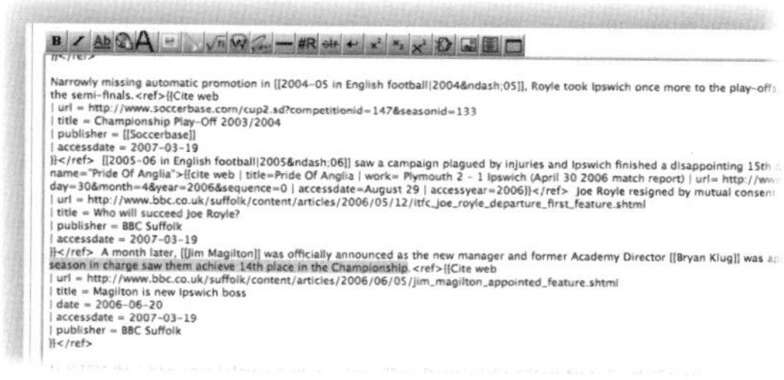
Narrowly missing automatic promotion in [[2004–05 in English football|2004–05]], Royle took Ipswich once more to the play-offs
the semi-finals.<ref>{{Cite web
| url = http://www.soccerbase.com/cup2.sd?competitionid=147&seasonid=133
| title = Championship Play-Off 2003/2004
| publisher = [[Soccerbase]]
| accessdate = 2007-03-19
}}</ref>
| url = http://www.bbc.co.uk/suffolk/content/articles/2006/05/12/itfc_joe_royle_departure_first_feature.shtml
| title = Who will succeed Joe Royle?
| publisher = BBC Suffolk
| accessdate = 2007-03-19
}}</ref> A month later, [[Jim Magilton]] was officially announced as the new manager and former Academy Director [[Bryan Klug]] was
season in charge saw them achieve 14th place in the Championship.<ref>{{Cite web
| url = http://www.bbc.co.uk/suffolk/content/articles/2006/06/05/jim_magilton_appointed_feature.shtml
| title = Magilton is new Ipswich boss
| date = 2006-06-20
| accessdate = 2007-03-19
| publisher = BBC Suffolk
}}</ref>

- The HTML code behind the article appears in the edit window. (Knowledge of HTML is by no means a necessity to edit a Wikipedia article. If you are unsure, to be on the safe side, avoid interfering with any of the "tags"—the commands found within the arrowed brackets.) Edit your text.

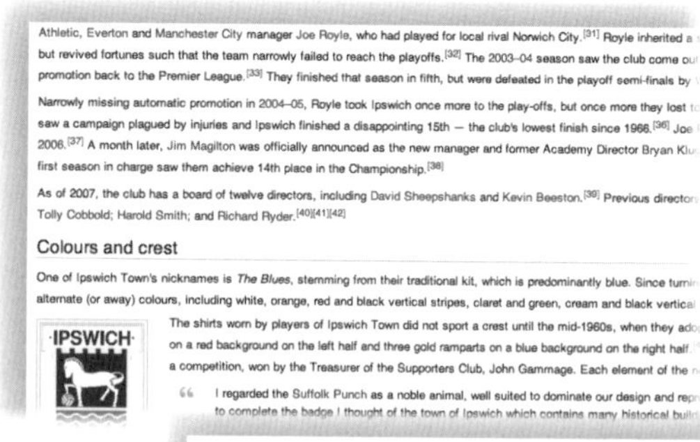
Narrowly missing automatic promotion in 2004–05, Royle took Ipswich once more to the play-offs, but once more they lost
2006. A month later, Jim Magilton was officially announced as the new manager and former Academy Director Bryan Klu
first season in charge saw them achieve 14th place in the Championship.
As of 2007, the club has a board of twelve directors, including David Sheepshanks and Kevin Beeston. Previous director
Tolly Cobbold; Harold Smith; and Richard Ryder.
Colours and crest
One of Ipswich Town's nicknames is The Blues, stemming from their traditional kit, which is predominantly blue.
IPSWICH
The shirts worn by players of Ipswich Town did not sport a crest until the mid-1960s, when they ad
a competition, won by the Treasurer of the Supporters Club, John Gammage. Each element of the
I regarded the Suffolk Punch as a noble animal, well suited to dominate our design and rep

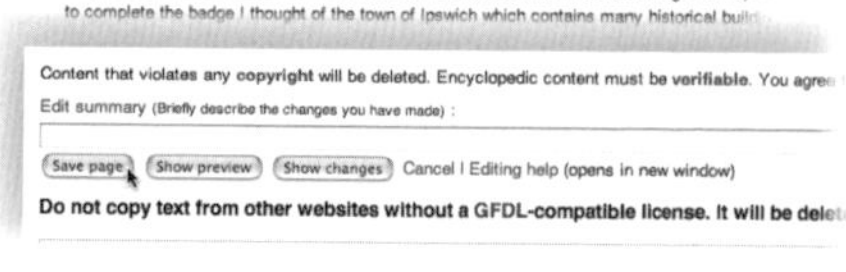
Content that violates any copyright will be deleted. Encyclopedic content must be verifiable.
Edit summary (Briefly describe the changes you have made) :
Save page
Show preview
Show changes
Cancel | Editing help (opens in new window)
Do not copy text from other websites without a GFDL-compatible license.

- To see what your edit will look like, click on the button marked **Show Preview**.

- If you wish to put your changes "live," click on the button marked **Save Page**.

Article History

There is a facility that enables us to view the changes that have taken place during the lifespan of an article, and compare past versions with the one currently on view.

- At the top of the screen, click on the tab marked **History**.

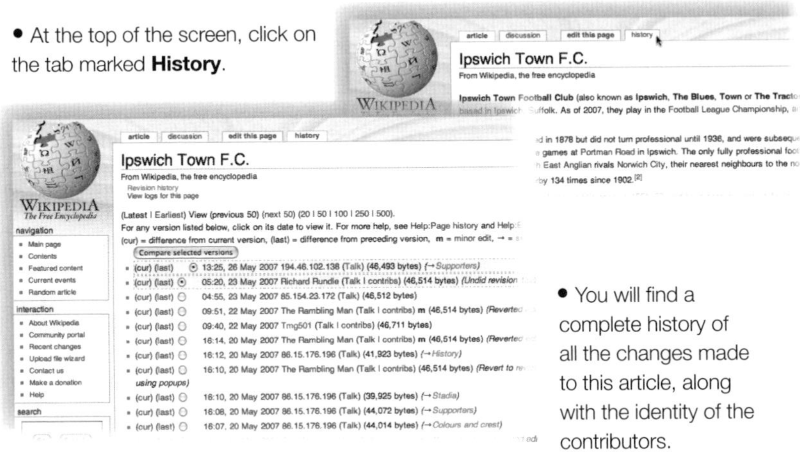

- You will find a complete history of all the changes made to this article, along with the identity of the contributors.

Discussing an Article

One of the most vibrant parts of Wikipedia is the **Discussion** area that every article has. Here users may argue their reasons for making alterations; in some cases this can result in so-called "edit wars," where "Wikipedians" revert articles back and forth between versions.

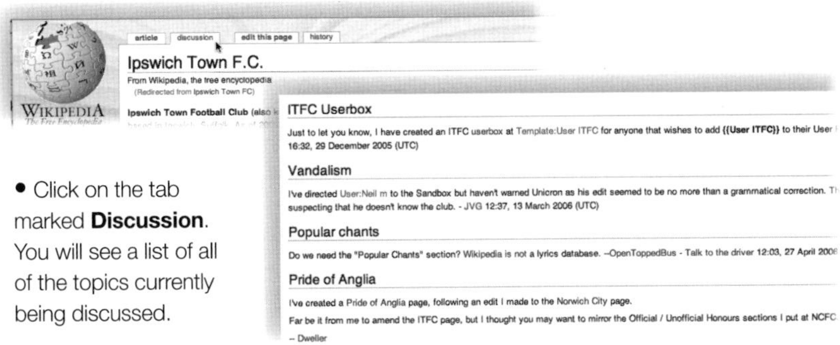

- Click on the tab marked **Discussion**. You will see a list of all of the topics currently being discussed.

Wikispaces

http://www.wikispaces.com

California-based Wikispaces is a product of a company called Tangient. It enables users to set up their own wikis very simply and very quickly. So let's look at setting a basic wiki-style web page.

• Enter the URL: **http://www.wikispaces.com**. Complete the registration details on the front page, and click on the button marked **Join**.

• The next screen you will see is your **Welcome** page. To start your wiki, click on the button marked **Edit This Page**.

• You can now begin typing text into your wiki page. If you want to add a picture, click on the **Add Image** icon (*see right*).

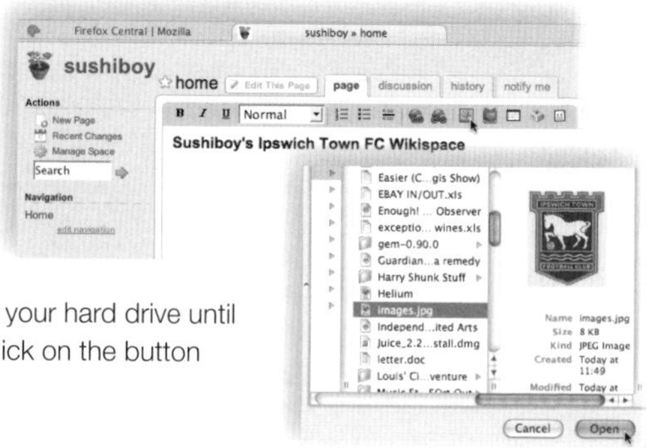

• In the pop-up window that follows, navigate through your hard drive until you find your selected files. Click on the button marked **Open**.

- In the **Images & Files** window, click on the **Upload** button. It's also possible to "point" to an image elsewhere on the web—to do this, type in the URL of the image and click on the **Load** button.

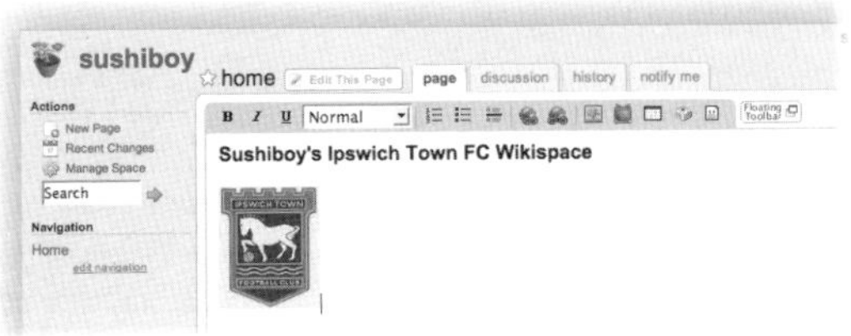

- Your wiki is now complete—it can now be viewed by anyone.

Wikihow

http://www.wikihow.com

Wikihow was launched with the intention of creating the world's largest "how-to" manual. To get a flavor of the information you'll find, go to the **Toolbox** window and select **Random Article** from the drop-down list.

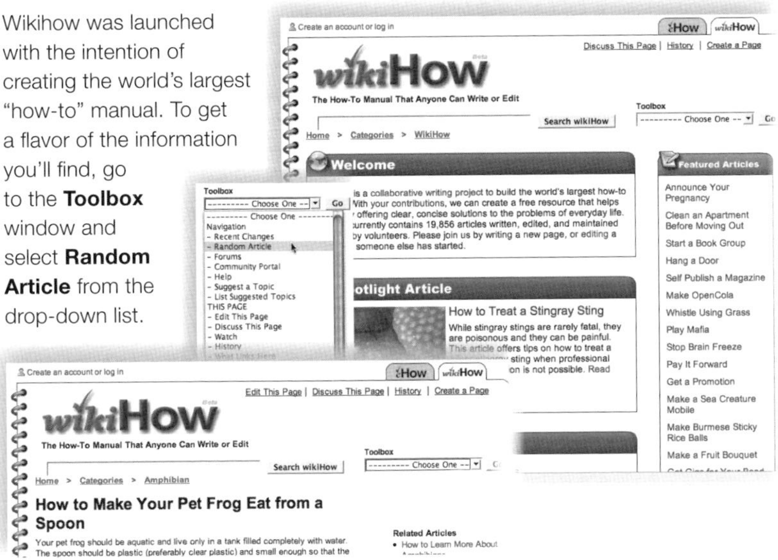

Editing an Article

Now let's look at making a simple edit using Wikihow.

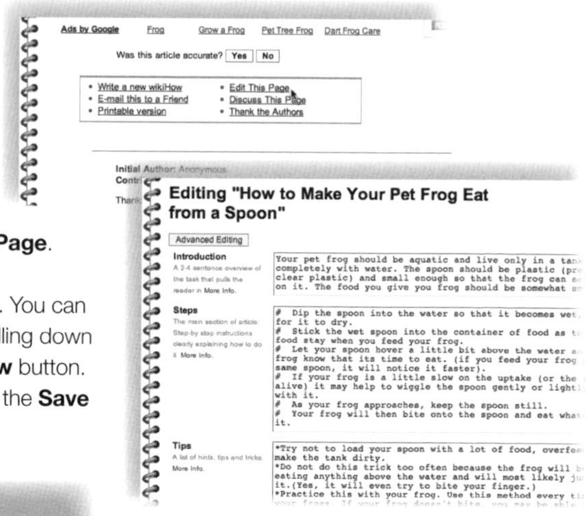

• Scroll to the bottom of the article and click on the text labeled **Edit This Page**.

• Alter the text as required. You can see how it will look by scrolling down and clicking on the **Preview** button. To retain your edit, click on the **Save Page** button.

Wetpaint

http://www.wetpaint.com

Wikis may be extremely easy to create and edit, but they are often not very pleasant from a visual point of view. Wetpaint addresses this issue by providing a series of layout templates.

• Enter the URL: **http://www.wetpaint.com**. In the main window, click on the large green button marked **Create Your Own Wetpaint Wiki Now!**

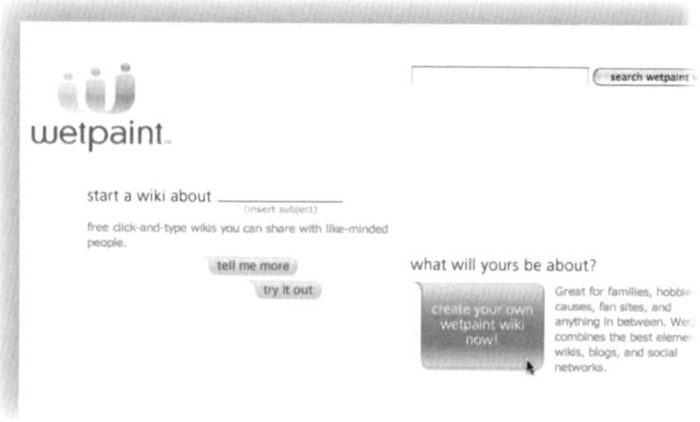

• Wetpaint uses three different set-up screens to create a wiki. In **Step 1** (*see top right*), create a name for your wiki, give it a URL address, and select a category from the list. You can now set your chosen level of privacy—

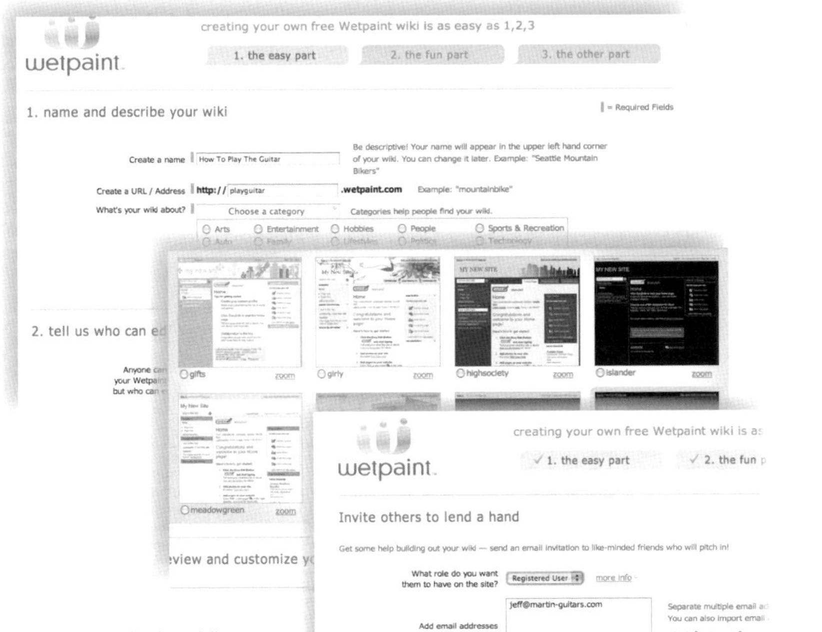

you can make it public, open to anyone with a wetpaint account, or by invite only. When you've finished, click on the button marked **Continue to Step 2**.

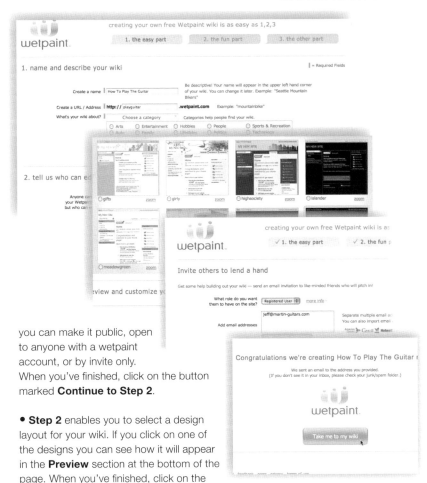

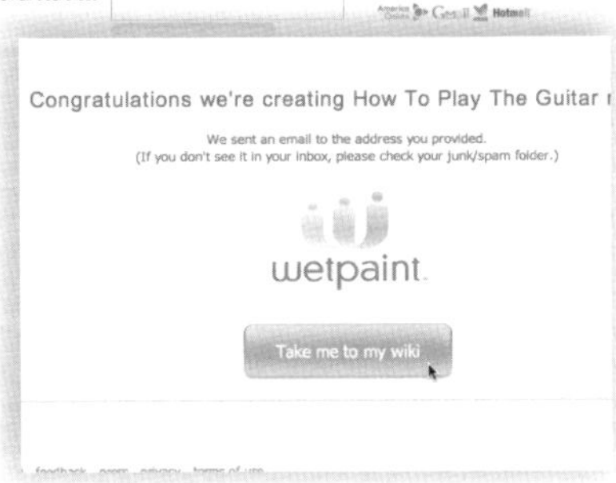

• **Step 2** enables you to select a design layout for your wiki. If you click on one of the designs you can see how it will appear in the **Preview** section at the bottom of the page. When you've finished, click on the button marked **Continue to Step 3**.

• In **Step 3** you can invite others to participate in the creation of your wiki. Click on the button marked **Send the Invitations and Create My Wiki**. Finally, click on **Take Me to My Wiki**.

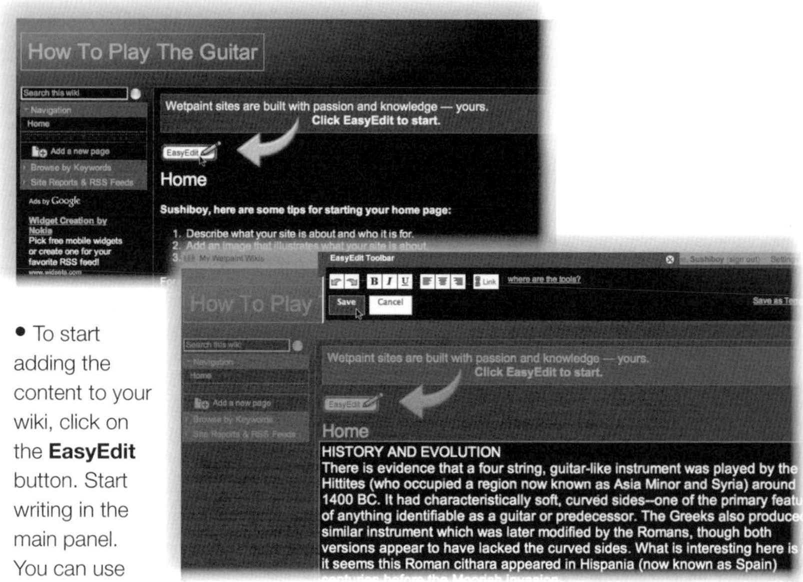
How To Play The Guitar
Search this wiki
Navigation
Home
Add a new page
Browse by Keywords
Site Reports & RSS Feeds
Ads by Google
Widget Creation by Nokia
Pick free mobile widgets or create one for your favorite RSS feed!
www.widsets.com
Wetpaint sites are built with passion and knowledge — yours.
Click EasyEdit to start.
EasyEdit
Home
Sushiboy, here are some tips for starting your home page:
1. Describe what your site is about and who it is for.
EasyEdit Toolbar
where are the tools?
Save
Cancel
HISTORY AND EVOLUTION
There is evidence that a four string, guitar-like instrument was played by the Hittites (who occupied a region now known as Asia Minor and Syria) around 1400 BC. It had characteristically soft, curved sides--one of the primary featu
of anything identifiable as a guitar or predecessor. The Greeks also produce
similar instrument which was later modified by the Romans, though both versions appear to have lacked the curved sides. What is interesting here is
it seems this Roman cithara appeared in Hispania (now known as Spain)

- To start adding the content to your wiki, click on the **EasyEdit** button. Start writing in the main panel. You can use the **Type Style** and **Justification** buttons to position your text. When you are ready, click on **Save**. Your wiki is now live.

Glypho

http://www.glypho.com

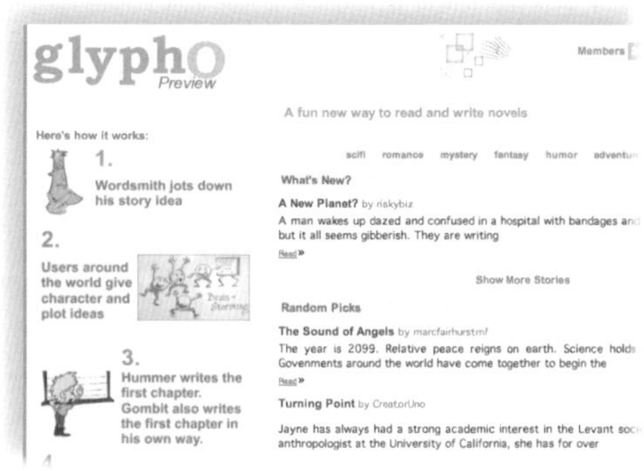
glyphO
Preview
A fun new way to read and write novels
Here's how it works:
1. Wordsmith jots down his story idea
2. Users around the world give character and plot ideas
3. Hummer writes the first chapter. Gombit also writes the first chapter in his own way.
scifi romance mystery fantasy humor
What's New?
A New Planet? by riskybiz
A man wakes up dazed and confused in a hospital with bandages and but it all seems gibberish. They are writing
Show More Stories
Random Picks
The Sound of Angels by marcfairhurstmf
The year is 2099. Relative peace reigns on earth. Science holds Govenments around the world have come together to begin the
Turning Point by CreatorUno
Jayne has always had a strong academic interest in the Levant anthropologist at the University of California, she has for over

Glypho is an interesting experiment that takes an extremely literal approach to collaborative text—in fact, the idea is to create collaborative fiction. Any individual can submit ideas, characters, and plot lines, or add to works that are already in progress. And anybody inspired by what they see can get on with the job of writing.

Projects in progress are listed according to their categories. If you click on your chosen genre you'll see the most recent projects. Click on the title of any story in the list to see a more detailed description of its current status.

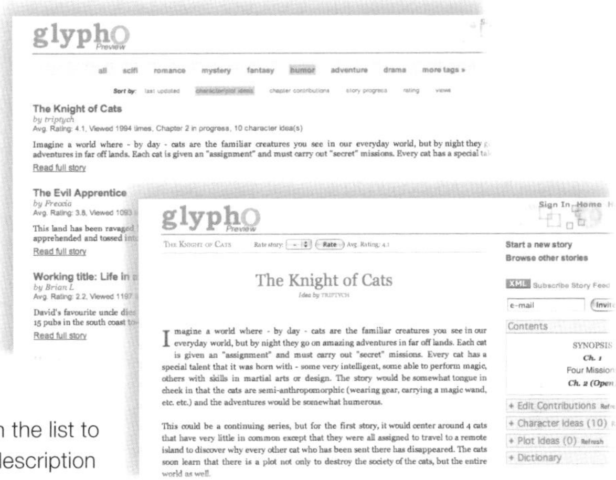
glypho Preview
all scifi romance mystery fantasy humor adventure drama more tags »
Sort by: last updated character/plot ideas chapter contributions story progress rating views
The Knight of Cats
by triptych
Avg. Rating: 4.1, Viewed 1994 times, Chapter 2 in progress, 10 character idea(s)
Read full story
The Evil Apprentice
Working title: Life in
by Brian L
Sign In Home
The Knight of Cats
Start a new story
Browse other stories
Subscribe Story Feed
e-mail
Contents
SYNOPSIS
Four Missions
+ Edit Contributions
+ Character Ideas (10)
+ Plot Ideas (0) Refresh
+ Dictionary
Imagine a world where - by day - cats are the familiar creatures you see in our everyday world, but by night they go on amazing adventures in far off lands. Each cat is given an "assignment" and must carry out "secret" missions. Every cat has a special talent that it was born with - some very intelligent, some able to perform magic, others with skills in martial arts or design. The story would be somewhat tongue in cheek in that the cats are semi-anthropomorphic (wearing gear, carrying a magic wand, etc. etc.) and the adventures would be somewhat humerous.
This could be a continuing series, but for the first story, it would center around 4 cats that have very little in common except that they were all assigned to travel to a remote island to discover why every other cat who has been sent there has disappeared. The cats soon learn that there is a plot not only to destroy the society of the cats, but the entire world as well.

More Wiki Sites

Bbbuddy	http://www.bbbuddy.com	SemaPedia	http://www.semapedia.org
Bibli	http://www.bibli.ca	Serversidewiki	http://www.serversidewiki.com
Citeulike	http://www.citeulike.org	Sharingpoint	http://www.sharingpoint.net
Cluebacca	http://www.cluebacca.com	Socialtext	http://www.socialtext.com
EditMe	http://editme.com	Sportiki	http://www.sportiki.com
Epictrip	http://www.epictrip.com	Stikipad	http://www.stikipad.com
Foopad	http://www.foopad.com	TagBud	http://www.tagbud.com
Ilovetravelstories	http://www.ilovetravelstories.com		
LittleWiki	http://littlewiki.com/wiki	Tiddlywiki	http://www.tiddlywiki.com
Lumrix	http://wiki.lumrix.net/en	Wikihost	http://wikihost.org
Ottowiki	http://ottowiki.com	Wikimatrix	http://www.wikimatrix.org
PB Wiki	http://pbwiki.com	WikiMusicGuide	http://www.wikimatrix.org
Product Wiki	http://www.productwiki.com	Wisdomark	http://wisdomark.com
Qwika	http://www.qwika.com	World66	http://www.world66.com
Reader2	http://reader2.com		
Readitswapit	http://www.readitswapit.co.uk		
Schtuff	http://www.schtuff.com		
SeedWiki	http://seedwiki.com		

Glossary

aggregator Software or online service that uses a web feed to retrieve syndicated web content such as weblogs, podcasts, vlogs, and mainstream mass media websites.

AJAX Abbreviation of Asynchronous JavaScript and XML, a development technology for creating interactive web applications. Works by making web pages seem more responsive by exchanging small amounts of background data with the server. Therefore the full web page doesn't have to be reloaded each time, thus increasing interactivity, speed, and usability.

avatars Graphics used to represent people in virtual worlds. It is possible to build a visual character with the body, clothes, behaviors, gender, and name of your choice.

back-channel communications Private e-mails or other messages sent by the facilitator or between individuals during public conferencing.

blog An abbreviation of "weblog," a term used to describe websites that maintain an ongoing chronicle of information. A blog is a frequently updated personal website featuring diary-type commentary and links to articles or other websites. Blogs range from the personal to the political and can focus on a specific subject or a whole range of subjects.

blogroll A list of recommended sites that appears in the sidebar of a blog. These are typically either on similar topics, sites that the blogger reads regularly, or sites that belong to the blogger's friends or colleagues.

bookmarking Storing the URL address of a website either in a browser or on a social bookmarking site such as Del.icio.us.

boolean logic A method of combining terms using operators such as "or," "and," or "not" in a search engine.

browser Computer software used to view websites. The most popular examples are Microsoft Internet Explorer, Mozilla Firefox, Netscape, Camino, and Safari. Multiplatform versions exist for many of these programs.

bulletin boards Early mode of online collaboration still used in forums. Users connect with a central computer to post and read e-mail–style messages. They could be thought of as the electronic equivalent of public notice boards.

categories Keywords under which to organize content. (*See tags.*)

comments Blogs and other types of applications may allow readers to add (or provide a feed for) remarks on specific items.

community building Expanding the number of people in a network by recruiting potential network participants with shared interests and goals. With more people brought into a community, the importance of the network and its usefulness to members increases.

connection The speed and nature of available Internet connection determines what tools can be used. High-speed broadband is a basic necessity for many modern web applications.

content Text, pictures, video and any other meaningful material found on the Internet.

content management systems Suites of software enabling the creation of static web pages, document stores, blogs, wikis, and other tools—the Swiss Army knives of social media.

copyright The rights of an artist or owner of a work in respect to its use. Much of the content found on websites such as YouTube infringes copyright. Specific laws differ from country to country. For example, some of the most popular BitTorrent search engines are based in Tonga, which does not seem to enforce any such regulations.

crawler Computer robot programs (also known as "spiders" or "knowledge-bots") used by search engines to roam the Internet and catalog information.

Creative Commons A copyright license that enables an individual to allow certain controlled freedom to the sharing or re-use of their content. For example, a musician may give the end-listener the legal right to download and share a piece of music, but retain the copyright with regard to its commercial distribution. Or a song may be freely sampled by another musician so long as attribution is given in any new piece of music.

default "Out-of-the-box" settings for any piece of software—can be customized to meet personal requirements.

democracy One of the buzzwords of social networking and media among those who claim the Web's potential for enabling individuals to discuss, deliberate, and take action on issues of common interest.

download To retrieve a file from a website to your computer or other device.

e-mail lists Networking tools that offer the facility to "starburst" a message from a central postbox to any number of subscribers.

face-to-face (f2) Meeting people offline.

feeds The means by which you can read, view, or listen to items from blogs and other RSS-enabled sites without visiting the site, by subscribing and using an aggregator or newsreader. Feeds contain the content of an item and any associated tags without the design or structure of a web page.

folksonomy A term used to describe the categorization and retrieval of web pages, photographs, links, and other items using open-ended labels called tags (*See tags*). Folksonomic tagging is intended to make a body of information easier to search, discover, and navigate over time.

forums Discussion areas on websites where people can post messages or comment on existing messages asynchronously—independent of time or place.

friends On social networking sites, friends are contacts whose profiles have been linked to your own profile.

instant messaging (IM) Online chat with one other person using IM software such as AOL Instant Messenger, Microsoft Live Messenger, or Yahoo! Messenger. An ideal alternative to e-mails for a rapid-exchange conversation.

links Highlighted text or images that are used to navigate from one web page or item of content to another. Bloggers make frequent use of links to reference their own or other content. Linking is another aspect of sharing, by which you offer content that may be linked, and acknowledge the value of other people's contributions by linking to them.

"listening in the blogosphere" The art of "skimming" feeds to see what topics are becoming fashionable.

logging in The process of gaining access to a website that restricts access to content, and requires registration.

lurkers Individuals who read forums but don't contribute. Estimates have suggested that about 1 percent of readers contribute new content to an online community, a further 9 percent comment, and the remainder lurk.

mapping By looking at the physical connectivity of a network, mapping enables you to identify the main connecting people, and those with whom they communicate most frequently. In this way it becomes possible to evolve an online community or network from an existing "real world" network.

mash-up A new hybrid of web-based applications that mixes different services from disparate—even competing—websites. An example of a mash-up might be integrating traffic data from one source on the Internet with maps from Yahoo!, Microsoft, or Google.

membership Belonging to a group or network.

moblogging Abbreviation for "mobile blogging." Refers to posting blog updates from a cell phone, camera phone, or pda (personal digital assistant). Mobloggers may update their websites more frequently than other bloggers, because they don't have to be at their computers in order to post.

networks Structures defined by nodes and the connections between them. In a social network the nodes are people, and the connections are the relationships that they have.

newsreader An application that gathers the news from multiple blogs or news sites via RSS, and allows readers to access all their news from a single website or program. Online newsreaders (like Bloglines, Pluck, or Newsgator) are websites that let you read RSS feeds from within your web browser. Desktop newsreaders download the news to your computer, and let you read your news inside a dedicated software program.

online Connection to the Internet.

open-source software (OSS) Any computer software whose source code is available under a license (or via the public domain) that permits users to study, change, and improve the software, and to redistribute it in a modified or unmodified form. It is often developed in a public, collaborative manner.

participation Key word in social media culture used to describe the way in which people share and collaborate.

peer-to-peer (P2P) Direct interaction between two people within a network. In that network, each peer will be connected to other peers, opening the opportunity for further sharing and learning. Napster, Gnutella, and BitTorrent are examples of P2P systems.

permalink The URL address of a specific item of content, such as a blog post, rather than a website which may contain large amounts of varying content.

photosharing Uploading images to a website such as Flickr. Tags may then be added enabling others to view, comment, or even re-use those photographs.

platform The framework within which an application is able to operate. This can refer to the type of hardware used (computer, cell phone, PDA); the specific operating system (Windows, Linux, Apple Macintosh); or the nature of the application (blog, forum, or wiki).

podcast A media file distributed over the Internet using syndication feeds, for playback on portable media players and personal computers. Although podcast content may be available as a direct download or streamed from a website, a podcast is distinguished from other digital audio formats by its ability to be downloaded automatically, using software capable of reading feed formats such as RSS or Atom.

podcaster The host or author of a podcast.

post An item on a blog or forum.

profile The information that any individual provides about themselves when signing up for a social networking website. This may include photographs, basic information, personal opinions, and tags that can help people searching for like-minded individuals.

proprietary software Unlike open-source software, proprietary software is owned by an organization or individual developer.

registration (*See logging in.*)

relevancy rating The most common technique for determining the order in which search results are displayed within a search engine. Each tool uses its own unique algorithm.

remixing Social media enables different items of content to be identified by tags and published through feeds, and combined in different ways.

RSS A family of web feed formats, specified using the XML language and used for web syndication. RSS is used by news websites, blogs, and podcasting. RSS is widely considered to be a mnemonic of "Really Simple Syndication." (However, it has also been defined as "Rich Site Summary.")

search engine Information on the Internet can be found using a search engine. As well as searching by keywords or phrases, it may also be possible to search using tags that others have set up.

social bookmarking A web-based service or application aimed at sharing Internet bookmarks. Social bookmarking sites such as Del.icio.us are a popular way to store, classify, share, and search links through the practice of folksonomy techniques. Some social bookmarking applications allow users to subscribe to feeds based on tags, thus enabling subscribers to become aware of additions on a given topic as they are created.

social media A term used to describe the tools and platforms—blogs, wikis, podcasts, photosharing websites, bookmarks, etc.—used to publish and share content online.

social software A type of software or web service that allows people to communicate and collaborate while using the application. E-mail, blogs, and even instant messaging are all examples of social software.

startpage Web service, such as Pageflakes or Netvibes, that can be configured to pull in content from a range of web-based services, such as e-mail, feeds from blogs, and news services. It is a multi-purpose aggregator.

subscribing The process of adding an RSS feed to your aggregator or newsreader. This is the online equivalent of signing up for a magazine.

synchronous communications Those occurring in real time, such as chat, audio, or video. Face-to-face communication is synchronous in the same place; talking by telephone is synchronous, but in different places, the Internet extends the scope for both types of communication.

tag A keyword or term associated with a piece of information. An item will typically have more than one tag associated with it. Tags are chosen informally and personally by the author/creator, not necessarily as part of some formally defined classification scheme.

taxonomy A formal method of classifying content, such as that used in a library.

teleconferencing A meeting that takes place using a network connection without being in the same location.

threads Strands of an online conversation, whether in an e-mail, instant messenger, or via comments on a social networking application.

URL Universal or Uniform Resource Locator: the address on the Internet of a website or specific piece of content held on a web server.

virtual worlds Online "worlds," such as Second Life, where individuals can create representations of themselves (avatars) and socialize with other residents.

voice over internet protocol (VOIP) The use of a computer or other Internet device to make and receive telephone calls. The best-known VOIP tool is Skype.

Web 2.0 A phrase coined by O'Reilly Media in 2003 referring to a perceived second generation of web-based communities and hosted services—typically, social networking sites, wikis, and folksonomies that facilitate collaboration and sharing between users. It does not, as the name suggests, indicate any update to the technical specifications of the World Wide Web, but to changes in the ways systems developers have used the web platform. As the term has reached the mainstream, its specific meaning has become increasingly vague, and is now often used as little more than a marketing buzzword to evoke the idea of technical innovation.

web-based tools Applications that function as part of a website rather than as software running on a computer.

widgets Stand-alone applications that can be embedded in other applications, such as a website or a desktop, or viewed on their own on a PDA. These may help you to do things like subscribe.

whiteboards Tools that enable users to write or sketch on a web page. Useful in online collaborations.

wiki A collaboratively edited web page. The best known example is Wikipedia, an encyclopedia that anyone in the world can help write or update. Wikis can be used to allow people to compose documents together or to share reference material.

Index

Acknowledgments

I'd like to thank the following people who helped out in some way with this project: John Bowers, Steve Elsey, Luke Griffin, Roland Hall, Martin Howells, Piers Murray Hill, Rachel Price, and Alex Sanders.

I'd also like to thank everyone connected with the various websites dotted throughout the book who gave their assistance or permission to use their content.

Finally, I'd like to dedicate this book to my four-year-old son, Louis, who tried his hardest to prevent me writing it at all.

Terry Burrows (www.terryburrows.com)